BECOMING
PARENTS

BECOMING PARENTS

*Preparing for the Emotional Changes
of First-time Parenthood*

Sandra Sohn Jaffe

AND

Jack Viertel

New York **ATHENEUM** 1985

Library of Congress Cataloging in Publication Data
Jaffe, Sandra Sohn.
Becoming parents.
Includes index.
1. Parenting — United States — Case studies.
I. Viertel, Jack, joint author.   II. Title.
HQ755 5.8.J33   1979   301.42'7   79-63794
ISBN 0-689-70685-5

Published simultaneously in Canada by McClelland and Stewart Ltd.
Manufactured by Fairfield Graphics
Fairfield, Pennsylvania
Designed by Kathleen Carey
First Atheneum Paperback Edition

FOR

Our Parents, Our Partners, and Our Children

ACKNOWLEDGMENTS

The authors would like to thank the following people for their encouragement, time, information, and inspiration before and throughout the writing of this book: Phillip Brooks, M.D., David Colker, Irwin Frankel, M.D., Phillip Goldberg, Rory Halperin, Gunilla, Joseph, and Eric Horacek, Bruce Jaffe, Jerry Jaffe, Bruce and Chrystie Jenner, Donald A. Lackey, M.D., Sandra and Malcolm Musicante, Celia Sockett, and Stanley Warner, M.D. In addition, Linda Viertel, a dedicatee of this book, ought to be acknowledged for round-the-clock proofreading and other tasks too numerous to mention in connection with the final preparation of the manuscript. To the couples and single parents who gave us their time, their carefully considered self-analysis, and their trust, we, of course, owe everything. They *are* this book.

ACKNOWLEDGMENTS

CONTENTS

THE SECOND FAMILY
Doug and Casey Sterling, and Leora

THE THIRD FAMILY
David and Ellen Welles, and Edward

THE FOURTH FAMILY
Alan Sheinman and Nina Degarmo and Lauren

THE FIFTH FAMILY
Hal and Susan Bradford, and Eric

THE SIXTH FAMILY
Ben and Sally McCadden, and Brian

PREFACE

By Allan Fromme, Ph. D.

Author of *The ABC of Child Care* and *The Ability to Love*

Becoming parents is almost as inevitable as growing up. We've hardly needed the moral urging to be fruitful and multiply. It's all so natural that until recently, few, if any, of us questioned our qualifications for the role. In trying to learn how to become *good* parents, however, increasing numbers of men and women are studying psychology at college, participating in prepared childbirth classes as the time grows near, and immersing themselves in baby and child-care books once their young hopeful arrives. All this, of course, helps them to understand babies better.

Human behavior is shaped only in small part by such reasoned, cerebral elements, however. Even when we try, and know we know better, we are frequently disappointed with the results. More often we're moved by the unrelenting pressure of needs and desires, often in conflict, often tied up in habits and a vague, unclear image of ourselves.

Our feelings and emotions will always be part of the vitality

and quality of our lives. For better or worse, our mental outlook rubs off on our children and is probably the most potent
force of all in shaping their emerging humanity. Put more
simply, what counts is not so much *what* we do, but *how* we
do it. The child's overall personality development is not the
simple end result of all the right answers we get from books.
Our effectiveness as parents also depends upon the emotional
ambience of the home. How we feel (and act) about life, ourselves, each other, our home, work, friends, parents, *and* the
baby are even more important in the long run than specific
bits and pieces of child-care knowhow.

What this means is that parents are not simply people who
have a baby. They are also people with private, marital, occu-
pational, and social lives. These various facets of their being all
influence each other. The first child, even before its nearly
traumatic, or at least spectacular, appearance is not just one
more side of our lives. The whole gestalt gets shaken up. The
order of our priorities gets bounced all over the place. What
has emerged slowly over the years and finally congealed into
the daily routine of habit suddenly is exploded. Outside, everything remains the same. Inside, there is chaos. Taking care of
the baby is one thing; what are we to do about ourselves?

It's high time some of our learning and preparation dealt
with this problem. *Becoming Parents* is a sensitive, modest ex-
ploration of many of the demands and problems associated
with this change of life. It is realistic and instructive without
being didactic or discouraging. Most of all, it provides us with
a good deal of furniture for our minds to accompany the efforts
we make for the baby's room. We see with astonishing clarity
how very much the whole house is involved.

INTRODUCTION

Nearly every child-care guide ever written contains a well-buried land mine somewhere in its early pages, an innocuous paragraph to the effect that bringing a newborn home requires a "period of adjustment" for the parents. The anxious mother and father, loaded down with information about feeding, burping, changing, comforting, and otherwise protecting the newborn, are encouraged to let this "period of adjustment" run its course, like a head cold. Baby is so much more important. And so it is that millions of parents embark on an uncharted course with neither sail nor compass, amid disturbingly unstable winds.

Suddenly everything is different. With the focus of attention heavily centered on the baby, the couple relationship tends to be ignored at exactly the time when it most needs looking after. Becoming a family reshapes every facet of every relationship, and the "period of adjustment," so casually mentioned, can take months, even years. Bringing home a newborn can be a frightening proposition, and, ultimately, a lonely one. For most parents, who temporarily disassociate themselves from their social acquaintances, it is a period of living on the edge of life, a short fall away from familial anarchy. The emotions are overtaxed equally by the good times and the bad. Life becomes surprising, unstable, exhilarating, depressing, incomprehensible, and, at the same time, all too predictable. The separation and divorce rate runs high during the first year of parenting.

It was not always this way. There were days when generations of the family lived together, or at least in close proximity. Family traditions, family gatherings, and family decisions were a way of life. Within these tightly knit organizations, grandparents and grandchildren leaned hard on eath other; new parents had varied sources of instruction, psychological advice, and confidence. The responsibility for a child never rested solely on one person, or even on one couple. In addition, there was the ever-present comfort of knowing that many surrounding family members had gone through the first year of parenting and all had survived.

Our parents and grandparents are not so much with us now. We have come to appreciate the freedom distance has given us; we tend to think of the impulse to strike out alone, away from the family, as a healthy one. But, undoubtedly, something has been lost. With freedom comes the responsibility to create our own support systems, and we have no instructions.

The problem is complicated by the changing role of women in our society. What little tradition we *have* carried with us holds that child care and family preservation are the private provinces of women, but just as the extended family has been shaken, so has the traditional role of women. As society adjusts to women's demands for careers, new professional stature, and a new kind of respectability, men are being called into active duty as parents, something for which their upbringing never prepared them.

Even the most eager new fathers find aspects of the job baffling. Many find thir psychological reactions to parenting rather discomforting. They discover, with appropriate guilt, that they don't *like* doing something which their wives do better. They would rather not do it at all. This private revelation tends to be closely guarded. Secretiveness leads to stress, and stress breeds frustration. In this world of heightened emotion, mates examine each other's character with a suddenly critical eye; trivial aspects of behavior begin to balloon in importance. There is a potential disaster here, one that nearly every couple senses at some point during the first year of parenting.

All sorts of attempts have been made to explain the dangerous ground trod by first-time parents. These attempts take the form of advice dispensed by a trained professional. The advice is theoretical, and it grows from study and thought. However, there is no special discipline that completely covers parenting. Parenting is not simply a matter of psychology or pediatrics, family counseling or consciousness-raising. It is a discipline unto itself, involving all the above and more: soap opera, slapstick, and diplomacy. Only parents know how to do it.

On the theory that experience is the best teacher, we have gathered a year's experience from six new families. Practically the only thing that these parents have in common is their lack of accurate prediction. No one knows what to expect.

It must be emphasized that *Becoming Parents* is *not* a book about babies or child care. It contains no information about feeding schedules, infant diseases, toilet training, or flammable sleepwear. These are healthy, important topics, but they are well treated in other books. This book is about parent care. It is about how parents treat each other, their friends, their own parents, and themselves. It is about the unexpected changes parents find themselves going through—sexual changes, behavioral changes, emotional changes. It is about the traumas suffered by parents—guilt, distrust, and frustration.

It is not a horror story; most parents find this year an exhilarating time of life. But they also find it bewildering and exhausting. *Becoming Parents* is an attempt to find a common ground for parents, a reference guide for their emotions.

The six couples come from varied walks of life. Their incomes, life-styles, and occupations differ vastly. Each represents a unique relationship, and each had its own reason for having children. The six have been selected from a much larger pool of candidates, with an eye to displaying the widest possible variety of life-styles and problems. They do have certain things in common, however.

They are all from the Los Angeles area and reflect, for the most part, an urban existence. Each had taken some part of a Lamaze prepared childbirth course. They all delivered their babies at a hospital where the father is allowed to be present at delivery whether he has taken any classes in childbirth preparation or not. However, these factors are not nearly as limiting as they may sound. The Lamaze prepared childbirth class attracts a wide variety of people from all backgrounds, as our six families demonstrate. Cedars-Sinai Medical Center, where nearly all mothers in our sample delivered, provides services for the entire Los Angeles community. Our sample included couples living on relief and couples making in excess of $60,000 annually. It included electricians, executives, nurses, attorneys, striptease dancers, and the unemployed. It included blacks, whites, Asian-Americans, and Orthodox Jews. From the sample, six stories emerged as the most telling, the most surprising, the most common in their emotional basis, the most unusual in their narrative paths.

We interviewed each set of parents slightly before the baby's due date. All were encouraged to envision the future as they hoped it would be, and as they expected it to be. In subsequent interviews throughout the year following birth, these dreams, fears, and expectations were held up to the reality of the parenting experience. Interviews were held one month, three months, six months, nine months, and one year after the actual delivery date. They were openended, free-flowing conversations in which the parents were encouraged to talk about anything that interested them.

In imposing ourselves on the information our subjects gave us, we have tried to be very careful. Some had successful years, some did not. We have spent a good number of hours picking

apart the details of every action each parent took, trying to find
the reasons for success or failure. What we have found should
have been evident from the beginning: there is no "right" way
to confront the first year of parenting, and what you do depends
upon who you are. What works for one couple may lead to
catastrophe for another.

In order to preserve the independence of each family's first
year, we have given each its own place in this book. We report
what happened at each time interval, and we try to figure out
why it happened. To protect the identity of our subjects, so they
could feel free in talking to us, we have taken care to disguise
them. We have changed their names and certain other details
about their lives. We have drawn upon comments and incidents
from interviews with other couples when appropriate, and tried
to shape the mass of material into a naturally flowing, inte-
grated whole.

In the process, we hope to lead the reader through the
first year on a guided tour of the carnival, stopping at every
attraction in the park for long enough to give her or him
some idea of what to expect. Undoubtedly, with six families acting as demonstrators, there will be contradictions, differences of opinion, and multiple solutions to the same problems. They are all there for the choosing. By the end of *Becoming Parents*, the reader should have a pretty good idea of
the first year: how it works, how it doesn't work, what can be
realistically expected, and what must be recognized as fantasy.

This book is based on hundreds of actual interviews. All the
incidents are real. The judgments and interpretations of incidents and emotions are those of the authors.

To say that we have tried to be objective would only be
stretching the truth a small amount. To say that we have
succeeded would be preposterous. Both the authors are parents.
One had children of seven, four, and one when this book was
begun. The other witnessed the birth of a first child at practically the same moment the first draft of this introduction was
rolling off the typewriter. In the year that has intervened between first and second draft, an enormous amount of personal

concern has filtered its way into these pages. This book is full of personal opinion: we have said what we believe to be true. That nothing we say should be taken as fact, or gospel, or advice from the world's foremost authorities is, we hope, obvious. We are, after all, merely the seventh and eighth families, and while we have collected and edited all the information, our solutions to the problems are only our own. They are designed not to provide easy answers, but merely to banish fear and to encourage discussion. If nothing else, this book should allow you to spend your first year as a parent in sympathetic company, with a map of the territory near to hand.

THE
FIRST
FAMILY

Frank and Betsy Scheflin

AND ANDREW

EARLY DECISIONS

Nursing and Sex

IT WAS frightening to set up a nursery for a person who did not exist. The implications were ghoulish. So Frank and Betsy Scheflin maintained an empty white room in their newly rented house in California. They refrained from referring to it as "the baby's room." They bought no bassinet, no crib, no layette, and no stuffed animals.

Days before, the van from Abbey Rents Furniture had pulled up at the drive and deposited two thick-waisted men in T-shirts. The men had unloaded what amounted to a brand-new life for Frank and Betsy—six and a half roomfuls of furniture hastily picked out of a store display. In an hour, every room in the house looked like a waiting room. Sofas stood by tables, almost new, piteous in their lack of personality, like small men waiting alone at a cocktail party. Betsy just shook her head. Everyone in New York had told her that Los Angeles was a huge motel. The Scheflins were doing their part to make a myth come true.

The moving van men were nervous. It was the end of the day for them, and they seemed to have come up one room short on this order. They hated like hell to go back to the warehouse at this hour. And so it was that Frank Scheflin came home from the first day of work and found his wife explaining to two goons in T-shirts about not furnishing the nursery. It was all quite bewildering.

The move was sudden, and they had not asked for it. But it meant $50,000 a year for Frank, and he was in no position to turn it down. The advertising world needed new blood on the West Coast; the agency paid for the move. Betsy never protested. She was proud of Frank, and she liked the money, but she missed everything: friends, family, Central Park, decent pastrami, and, most of all, her own career.

She had taken her M.B.A. at Columbia and was building a reputation as an investment banker, bringing in a good salary, when Frank's promotion brought her professional life to a halt. Work had made her free, had made them a young, independent, New York couple, taxiing to important events in Manhattan's night. She felt nourished by that mainstream of electric activity. For the five years of her marriage, she had been what and where she wanted to be.

California was quiet, by contrast, and an empty breeze seemed to be blowing. Betsy said all the things about California that New Yorkers always said. She thought it was fair; she had to weather her new acquaintances' running assaults on New York.

No new job awaited her in Los Angeles, and it was senseless to look. The baby was only three months away when they moved. Betsy took the *Wall Street Journal* and kept up. Frank's new, bone-crushing schedule left her alone in the unfamiliar house to contemplate her all-new life that was to be. The furniture seemed lonely in the redwood-beamed Spanish-style house. There was a coldness to the red tile floors and gas fireplace. From time to time Betsy would toss magazines around the living room, but it never looked as if anyone had been there. She didn't know a soul.

It was the women's movement that had inspired her to take

her graduate degree; it was the women's movement that had nudged her out into the job market. Now the rhetoric of that movement rattled around in her head as she padded the bedroom's shag carpet in fluffy slippers, moving paintings from one wall to another and dumping ashtrays. She felt she was living someone else's life, in someone else's house. It gnawed at her not to get up in the morning and go to work; guilt came easily to Betsy. No matter what she did, she felt like she was getting away with murder.

Her parents had always had one too many black maids or laundresses, just picking up after Betsy, or feeding her, or making her bed. She resented all the help, but she resented more that she had never turned it down. Sometimes she felt that the civil rights movement and the women's movement had secretly joined forces and were conspiring to drive her crazy.

On those rare occasions when Frank got home for a regular dinner, they would look in the doorway at the empty nursery and wonder what would take place there. They refused to fantasize. The echo off the walls put them in mind of just how much was unknown about the future. Great developments were beginning to jockey for position in Betsy's womb. They were not to be second-guessed by the expectant couple. Night life went on as usual—not as hectic as the New York life but of the same stripe: late dinners at Dan Tana's when Frank couldn't get home, whatever shows the theater cared to mount. But somehow it just wasn't the same without the street noise and the friends who always turned up if you waited long enough at P. J. Clark's or Michael's Pub in New York.

They didn't look right for a California couple either. Frank's thick black hair and angular features, his soft skin and deep eyes made him appear too pensive for tennis and sailing, although he was an expert at both. Betsy's heart-shaped face and strong mouth would have looked silly under blond hair. She was a job woman and looked it. The hair was brown, and it would stay brown.

Even so, Frank began to notice that when he finished telling her about his day, she had nothing much to offer in return. Little encounters on the freeway, a funny comment overheard in the supermarket, and then nothing. But soon there would be the baby. Whatever it was now, life would all be different then; there was no point in prying around the dark corners of an emotional situation that was so temporary.

Frank worked day and night, partially because he loved it, as much because the advertising world was a jungle. The competition was savage and could be venomous. Frank found it invigorating to win, worth the risk of losing. He had always been an athlete, and tough-mindedness came naturally to him. He was an advantaged kid who had tightened his grip on every advantage. His family's reputation and social circle—old Jewish New York money—helped, but Frank worked for everything he got. A Harvard education helped, but the instinct for success had been implanted long before college. Nothing was holding him back.

In his moments of solitude, Frank worried about Betsy's future, her emotional upheaval at leaving the city, at leaving work, at taking on this new role, but he couldn't *be* Betsy. She had the brains and the stability to banish these demons, and no one could do it for her. He wanted badly for things to settle, but could fathom nothing that would calm the waters. He felt quite distant from the turmoil within her. When they discussed it, which was often, he listened to each word, to each tonal shift and pause in her voice, but when the conversation was over, he was still locked outside, looking in by dim light.

Still, there was nothing seriously wrong with the relationship—just a couple of mildly neurotic people making adjustments. Most of the time there was work for him, domestic duty for her, dinners out, tentative ice-breaking evenings with new acquaintances from the agency, and bed. Betsy never felt that Frank was inattentive or insensitive. He simply didn't have the equipment to help her at the moment. She understood the gruelling complexities of his day and tried not to interfere. The marriage was like a car that would not stay in tune, but remained driveable.

Their refusal to furnish the nursery made people laugh, but it had its dark side. Frank and Betsy spoke openly of the possibility that there might be no living baby at the end of this road, or, worse, that the baby might "have problems." The room served as an emblem of their hopes and dreams. Cautious pains were taken to keep it empty, in limbo, offering no promise that might have to be broken by tragedy.

Frank was particularly obsessed by these fears as he watched in awe, and with not a little fear, as his wife's body went through metamorphosis. Somehow, his inability to make contact with the process and its emotional side effects generated these images of stillborn or malformed infants. The unknown bred fear in him, and the more he looked at Betsy's new body, the less he knew. He had seen the encouraging statistics, but he didn't think of himself as a statistic. He thought of himself as the only prospective father in the world. It was a grave responsibility.

In line with their attitude about the nursery, Betsy refused to prepare herself for motherhood in any other way. She would not read books; she would be guided only by instinct. They would have a live-in baby nurse who would show her how to bathe, hold, change, and feed when the time came. The nurse was chosen from the yellow pages, her competence confirmed by a brief telephone interview. Because the nurse would feed the baby at night, Betsy elected not to breast-feed. She did not want to be unwillingly attached to the baby, and she did not want to worry about dripping for nine months or a year. Frank was vaguely relieved by the idea of a bottle. Betsy's body was already distressing to him. When it returned to normal, he wanted it to be perfect, not damp with unwanted secretions from her breasts.

Their lack of involvement in the approaching birth scared them a little, so they enrolled in the Lamaze prepared childbirth classes.* They hoped to ease themselves into readiness for

* The Lamaze prepared childbirth course is a six- to eight-week class which generally involves expectant mothers *and* fathers in learning about the experience of childbirth and prepares them for labor and delivery. The fathers function as "coaches" during the practice sessions and the actual event, at which they are present. When the father is not available, or doesn't wish to be involved, another person of the mother's choosing becomes the coach. Thousands of hospitals now consider Lamaze deliveries common procedure.

the due date. At the first class, Betsy was the only one who forgot to bring the two pillows requested in the class brochure. Frank arrived late, direct from work, bushed and hungry. During the third class, Betsy cried briefly after failing to remember a basic breathing exercise. She could not make the preparation happen. She could not take the experience seriously. Getting ready for childbirth, for motherhood, seemed like a joke. It was supposed to be a natural adjustment, not something you went into training for. Betsy looked around the classroom at the serious faces creased with concentration, and it was all she could do to keep from laughing. The profound emotion seemed to be self-generated by her classmates, but it was not happening for Betsy. She just couldn't make the baby seem real. The classes were like an adult session of "let's pretend."

The due date hurtled toward her. Two days before it, she awoke, nauseated, at two o'clock in the morning. She vomited and felt what she thought was a painful contraction. She felt awful. She awakened Frank and described the pain, the nausea. The Lamaze class had prepared her for the procedure that would follow if this was really labor. But she could not say for sure that it was. She had suffered no sickness, no pain, for the first eight and a half months of her pregnancy. So this must be labor. On the other hand, she was not feeling regular contractions, her water hadn't broken, and she had no vaginal bleeding. She made coffee. Frank put a roll of dimes in his pants pocket for phone calls, in case they went to the hospital. They sat in the dinette to wait, either for real labor or for recovery from the pain. They waited for fourteen days.

There is no typical couple, no typical mother or father, and no typical baby. Certainly the Scheflins are not typical: they have more money than most of us, more education, and a longer tradition of financial success in their backgrounds. They are upper-class people. What is typical—almost universal—is the nature of their hopes and fears as parenthood approached them.

Becoming a parent for the first time involves the unknown, and most of us aren't as eager to greet the unknown as we think we are. We like it in books and especially in movies, but in real life it's more disconcerting than anything else. One of the biggest surprises expectant couples come up against is that when it comes to hopes and fears, the fears can run neck and neck with the hopes. Sometimes they can jump out to a clear lead. Anxiety is the common property of pregnant women and their mates—anxiety about everything from money to birth defects to loss of personal liberty. The last hours of freedom may seem to be ticking away like a two-dollar wristwatch. The possibility of having all your dreams shattered with the birth of an imperfect baby remains ever-present in the minds of many an expectant parent. Along with this there is, of course, an uncommon level of anticipated delight, excitement, and high expectation. These things are easy to celebrate and don't need to be talked about in this book, since they pretty much take care of themselves. The anxiety is another matter, however.

People don't like to talk to each other about the negative side of being pregnant, and, as a result, no one seems to know that whatever bad feelings he or she is having are as universal as the good feelings, and as impossible to control.

The Scheflins did a number of things to separate themselves from the approaching event, possibly in the subconscious hope that they could quell their fear if they could ignore the pregnancy. They didn't furnish the nursery—a symbolic act—and they quickly arranged for a baby nurse so that their freedom would be preserved. The empty nursery is a common Jewish superstition, probably a buried part of the Scheflins' upbringing, although neither of them could remember such a thing. The nurse is at least a somewhat common addition to upper-class households at the time of a first birth. The ramifications of having one will be discussed in the next chapter.

The prebirth decision that was most important to this couple, and to every couple, was whether or not to breast-feed. Nursing is perhaps *the* hot topic of conversation during pregnancy, and if it's not, it ought to be. Of all problems and emotional upheavals in this book, a disproportionate number of them relate in some way to breast-feeding. A discussion of the nutritional advantages or disadvantages of breast-feeding belongs in some other book, and can be covered by your doctor or any one of a number of people. We are concerned with the emotional and sexual implications of breast-feeding. Betsy Scheflin knew that her husband was worried about his own reactions to her pregnant body, and more worried about what would happen when and if she started nursing. She herself wasn't crazy about the idea of becoming a lactating mammal— the image smacked of barnyards to her. We can't say this is a particularly healthy attitude, but at least she recognized it and acted upon it. She decided not to breast-feed, and it's probably a good thing. Breast-feeding is a simple activity with a complicated set of related side effects that should be taken into consideration. All of them have emotional, as well as physical, components.

1.) *You leak, especially when your breasts are stimulated.* Your breasts don't distinguish between baby and lover. They will leak on anyone. Men have to get used to this. Many of them worry about it, but few are affected adversely for any length of time. You are, after your delivery, a somewhat different creature, sexually, than you have ever been before. Your lactating breasts, your stretched vagina, and your reshaped body will all be new to a lover who has known you only one way. You *will* get back to normal, but it can take months, and your breasts will produce milk for as long as you nurse. In asking men about this period in their sex lives, we found a neat split between those who were intrigued and excited by their wive's tendency to lactate and those who were distressed and reluctant to become involved with the upper half of their wives' bodies. It's a guessing game. Many of the men interviewed were surprised by their own reactions, both positive and negative.

2.) *Your sex drive may be greatly reduced.* There doesn't seem to be any cut-and-dried physiological explanation for this. Your hormones are doing different things while you are breast-feeding, and a great percentage of the women we interviewed said that their desire for sex was only occasional during the entire period when they were nursing. Somehow, breast-feeding seems to satisfy a sexual need in women, although it is not, in itself, a sexual act. Oddly, most men reported that they seemed to naturally adjust their own sex drive downward during this period. They could not explain how this happened. Men used to having sexual relations three and four times a week found themselves satisfied with less, a reaction which is unplanned, but helpful.

Breast-feeding is not, of course, the only cause of lessened sex drive in women. Many new mothers are exhausted by their new life and not completely comfortable sexually until the vagina has had several months to heal. Painful intercourse is common and makes each successive attempt at sex less and less carefree. However, one day you try it and there is no more pain. This requires faith. Please have it.

If all this sounds like an attack on breast-feeding, it is not intended as such. Both authors of this book are raising children who have been breast-fed, and we would not do it any other way. But we are lucky in that none of the above-mentioned complications proved especially bothersome. They weren't delightful, but we weathered them. Other couples in this book had greater problems, and in several cases the nursing decision was taken without enough consideration or understanding. It is a decision that must be made by the couple, not by the mother alone. The husband is definitely an active partner here: it is his sex life and his emotional security that may be threatened by the wrong decision. We should state that in almost every case, husbands were more frightened about breast-feeding *before* their children were born than when they actually saw the process in action. They adjusted to the sexual situation, and any damage that was done was temporary. Still, any husband who abstains from voting on the question deserves what he gets.

Of more concern to husbands is a directly sexual question: How will they look at their wives after witnessing birth? The prospect of seeing a woman's sexual parts put through physical contortions required for birthing worries a lot of men. This fear is darkly guarded, as are most fears of sexual failure. But it is a common enough fear. In prepared childbirth classes the most common reason men give for not wanting to attend the delivery is that they don't feel it's "right" for husbands to watch their wives give birth. They make jokes about fainting, but when the discussion is extended for any length of time, a great many of them confess that they are worried about how the experience will affect their sexual attitudes toward their wives and how those attitudes will change.

The fear is common beforehand, but the change in attitude rarely materializes, and when it does, it rarely lasts. We're not sure why this is so, but part of the reason seems to be this: in the delivery room, the circumstances are so special that husbands don't tend to relate them to anything in the outside world. They are concentrating on the activity at hand. The association between the vaginal process of delivering a baby and the vaginal process of the sex act is simply never made. We cannot speak for all cases, of course. There must be men who *do* face a sexual confusion after watching their wives give birth. But for all the worry many of them expressed, not one of them turned up in our sample.

AT ONE WEEK

Help at Home—The Question of the Nurse

MORE than anything, Betsy Scheflin didn't want to be sent home from the hospital with false labor. She didn't want to appear a fool. She made certain that she was in labor before she and Frank made the ten-minute trek and took the elevator to the third floor, marked MATERNITY. As a result of her wait, she was suffering by the time she arrived, and, within moments, the pain became worse than anything she had ever imagined.

"I wouldn't recommend it," she told a friend, shortly after the birth of Andrew, six pounds, eleven ounces. "It's horrendous." But, when pressed, she could only remember about a half-hour of severe pain, and Frank was with her, nudging her, encouraging her, and rooting for her.

Following the euphoria in the delivery room, pure exhaustion set in. Betsy loved her baby; she wanted to look at him, watch him sleep. But she didn't want to feed him, or learn to bathe him, or clean his umbilical wound. She just wanted to rest and think. Frank watched her, dozed in a chair, then went home to bed.

Home was still empty. While Betsy spent a final day in the hospital, Frank called some stores. A bassinet and a changing table turned up on the doorstep, along with the nurse. She was a woman of thirty-three, soft-spoken and plain, with reddish, lusterless hair and a broad, Scandinavian face. Just this side of shy, Frank thought, and eager to be helpful. He dispatched her with his Master Charge card for whatever else was needed. She had experience. She knew how many crib sheets and receiving blankets, and what kind of powder and ointment. She was frugal with the Scheflins' money, too. Frank was enthusiastic.

Betsy was less so. She arrived home expecting to find a matron, someone with comfortable shoes and endless patience, a thick little gray lady with bifocals. She was somewhat cowed to be taking instructions from a woman not much older than she, surely too young to be an expert. In silence she watched Andrew's daily routine. Even when she didn't watch, she could listen. Lying in bed with the radio playing softly, she could hear the nurse, humming as she gave the baby a bottle, singing and splashing at the little bucket of water she used for the sponge bath, cooing and clucking through the day. The nurse kept out of Betsy's way, except to bring in the baby every time a feeding was finished so that Betsy could hold him. And Betsy couldn't complain about discretion; the nurse always left her alone with the baby and made only the gentlest suggestions that Betsy might try a feeding every now and then. When Betsy said yes, the nurse produced a bottle ready and waiting, heated for the purpose. It was unnerving, this help.

When nurse and baby were occupied, Betsy sat at the telephone, finishing off the nursery from catalogues. Her orders arrived regularly; Betsy directed Frank, who moved things from one corner of the room to another until it looked right. In two days the room filled up while she watched. The baby slept, ate, was bathed and changed in her view. Sometimes she helped. It was all going on around her, near her, but not inside her.

It was at dinner on the second night that the nurse offered to bring her some mashed potatoes and she burst into tears. Sobbing piteously, she shut herself in the bedroom, leaving Frank and the nurse to finish dinner. Frank knew what was wrong. He wanted to give the nurse the rest of the night off, get the alien feelings out of the house, return to the family alone, but there was a problem: no one but the nurse could take care of the baby. The nurse was apologetic, but unruffled. She'd seen it all before. To her, it was part of the standard drama of bringing a baby home.

"I'm afraid to cuddle my own baby," Betsy told Frank. "I'm not afraid of *him*, I'm afraid of *her*. She does all the hard stuff. I'm afraid she'll resent me butting in. She's working so hard, I'm afraid to bother her. I'd hate me if I was her."

The guilt that was never out of reach for Betsy had blossomed. Guilt over the servant problem, guilt over her own inactivity, and the gnawing feeling that somehow this little infant had an operating consciousness and knew, knew all too well, that it was being neglected by its real mother.

"He'll never even *know* me," she said. "He won't even know my name." She knew she was being ridiculous. She belittled herself, laughed about it, and went to bed early. But it wouldn't go away. This time, she thought, I've really gone crazy.

In the morning things looked a little brighter. Frank had a talk with the nurse. Betsy spent the day learning everything. Andrew was light, trouble free, and sleepy. The nurse watched Betsy work, commented here and there, and tried to be friendly. By the end of the morning, Betsy had gained a moderate amount of confidence, and, at three o'clock, the nurse went on a twenty-four-hour furlough. Frank returned home from work to find his wife calmed, his son sleeping, and the house immaculate. The pulse had slowed. Everything seemed to be all right.

At 3:00 A.M. Betsy heard a muffled squeak from the bassinet by the side of the bed. The tiny sound shot through her like a lightning bolt. Andrew was wide awake, ready to eat. Half-asleep, she sprang from the bed, elbowing Frank in the throat.

Andrew took a full bottle, but he was not sleepy. He wanted to stay awake. For an hour she humored him. She took him from the bedroom, waltzed him, and did some singing. She changed him and gave him a massage. Then she tucked him into the bassinet and he began to wail, a wild resentful cry that drove right to her center. She left him there long enough to bring Frank up from a good slumber, and when his eyes crept open, she said to him, "I think babies and nurses are in the same union."

"What's wrong with him?" Frank asked.

"Not sleepy," she replied. By this time Andrew was back in her arms, where he stayed for three hours. At six-fifteen he fell into a sound sleep. She had survived. When he awakened her at nine o'clock with his cry of hunger, Frank had already gone off to work. The two were alone, and the day was beginning again. She dozed with him throughout the morning and into the afternoon. She was feeding him at two when she noticed a sudden blossoming of red bumps, tiny pimples covering his forehead. Only one thought brought her up short. These had to be gone by the time the nurse returned. How could her incompetence be demonstrated more clearly. Then a more serious fear dawned: What if this rash leaves a scar? Then what? An imperfect baby, ruined by its own mother. The insanity had returned. Betsy knew none of this could really be true, that she could not be serious, but still her stomach churned. She gave the baby the second bath of the day. Then, while he slept, she read Doctor Spock on rashes and pimples, regaining some measure of composure. Nevertheless, it had been a hell of a twenty-four hours.

Betsy welcomed the nurse back with open arms. She handed Andrew over, had two glasses of white wine, and slept through the night. The process had become real to her, but she was dogged by her lack of competence. Here was this high-powered person, a successful investment banker and a well-trained model of organization, brought to her knees by a six-and-a-half-pound infant who was only awake five hours out of twenty-four. She just didn't understand it. Frank's work load had be-

come overwhelming, and she refused to ask him to help, except to listen to her, which he always did anyhow. He brought
dinner home, too. It was usually corned beef sandwiches, pale
imitations of New York deli, but anything was appreciated. In
the morning, when Frank left, Betsy took to making an enormous bowl of oatmeal for herself, with brown sugar and milk.
She had not had any taste for this combination since she was
nine. Now she craved it, and it didn't take long to figure out
why. Nine was a good age. There was certainly nothing wrong
with being nine.

On the fourth morning, Betsy got a grip on herself. She sat
down in the breakfast nook with her oatmeal and made lists
with paper and pencil. The lists would have made anyone
laugh. One read, simply: feeding, changing, bathing, cleaning
navel and circumcision. That was her baby list. There was a
house list: cooking, making bed, organizing laundry and cleaning. There was a personal hygiene list and a list of thank-you
notes to be written. Each list was modest, no more than three
or four items. All the lists together constituted what seemed
to be a relatively easy day. Betsy put approximate times beside
every item—when to do it, how long it would take to do it.
There seemed to be time to spare. Betsy washed the dishes
and checked on the nurse. She was supposed to lie down a lot,
so that her stitches would hold. The nurse was reading, Andrew sleeping soundly by her side. Betsy took the opportunity.
She was exhausted, seemingly from writing out lists.

As little as a week later, the first four days of Andrew
Scheflin's life had gone from being a crazed nightmare to a
pretty good cocktail-party story. Betsy recovered quickly. The
strange twists and turns taken by her inner resources became
milder as the days went on, and one day they were gone. This
happens to new mothers not always, but often. A combination
of hormone changes, exhaustion, and emotional overload
causes measurable alterations in behavior. For Betsy, the focus
of her bewilderment was not her baby, but the nurse.

Much has been said, pro and con, about baby nurses. They were once, in cheaper times, a common addition to any middle-class household, but this is no longer the case. Unlike our parents' generation, ours seems to have quite a bit of guilt about "servants," and many of us feel an obligation to make them part of the family, or, worse, to treat them as guests.

The theory is that the nurse will give the couple some peace and quiet during the tough days of recovery and adjustment. She will ease you into the chores of child-rearing, acting as a teacher, assistant, and emergency adviser. In practice, things can get much more complex. A nurse's presence may bring a sense of foreignness to the house, may make parents more formal with each other, more concerned about the appearance of things, and more distant from their newborn than they would like to be. To a great extent, your reaction to the nurse depends upon who you are. If you are used to having regular help—maids, laundresses, or housekeepers—in your home, you may have no trouble adapting to a nurse. But if the nurse is the first "servant" you have ever hired, there is a good chance you will have some difficulty adjusting to her presence.

That was Betsy's problem. She had *always* felt guilty about the help in her parents' house. Now her guilt had a new dimension. She felt that the nurse, who did all the "hard" work, was entitled to control the baby, and she felt that the baby somehow knew, subconsciously, that he was being ignored by his real mother. Neither of these ideas had any basis in fact. They were products of the way Betsy looked at the world, and that brings up an interesting point about this book.

We have tried to keep this book relatively free of direct advice. Do this. Don't do that. Each parent behaves according to his own beliefs, his own upbringing, and his own attitude toward things. The people we interviewed had relatively little in common, and what was right for one of them was always wrong for another. So when we report Betsy Scheflin's trouble with the nurse, we do not wish to imply that hiring a nurse is, or ever was, a mistake. It was a mistake for Betsy. For you, it might be the perfect solution to a problem. For Betsy, guilt

was a big issue. She was uncomfortable around hired help, and
she didn't like the idea that *anyone*, hired or not, was working
harder than she was. So when the nurse came and took over,
she fell apart. The lesson here is not that nurses are a bad
idea, but that hiring one is a very personal decision. It doesn't
seem like a personal decision because it's clothed in business
language: How much will it cost? What will be the hours?
Who will have what duties? But the personal question is really
the question with which to begin: Do I want another person
living in my house, taking care of my baby? What the woman
down the street, or your best friend, or your own mother did
about this issue is really not very important. You have to
decide what *you* want.

The first week is a hard week. You will almost certainly need
help, even if both parents are home all the time. It is important to decide which tasks you wish to delegate and which
ones you expect to reserve for yourself. You have three basic
choices here: You can hire a maid, who will cook and clean;
you can hire a nurse, who will care for the baby; or you can
get a family member to move in for a week (we'll discuss this
option more fully in chapter 10). In general, we have found
(remember: this does not necessarily mean you) that the
couples we talked to who had the least troublesome first weeks
were the couples who kept the baby care to themselves, who
had either a maid or a mother/mother-in-law handling the
housework and cooking. Several couples who felt they needed
privacy got up the courage to tell relatives *not to come* for
the first week so that they could work things out within the
family, before adding to the size of the household. In every
case, these people reported that they were glad they had done
so. Couples who had live-in help, either paid or volunteer,
reported mixed results, at best.

AT ONE MONTH

Isolation

THEY were smiling at Frank Scheflin down at the office. By three o'clock in the afternoon, he was glazed, his mind drifting at the slightest lapse in conversation. They were sympathetic. They brought him coffee hourly. The whole thing was a big joke. But Frank knew what they meant. Nothing remains a joke for long in the advertising business. Frank was only as good as his ability to think on his feet, his moment-to-moment inspiration, his innate sense of salesmanship. All three were flagging. At the time, Andrew Scheflin was three weeks old, and the nurse had been gone for a week.

Here was the schedule: Andrew had day and night reversed. He was up from shortly after midnight to two in the morning, then from four to seven, and from nine until noon. Frank and Betsy went to bed, too tired to kiss good night, at ten-thirty. At midnight, Betsy would get up with Andrew. At one o'clock, Frank would become aware of her absence, start to feel sorry for her, and wake himself up. He would be up for a half-hour, asking if there was anything he could do, wanting desperately to go back to bed. Betsy knew he needed his sleep. She would tell him so. He would lie awake until two, trying to put the whole situation out of his mind. At four, the process would begin again. Usually Betsy cried a little on the four-o'clock shift. Nothing serious, just tears of exhaustion and frustration. The tears kept Frank awake from four until just before six. At eight, he would drop some instant coffee on an already rebellious stomach and drive into Century City to begin the day. His co-workers found this hilarious, and Frank smiled a lot about it, but he knew it would not be long before they began to use it. It needed talking about at home, but every evening Frank would find the bedroom darkened upon his arrival and his exhausted wife and innocent son lost in sleep. Where Betsy worried about estrangement from her baby during the nurse's tenure, Frank began to worry about it now. He never saw Andrew on some days, except as a curled bundle in the bassinet, making an occasional gurgle. At night he heard him wail, but only saw a darkened shape in Betsy's arms being waltzed out of the bedroom and away so that he could enjoy the sleep that would not come. Most of the time he did not know what was going on in the house. Strangers were living there.

Betsy was the kind of person who liked to get up and get going. Shower, dress, and get out. This was an average schedule: getting up—she was never certain when she was getting up. If she got up at seven to give Andrew a bottle, she could not stay up for the day. She went back to sleep, vowing to get up for sure the next time he got up. That was, say, nine-thirty. At ten-fifteen, he would be finished with a bottle, have a new diaper on, maybe even have had a sponge bath. She would get into the shower, turning it on and off to hear if he was crying or not. By ten-forty, shivering but clean, she would start the blow dryer. Again, she had to flick it on and off every minute or so to listen for Andrew. Finally, clean and dry, but not yet dressed, she would now attack the dinner dishes from the night before. She could go no further without coffee, and this usually took her up to Andrew's next wakeful period. Propped up in his infant seat on the closet floor, he would watch her dress. He could not move or reach for anything, but the closet still made Betsy uncomfortable, with its plastic bags and wire hangers. She felt disaster lurking there, but it kept Andrew quiet to watch her. The final hairpin would be inserted at about ten past noon on an uneventful morning, and Betsy would be ready to start the day. The lateness of the hour burned her up. She made little trips to the supermarket, to the dry cleaner, and then home again. It became apparent how isolated she was in Los Angeles. She had no friends to see, no relatives to lean on.

At home, after errands, she would put Andrew down, and if by chance he should nap, she would doze by his side. If not, she would hold him, show him the mirror, the wallpaper, play him some music, anything until his eyelids would slowly drop and she could nestle him into the bassinet.

Her own sleep was fitful. As worried as Frank was about being apart from his son, he could not match Betsy's sense of guilt over having deserted her husband. She could see him in her dreams, pacing the upper stories of tall buildings, involved in things that made the world go round while she wallowed in an intellectual and cultural rot that had begun to stink up the whole house. Betsy didn't like it. Andrew (he was slowly becoming Andy) was doing just what they swore he would never do: he was driving a stake into their intimacy. There were not enough hours in the day to accommodate three people. There was no time to talk, which Betsy saw as a possible blessing in disguise; she saw herself rapidly becoming the most uninteresting woman in town.

It could not go on for long. Frank and Betsy had been married for five years. They knew each other well enough to know they were in trouble. The saving grace of their problem was that each felt terrible for the other. As alarmed as they were, they were not angry. Frustrated, distressed, but not angry, at least not at each other.

Betsy called a baby-sitting agency. She arranged a twelve-hour sitter for the coming Sunday. She had no ideas about making it a "Big Event," neither a celebration nor an emotional outpouring. It was just supposed to be a day off. It happened to be Andy's first-month birthday.

The couple slept until noon. Betsy had to get up and let the baby-sitter in at nine, but now she had been two weeks without help, and most of her guilt on that score had worn away. She slept gratefully, almost ravenously, sucking in enormous breaths of air in her unconsciousness. At one o'clock they were dressed, the day half gone, as usual. It was late autumn. They drove to the beach, and did all the things people in old movies do—played skeeball on the pier, walked along the shoreline alone in their sweaters. It was a dumb day, all paralyzingly foolish and romantic, and it should have been perfect, but they couldn't start talking, and seconds were ticking away. They tried drinking in a fishnet-decorated bar near Malibu, but they drank in silence. Both of them recognized the scene. It was a scene where you break up at the end, where the romance is over. Not what they intended at all. But it was a crucial scene, proving an important point: the romantic solutions had stopped working, possibly forever. Frank broke it with a toast.

"Let's just get a divorce and be done with it," he said.

The sun was down by the time they finished talking. They hadn't really said anything much. Each had tried to create a picture of the previous four weeks, autobiographically, as best as he or she could. Guilt and isolation were the main topics, but there weren't any great revelations. The greatest was that they'd never told each other anything, never dared to burden the other with all that mundane misery. Each knew about the other, of course. But it was in the physical telling, the actual act of communication that the relationship began to trickle back to them. It wasn't what they said, but simply that they talked.

There was something besides emotional isolation bothering them, too. There was physical isolation: sex. Never the main problem, but always there.

Betsy had stopped feeling comfortable enough to make love

about two weeks before the baby was born. That brought the total weeks of abstinence up to six. Nobody knows what that does to a relationship—sometimes nothing, sometimes a lot. It changes it at the core. Sex may not be what a relationship is all about, but it's generally one of the structural pillars. The Scheflins had been waiting for clearance from Betsy's doctor, but they were not above taking the law into their own hands.

At home, with Andrew asleep and the sitter gone, Betsy found herself unexhausted for the first time since delivery, and Frank knew it. He was tentative, extremely delicate at the beginning, alert to signs of pain, discomfort, mental unreadiness. But there was none of it. It sort of seemed like old times. Facing it later, it did not seem like one of the greatest sexual experiences of his life, but it really wasn't too bad. Betsy liked it, too. They weren't used to being unused to each other, and responses were a little off-time, almost stuttering. But it was sex, and there'd been conversation, and the isolation was banished, at least for a day. Their renewed unity made the problems seem comprehensible for the first time.

A week after the trip to the beach, Betsy was interviewed for this book. When asked how she was doing, she gave a strange response.

"Things are marvelous," she said. "Everything's completely different." She then proceeded to tell the story of the month that had gone by. The exhaustion, the loneliness, the break in communication, and even the little self-help session at the beach, which she considered a relatively minor breakthrough in a wall of problems still unsolved.

"How can you say things are marvelous?" we asked.

"I don't know," she said. "They just seem to be."

Marvelous may be something of an overstatement as a description of the Scheflins' life at the end of their first month as parents. But certain victories had been won. The several problems they faced during the month were really all the same problem: isolation. It came about for two distinctly different reasons, explained below.

HUSBANDS WORKING

Most husbands have jobs. Frank was an extreme case—a highly competitive man in a tough business world. But at some level, most new fathers go through the same tangle as Frank. If you work, and you have responsibilities to your career, those responsibilities do not change because of fatherhood. Artist, lawyer, factory worker, you still have to perform. People depend upon your performance and so does your success. Naturally, there's a conflict. A new mother is overwhelmed with work, menial labor she may not be up to, as well as emotional taxation of a high order. As a working father, you may have no way of physically lightening her load. However, you serve no one by staying awake worrying about the situation. That doesn't mean you won't do it, but remember—it doesn't help. Frank Scheflin took the worst possible exit here: he let his guilt isolate him, cutting off any emotional communication. Not only was he not helping, he was unavailable as a sympathetic ear—he was afraid of finding out just how bad things were. Men, at least most of the men we've talked to, come painfully close to fitting the stereotype that has come to represent them. They shy away from the emotional side of things. The first month of parenting is a highly emotional time, and men could stand to get a little wetter than most of them care to. We doubt that this statement will revolutionize the situation, but there it is. We cannot teach you how to become emotionally involved, but we can offer this warning: the new father with a heavy career responsibility is a man with a dilemma on his hands. He who crawls into a cocoon to wait for the hard times to be over does so at his own peril.

BEING ALONE

Betsy Scheflin was alone in a serious way. She had given up a job to become a mother, she was new in town, she knew no one, her parents were 3,000 miles away, and her husband was

gone all day. Other women may have more fortuitous circumstances surrounding the birth of a first child, but chances are
they will feel alone a good deal of the time. Stuck in the
house with an infant, no energy, and a television for a companion, life can begin to seem quite an unlikely proposition.
If your friends are remaining active and are without children,
you may find yourself envious as well as lonely. Babies under
a month old are almost totally unresponsive. They eat and
sleep and cry, and give back nothing. It takes faith and endurance to wait for the first smile. It's harder if you're doing it
without companionship.

Betsy found this out and made a crucial mistake. She responded with silence. Never confiding in Frank for fear it
would burden his already overworked mind, she whispered
herself into a solid depression. There was nothing she could
do to change her day-to-day routine. She was drained of energy,
and she didn't want to be away from her baby, but she needed
to talk to someone. She wouldn't talk to Frank, and he didn't
want to know. He made himself busy and hated himself for
doing it.

Mates are made to lean on. In any relationship, the test
comes at the stress points. Having a baby qualifies as one of
the rare, exclusive, all-time high stress points in any marriage.
It is the wrong time to get shy with your mate, to try to
second-guess what he or she needs. Isolation between two
people only takes place when they stop talking, or stop listening. Lack of communication has become one of the clichés of
our psychology-soaked era, but nowhere is it a more crucial
problem than at the beginning of parenthood. At the moment
your baby is born, your relationship is tossed into midair. Two
becomes three, and chaos will surely reign unless a committee
is formed to confront the new shape of the relationship.

Our world moves too quickly. We are dependent upon the
social system working efficiently, and we live by the business
ethic of competition. In older societies, in simpler times, the
birth of a baby could be greeted with a shift in familial activity.
Father's work could be suspended, and the surrounding family

could become involved. Sadly, we cannot afford these simple virtues of a slower age. In most cases, father must work, and grandparents may be a long way away. A mother must be alone, with her newborn for company, and no encouraging view of the future. This is unfortunate, for the future may be quite lovely, and the grim first month, which seems to be an eternity, is, in retrospect, shockingly brief.

AT THREE MONTHS

Private Warfare—Irrational Action and Its Causes

At three months old, Andy Scheflin was all right. You knew when he was going to sleep, when he was going to wake up, and why he did what he did. He cried only in the bath or when he was hungry. He was settled and happy. Things were supposed to go back to normal. The reason they didn't was Betsy and her view of motherhood.

"About half the time I feel it's inspiring and really something worth doing," she explained. "Of course, the other half of the time I feel like a moron."

There was more to it than that. There was a trip to New York. They went back to the city for Christmas vacation and for meetings with an East Coast client of Frank's. It was a trip Betsy looked forward to as if simply touching Manhattan's concrete might change her life. Frank spurred on her anticipation. He wanted this for her, and until they left, it gave them common grounds for pleasant conversation.

It was a dream trip. Betsy's family, always close, wanted to take the baby from her, pass him around, feed him, change him, even get him up at dawn. Betsy gave in willingly the first two mornings. Saturday and Sunday she and Frank walked up Madison Avenue from Fifty-first to Eighty-sixth streets. It was twenty-eight degrees. They were dressed in clothes that each set of parents had kept in back closets. They crossed to Fifth Avenue to pick up some toys at F.A.O. Schwartz, and then back to Bloomingdale's on Lexington for a wool tie. The city was sharp-edged and clear. Throngs of Christmas shoppers made things pleasantly impossible.

To Betsy, it was a romance with the city reborn. The food tasted better. The traffic was livelier, more aggressive. She looked out the window and felt the inner core of sleepiness that was always with her in Los Angeles finally being wrung out. A fire engine, siren wailing, took a hard hop over a loose manhole cover and sent it spinning on Seventy-second Street at 3:00 A.M. In bed, Betsy smiled. No one understood New York.

Her eyes popped open at seven-forty on Monday morning. Time to go to work. Although Betsy hadn't had her job in almost seven months, the routine returned, and for a bleary moment before she sat up in bed, she really did think she had to get to the bank.

She wanted to go. She bundled Andrew into his Christmas snowsuit, pulled a wool hat down over his ears, and took him on a steamy subway to Wall Street. At rush hour people seem to bubble up out of the World Trade Center station and pour down the streets like first oil from a Texas gusher. Betsy was thrust up and out, around the corner, and in through the heavy glass doors of the Bradford Trust Company. There was, of course, another girl at her desk in her office, a Wellesley girl, two years her junior, somewhat taken aback to have a three-month-old in her office. The place was busy, even at nine-fifteen.

But her friends were there, and she caused quite a stir. Andrew went from hand to hand, with a tentative look of fear on his face, but no crying. He got points for blue eyes, for

his uncompromising baldness, and for his contented temperament, but Betsy didn't care how they appraised the baby. It
was her own image she was worried about. Among the career
women, she seemed to rate a mixed reception. And as she
spoke, she felt the magnitude of her own dullness with every
word that emerged from her mouth. He sleeps through the
night. He never cries. I'm tired a lot of the time. It's harder
than I ever dreamed, but more rewarding, too. Real conversation stoppers. She felt under the gun and depressed. A group
of women in their twenties, her friends of last year, were looking her over like a Hereford cow, each seemingly wondering:
Is this what I want to turn into? Is this a possible life? Everyone was far too curious.

Betsy wanted to spend the day at the bank, to look over the
last quarter financial reports, to check out the new computer
system. But would it be an admission that motherhood wasn't
enough? That she had gone the wrong road? To hell with it.
Andrew dozed in his stroller throughout the morning, nodding
contentedly at a filing cabinet from time to time, and Betsy
played the career girl.

They all went out to lunch. Afterwards Betsy wanted to go
back in the worst way, but it made no sense. She had nothing
to do there, and these people were busy. They all kissed good-
bye at the subway, and Andrew made his last go-round from
one to another. He was a smash hit. Betsy felt awful.

She was something of a masochist; she took the subway up
Broadway to Zabar's. This teeming shoebox of a foodstore is
a New Yorker's claim to native culture. Thousands of cheeses,
slabs of pastrami, corned beef, and Nova Scotia salmon, burlap
bags of coffee beans from around the world—to Betsy, Zabar's
smelled like God's stewpot. Crowds surrounded her. Total
strangers squealed with delight at bewildered Andy in his
stroller. Betsy didn't know why she had gone to Zabar's until
she got there. Perhaps, it was just for old time's sake, or to
torture herself, or to bring her parents a gift. She just wanted
to see the place again. But once there, she understood the
possibilities. She could take the stuff back to the coast. She
could borrow an overnight bag from her parents and bring

part of Zabar's back to let everyone taste. She began picking things out for everyone she knew: bagels, Nova, deep-brown Kona coffee beans, small copper bowls that were on sale. She was loaded down with bags and wax-paper packages and on her way to the cashier when she changed her mind; she wasn't going to give it away. She was going to keep all of it herself. Betsy spent $126.55 at Zabar's.

Frank thought it was fine. Funny, even inspirational. Betsy sulked. She wanted him angry, exasperated at her childishness, but nothing of the sort occurred to him. He was a little miffed about the extra baggage, and that was all. The trip had gone well for him, too.

Betsy's overnight bag stunk up the plane, and the stewardesses made jokes. Andy's ears hurt, and Frank was very good, walking him around, feeding him, trying to let Betsy rest. But Betsy couldn't rest. There was a knot in her stomach and her jaw was set. She was steaming. She had two martinis and a split of champagne all to herself, and by the time the baggage had come off the carousel, heartburn and a decent headache had set in for the night. It was after eleven when they got home through a spattering Los Angeles rain.

Into that pale, temporarily furnished house—Betsy couldn't believe they were there. She stared at the bleak view of the soaking city through the bedroom and fished through an open suitcase for a nightgown. Andy was not quite asleep in the next room. It had been six unacknowledged hours since she had spoken to her husband.

"I hate this," she said.

Frank looked at her as if it was news; she let him have it.

"You dragged me out here, I'm uprooted, no job, no friends, I never see you from day to day. There's no one I can leave the baby with, no family, I hate this house! I hate this life!"

Frank burned slowly.

"We spent so much time," he said, "thinking this through. We talked about it. We agreed. This was what we wanted."

"Well, it isn't fair," Betsy said. "I didn't know what it was when I agreed. I never knew. I want to go back. I hate this."

Frank stared at her, and, finally, his eyes were alive. He said nothing. He turned away. All his muscles tensed. With a fierce kick he sent his foot through the bedroom wall, shattering Sheetrock and stucco. Chunks of wallboard cascaded onto his ankle, others hung by paint alone. There was a gaping, foot-wide hole where he had attacked. Betsy looked down at the damage with satisfaction.

"Goddamn California house," she said. "Goddamn California walls."

There comes a moment when private war is declared, and until there is a cease-fire, all is lost. By private war we mean simply this: your possibly irrelevant anger, frustration, and unhappiness finally focus on a target, and you attack. All the preparation, the refinement, and the training for Betsy's attack went on inside her own head. Her husband, the unsuspecting target, witnessed none of the logical shifts or emotional steeple-chasing that led to the outburst. He *was* insensitive to the situation, and not especially sympathetic, but, in a sense, he was right and Betsy was wrong. What Betsy was really suf-fering from was not the specifics of a move to California, or a lack of friends, or even the loss of a career. She was vic-timized by something more general and more important: she had a baby without any idea of what she was in for. All Betsy's decisions were, in some sense, make-believe decisions. She had this terrific marriage to this terrific guy and a great job; every-thing seemed possible, even California and motherhood. Betsy's decisions were easy decisions. One of them was this: the baby would not control her life. They were unilateral decisions that did not take into account the unpredictable, or even the realis-tic. They were not, in other words, decisions of deep maturity. But it is only fair, after all, that when we bear children, we must stop *being* children. Frank and Betsy, for all their sophis-tication and their ambition, were really a husband and wife team playing Peter Pan. Betsy didn't want to grow up. When she found herself without any choice, she resorted to private warfare. And that's the poison of private warfare: it isn't properly or even logically directed. It's just a public explosion of private frustration. Usually it's aimed at the nearest target—usually a mate.

For Frank, this was all a mystery. He had vanished into his career as a means of certifying his own maturity. The responsibility of his position and the high degree of competitiveness seemed to offer a bona fide entrée into the real world. Frank found all aspects of his profession stimulating, which irked Betsy, who missed her own career. But she had known that *before* Andy was born, and before was probably the time when all these things needed to be dealt with. The source of the problem, the lack of decent psychological readiness, was visible from the beginning. Looking back, one could sight the inability of either mate to become involved in childbirth preparation even though they tried. The unfurnished nursery was a superstition with a history, but why had they embraced it? Frank and Betsy Scheflin spent the final weeks of pregnancy running in every direction to avoid the responsibility they had undertaken. When Andy was born they could run no more, and that's when the trouble started. Up until Andy, their marriage had been a series of choices, and lucky choices at that. Life had been easy, and there was nothing bad that couldn't be changed. But baby is the first item in a marriage that is guaranteed real and permanent. Babies require sacrifices (nasty word these days), and no amount of willful or positive thinking can alter this. You cannot have it your way—unlike the famous hamburger—at least not all the time. That may be a tough piece of news for the ME generation to swallow, but, as of this writing, it is unalterable.

AT SIX MONTHS

Careers and Guilt

FRANK SCHEFLIN was a man with a problem. As he saw it, his wife was having a very hard time adjusting to motherhood. He didn't really include himself in any of her frustrations. Even though she had directed her anger at him, and even though he had become angry enough at her to kick a hole in the wall, Frank didn't see himself at the center of the conflict. The problem of the hole in the wall was solved quickly: by the time it had been kicked, the Scheflins were on the verge of moving into a house they had purchased. The hole was left behind with the wretched house that Betsy hated so much. Frank thought this would help. He recognized his wife's uprootedness, that she had been torn from the physical surroundings she loved and separated from the career-oriented life that had satisfied her, but these were her decisions. She wanted a baby. She wanted success, wealth, and comfort. Frank even recognized that Betsy had a right to change her mind, to suddenly not want all these things. But she *hadn't* changed her mind. She liked the money and the success, and she certainly loved Andy. Mother and son were inseparable. So if Betsy couldn't live with the things she wanted, Frank didn't see that there was anything he could do about it.

Nonetheless, something had to be done. Frank was in the awkward position of finding his cool head, his unemotional approach to things, more of an annoyance to Betsy than a comfort. He could lay out the possibilities on a piece of paper —what Betsy could or couldn't do to change things. He saw the organization of life plainly. He was willing to talk. This was one of the things that made Frank such a good business-man. He could eliminate the irrelevant, emotional, fogged-in issues and cut to the chase. And he always said what he meant. Betsy's general sense of panic became all-pervasive, but Frank dismissed about 60 percent of her worries as mere hysteria. He had a talent for taking each day as it came, for approach-ing each problem individually, without regard for the pos-sibility that it was carrying a chain of related disasters behind it. He felt he could help Betsy solve any particular puzzle that troubled her, but as to the mystery of her life, he refused to acknowledge its existence. The idea that contradictory emo-tions could coexist, making simple solutions impossible, was useless for him to contemplate. He would tackle whatever came first into the line of vision, and, at the moment, it seemed that Betsy needed work—out-of-the-house, salaried, responsi-ble work.

Betsy suggested it shyly. To her it meant one very bad thing: motherhood was not fulfilling her in the way it was supposed to. Guilt again. She really wanted to do something else. The ambivalence made her angry.

"The women's movement really screwed me up," she said, "and I subscribe to it. I bought into it, and now I feel quilty every time I wash a dish or change a diaper. It's bad enough you have to *do* those things, you shouldn't have to feel *guilty* about them. I find myself going to parties, and when someone asks me what I do, I feel like I have to apologize for only being a mother. That's what girls are learning now—that being a mother is a subsidiary thing; it's an obligation, and you should get other people to do as much of it as possible for you. Because you have *more important* things to do. Well, that's how I feel part of the time, and it's an awful thing to feel because, inside myself, I know nothing's more important, and nothing ought to be."

Nonetheless, she was stuck with herself; so she took a job. Three days a week she paid someone to watch Andy, while she drove to an office and plunged herself into the financial management world. It was terrifying. Her impulse on the first day was to call home every fifteen minutes—thirty-two times in an eight-hour day. But she was new and wanted to make a good impression on her supervisors; so, instead, she didn't call at all and just went mad inside. Andy didn't seem to notice. He passed a placid day in his playpen, smiled wanly at his mother when she arrived home as if she had been gone ten minutes. Betsy heaved a high of relief and had two gin-and-tonics before dinner. Maybe this was a possible way out.

She hoped that Andy's contentment with the maid would teach her a lesson, that she'd be able to work now, free of anxiety. But even after a week of peace and quiet she was torn. She wasn't worried about Andy anymore. It was herself causing the trouble, as usual. She wanted to plunge into motherhood head-first, to throw all the anti-mother prejudice to the dogs. Mother triumphant—that was her goal. It wasn't working out. It would never work out. With hindsight, she began to see the cracks in the plaster. Where she had glutted herself on the literature and gossip of high finance, mother and baby stuff always seemed semiintelligent and suburban-dull. She could not bring herself to deal with it. Then there was the inability to get ready toward the end of her pregnancy. At the time she used philosophical arguments to defend her inactivity. But the reality might have been that she simply wasn't interested. The pattern began to crystalize—a sort of backsliding dishonesty with herself.

The job was a compromise, but then, everything was turning into a compromise. Three days a week she was a career woman, three days a week she stayed home. The seventh day was set aside—Frank marked it in his book—as a day for the couple. Trips were planned. Everything was organized: external solutions for internal problems.

The new house became important for Betsy. Having never been an intrinsic materialist, furnishings and style should not have mattered to her, but Betsy was re-creating herself, and everything counted. If she was going to be a mother in Southern California, instead of a banker in New York City, she was at least going to make this West Coast person in her own image.

The results were mixed. Betsy now felt guilty about absolutely everything, but less guilty about each thing. When she worked, she worried about Andy and about her inability to love full-time mothering. When she was at home, she questioned whether anyone could make anything of a three-day-a-week business career. She felt terrible that she was so poor a wife and lover that her appointments with her mate had to be penciled into a datebook like visits to the dentist. She even felt guilty about the house—about the care she lavished on her daydreams of furniture and fine art. But a certain amusement had set into the circle of guilt.

"You have to understand who I am," she said in an interview. "I'm a person who, when I was in New York, if I wasn't working, I couldn't get in a bus at ten o'clock on a weekday morning 'cause I was afraid I'd meet someone I knew, and they'd know I wasn't working. That's just me."

She did not wake up one morning and discover the pain was gone. Her solutions were small measures, each designed to chip away at the problem a little at a time. For a while nothing happened at all. Frank continued to lead his busy life, saving a half-hour in the morning, another at night, for the baby. Both parents lived with the rigor of a schedule for several weeks. They knew where they were supposed to be and when. Andy's six-month birthday passed smoothly, and the house began to look like something. The maid fell in love with the baby.

It was spring, and Betsy remembered the beach where she and Frank had their first summit meeting. Los Angeles's beach is empty on weekdays. Going to the beach on a weekday was for bums, the unemployed, and, Betsy reasoned, new mothers. Betsy thought she'd be brave. On a Tuesday, when even the parking lot attendant doesn't show up, Betsy took Andy to the beach, and they played. It wasn't easy. There was an unambitious crowd on the beach, except for the joggers. But Betsy sat with Andy and watched the waves going in and out, washing the sand back and forth, and she honestly felt relaxed. Not forever, God knows. Probably not even for the rest of the day. But according to her calender she was supposed to be at the beach. There was no work until Wednesday. They were going out to dinner. The shopping was done. She had scheduled relaxation for this morning. It wasn't easy, but Betsy got a tan.

Our society is structured for the overachiever. The American myth is the story of the inexhaustible toiler, the man who single-handedly builds a stairway to paradise. Competition in everything from lower-school soccer to high finance is revered in this country. We're not saying there's necessarily anything wrong with this view of life, but it does present certain problems. It's hard to become head of General Motors by working three days a week and bringing up a six-month-old baby at the same time. You may win the admiration of your friends and the amazement of your parents, but you simply won't be able to compete with the people who are working seventy hours a week. For highly charged career women, there is no comfortable solution to the job/baby dilemma.

Betsy took the obvious route: three days of job and three days of mothering. It is, to paraphrase Winston Churchill, the worst solution except for all the alternatives. It was, of course, worse for Betsy than for many less motivated women who simply want to be out of the house for a few days a week, to be challenged in some way, to be with adults, and to earn a little pocket money. But it's not the perfect solution for anyone, because women who want to work are made to feel guilty about leaving the task they were supposedly born for: mothering. And as more and more women work, women who stay home begin to feel guilty for not having a job. In short, traditional views of society, contrasted with the early view expressed by the women's movement, have created a Catch-22 that tightens like a vice around many new mothers. No matter what they choose to do, a little voice chirps into their ears that it is the wrong decision.

To put it bluntly, this little voice deserves nothing less than execution by firing squad, and the sooner the better. Life is tough enough on new mothers without asking them to face the vagaries of society's changing philosophy. We don't know exactly what to do to help shoot down this malicious voice, but perhaps two facts will be relevant in reducing your guilt. The first is that no evidence exists to suggest working mothers are harming their children by being out of the house. Babies need love, affection, and roots, but almost anyone can change their diapers and put them to sleep. Many women report that partial freedom from their babies drastically improved the time spent with them because the frustrations of the mindless hours were gone.

The second fact is that no one we interviewed was satisfied by being a full-time mother. Some took part-time jobs, some found regular recreation, some went back to school, some did nothing and just remained frustrated, *but not one mother really lived out what Betsy had dreamed*—that being a mother would satisfy everything.

So the problem exists across the board for all types of mothers, and as women advance, it becomes more acute. Not many years ago, Betsy would have been considered a highly unusual woman for wanting a full-time career. But the job market continues to widen for women. They can be as competitive, as striving, and as efficient as their male counterparts have always been. They can own as much of a piece of the American myth as anyone, but if they are mothers, they suffer for it as no man has ever suffered. Many of them want to work, not specifically for the money (although they use and enjoy it), but because they like to work. It means something to them that mothering does not. This is a modern dilemma. We have no tradition on which to rest. We don't know how to cope with the problem because our parents never coped with it, at least not in any number. There is a reason so many societies have kept their women uneducated and incapable. We are learning the price of having a free and educated female among us. Sadly, the price is highest for women.

The decision that Betsy should get a job was really Frank's idea. Far be it for us to suggest that the man did all the thinking in this relationship. It simply happened that Betsy was not thinking too clearly about anything after the hole-in-the-wall incident, and Frank, once he had cooled off, had to think for both of them. This is something important that both mates must understand about the early months of parenting. There often comes a time when one mate is just not functioning. Frequently it is the mother, because it is she whose life has been utterly disrupted. One mate's vigilance over the other's emotional state can be crucial at times like these. Vigilance was not one of Frank Scheflin's strengths. He let things slide until they could slide no further. It might have taken extraordinary perception to see Betsy's career/motherhood dilemma coming as early as the final weeks of her pregnancy, but an ordinary citizen on the lookout could have begun to see it as early as the third month after Andy's birth. Frank waited and waited. He retired to the office, hoping things would change, and he protested that it wasn't his problem. Quite obviously, it was his problem. Ultimately, he had to solve it.

One of the reasons that husbands tend to stay out of the line of fire when their wives begin to lose confidence is that they are busy and they don't want to admit that it is happening. They hope that if they hide, it will stop. A more important reason is their own guilt.

The average husband, working a forty-hour week (Frank

worked much longer, and this doesn't really apply to him),
must finally face the fact that—for a few months at least—
his wife is working longer, more inconvenient hours than he.
She is getting up several times at night, and again at daybreak.
Her exhaustion is evidence of the extent to which she seems
to be doing more than her share. Facing this situation is not
something husbands like to do if for no other reason than they
do not wish to be asked to contribute. They feel guilty about
not doing more, and they feel guilty about *not wanting* to
do more.

In some cases, wives turn on their husbands for the relative
ease of the working man's life. In a surprising number of cases,
this hits home with men. Men (at least the ones we talked to)
do seem to think they are getting off easily. We disagree. It *is*
true that mothers work a longer, less rewarding day than
fathers. But they do not have to suffer the pressure put upon
a man who must prosper in a tough business world, and who
must provide for the family by the success of his work. There
is no accurate way of measuring the relative hardness or easi-
ness of the lives of mothers and fathers. But we would guess,
pitting the pressure of the career against the endurance of
motherhood, parents tend to battle it out to an even draw.
In the average marriage, there is no reason for the amount of
guilt that is felt by both mates. It's a fruitless emotion on both
sides, and, in whatever way we can, we urge you to be rid of it.

AT NINE MONTHS

The Parents Take a Vacation

THE SCHEFLINS rented a cabin in the mountains. They made sure it had no phone. Andy was nine months old, and they left him at home. It was something they discussed for weeks before getting up the courage. They had taken one brief trip with him, at six months. Sharing a weekend in Yosemite with two childless couples was a trying experience; the comparisons were constantly flying up in their faces. Their well-rested, well-cared-for friends looked on with amusement as their room turned into a mountain of torn paper, broken toys, and wet diaperettes. Dinners were a catastrophe, and no amount of apology could assuage their embarrassment in restaurants where every condiment eventually found its way to the carpet. This time they were going alone.

They had five days of free time, and the mountains seemed like the place. They were hikers, fair trout fishermen, and they had no interest in lying on the beach at a Mexican resort. In addition, the mountains were close; they could get back in case of an emergency.

They didn't sleep the night before. Betsy kept creeping into the nursery to offer silent apologies to Andy, sleeping so innocently, who was about to be abandoned by his parents. There weren't even any in-laws to leave him with. The maid had agreed to live in for a week. There was no phone in the cabin because Betsy knew if there was one, she would be calling home eight times a day. There was a phone in the camp office, and each evening, when she was reasonably sure Andy would be asleep, she called and got a progress report. During the rest of the day, they were alone with each other outdoors, and several things became clearer with each passing hour. Frank had let nothing escape him about his son. Betsy was surprised to discover that all the little things she had made note of, all the progressions and developments she assumed Frank had never seen, were stored in his head, never mentioned. He was a sharp, but nonverbal observer. Now, with business off his mind, he was free to talk and reminisce about the areas of his son's development that Betsy thought had passed him by. He had theories about everything, from Andy's occasional midnight risings to his infant sense of humor. Frank was terrifically proud of this baby he had fathered, and proud of Betsy's success with him. More than once a day his attention would drift as they sat at water's edge, and he would think about where Andy was, what he would be doing. He never thought about these things at work.

Another shocking discovery made on the trip was that their sex life was terrible. They had considered it normalized, successful, and satisfying until they spent two days without Andy. For eight months they had been hopping in and out of bed like a couple of high school kids in a cloakroom. They were desperate to get sex out of the way before Andy either woke up, got hungry, or fell down. But with no place to go afterwards and no special time to get up in the morning, they behaved exactly the same way.

"Wait a minute," Frank said in the middle of a typical speed session, "we can keep doing this. We don't have to stop."

It took practice to break the habit. What had their sex life consisted of before?

"Suddenly it came to me," Frank recalled. "Foreplay. Fondling. All the things you read about before you're old enough to do any of them. We had gotten to the other side of the coin. We'd forgotten about them."

They did their best to remember.

They missed Andy constantly. The trip was fraught with guilty moments, but each night's phone call brought the same report: Andy didn't seem to notice they were gone. He was chortling the day through. He'd destroyed two plants and eaten a blue balloon, which turned up the next morning in his diaper. He was having the time of his life, as always.

There was nothing else to do but get into the rhythm of being a couple again, slower, smoother, with less adrenaline waiting to flow in case of emergency. By the end of the third day, they were reconciled, and mature. They recognized that things would never be this way for more than a few days at a time. They knew that the return home would be a return to the old pace, that there was no way to assimilate their current leisure into life with a baby. That was the lesson of nine months. They would simply have to make separate time for themselves, regular intervals of absence from their child, and, later, their children. Betsy had already begun to think about having another baby. Andy was no longer an extension of her; he was very much an independent character. And, despite all the memories of exhaustion, the guilt, the tears, and anger, Betsy missed the earlier stage when the baby was all hers, helpless, and dependent. She was aware that the trouble was not gone. Until now, she had been playing four separate roles, that of woman, mother, lover, and worker; and she could not bring those four into a unity that pleased her. Now, after nine months of parenting, she no longer felt that motherhood was dragging her along by the heels, or that the career was trumpeting its demand in her ear. She found she could be all four and still be a slightly schizophrenic self; she emerged a four-sided woman instead of four separate women. It was a small victory, but one to be celebrated. She constructed a theory of symmetry: nine months to create a baby, nine months to create a mother, and nine more for the adjustment to settle so that another baby might be created. She had made it through the first two periods.

Much has been written and said in favor of new parents getting away from their children, but parents seem frightened of the prospect. We cannot urge strongly enough that you make such an opportunity for yourself. A short trip accomplishes so many different things that its value is almost unlimited.

1). *It reunites the couple.* There is no way to overstress the importance of this. The dilemma of the first year is how to remain a couple while becoming a trio. After a few months of being three, it is important to get back to two, to isolate the relationship as it used to be, and to measure the changes. When children are grown and gone, you will, once again, be a couple. You are, first and foremost, a couple. The crucial, enduring number is two. Although this book does not cover anything beyond the first year of parenting, we would venture to say that couples should always, throughout the years of marriage, and whatever the obstacles, make time for themselves as a pair. If the marital relationship is ignored, it is sure to run down. It won't preserve itself without the attention of both partners. Invest in the couple and its strength will pay off all down the line.

2.) *It makes clear how independent your baby can be.* Most couples, especially mothers, imagine that their children are entirely unable to function without them. The truth (and it's healthy, if a little sad) is that children are resilient and will rarely miss you at this age. A familiar face—either grandparent, regular sitter, or even a maid—can provide affection, physical nurturing, and stimulation as successfully as a parent, at least for a limited time. Your ego may suffer with this knowledge, but your sense of security should be greatly increased, and a trip is worth it for that alone. Children, it should be remembered, are able to grow up despite enormous physical hardship, emotional trauma, tragedy, and terror. A one-week vacation from parents doesn't qualify as any of the above.

3.) *You can begin to set a pattern of privacy from your child.* To some extent, a child's habits are in your hands when he or she is small. You can exercise control. As the years go by, it will be a lot easier for you if your child is used to having you away for short periods of time. Babies do not see options. They accept the world as it is presented to them as if it were the only possibility. If you fit periods of absence into their world early on, they will come to see it as the natural order of things. They will also know to expect your return.

We do not wish to overstate the case in point. As children get older and become more aware, they will rebel more and more readily against your need for privacy. Probably no amount of early coming and going can prevent this, but it helps. It establishes a precedent and things can be much easier if your child never remembers a period when his claim on your time was 100 percent.

For the same reason, we advocate introducing a child into the mainstream of things early—taking him out, passing him from person to person, letting him get acquainted with constantly changing surroundings. He or she will become a good traveler, a painless companion, and less shy around strangers— all good qualities. But the major comfort will be yours. Knowing that you have the freedom to move about, to impose strange or different circumstances on your child without undue worry, eases your own ability to leave home and attend to your couple relationship when you need to, which you certainly will.

When the couple relationship comes into focus after nine months, it is a different relationship than it was before the baby's birth. There is, on the part of some couples, a futile effort to put things back the way they were. This is self-deluding, and the temporary euphoria of being two again can result in a crash landing at the end of such an experi-

ment. The trip away from the baby should be more for discovery than for re-creation. Having a baby is probably the
single most startling blow your relationship will ever suffer.
The marriage may not be weaker, but it will certainly be
different. There will be shifts in the strengths and weaknesses
of each mate. You will be pulling different weight than you
have been pulling in the past; your responsibilities will have
changed. Your relative levels of self-respect and respect for
your mate may also have changed. You may see the relationship in a different light than you have ever seen it before, and
your mate may be looking at it in yet a third light. A trip
away from your child, where there will be quiet and isolation,
is as good a place as any to find out what is going on. Sometimes the revelations can be quite unexpected. It's fair to guess
that after nine months of parenting you will be as distant in
communication as you have ever been in your marriage. You
will have been just too busy. The advice in this book remains
constant: talk and listen—especially listen.

AT ONE YEAR

New Fathering—Waiting for Interest to Awaken

THINGS slowed down. How to explain the organic, gradual reorganization that brings acceptance? Over the years, a tree that is butted up against a fence rail will allow its trunk to grow up around both sides of the rail. Eventually the rail will appear to have been driven through the center of the trunk and come out the other side like a branch. The tree incorporates it. In successful families, the same thing happens with children, and in many of them, the initial butting of fence rail to tree is not especially comfortable. In the early months, Frank and Betsy Scheflin acted on an untenable impulse: they tried to put things back the way they had been. But Andy was forever. There was no going back. There was also no idea of how to go forward, to reorganize. The organizational work was slow and not at all certain, but it got done and the Scheflins settled down.

Betsy remained a four-faceted woman, but she felt the facets beginning to meld. At least her four personalities recognized each other. Some days they battled. More often, they worked together without complaint. Frank found himself making jokes

about his new concerns—world peace, the meaning of existence, the future of mankind—but his concerns weren't jokes.
They were an embarrassed acknowledgment of what Andy had
done to him. Before Andy, nothing had mattered so much.
Frank's family needed the kind of attention he had never
before given to human beings, not to his wife or to his own
parents. For the first time, life was very serious. It had begun
quite innocently. Frank called from work one night at ten
past eight.

"How's Andy?" he asked.

"He's gone to bed," Betsy said.

Frank seemed fretful at the news. Betsy assumed he was
bringing home a toy or some piece of clothing for Andy.
It didn't sound like something Frank would do, but how else
could she explain it?

Frank arrived empty-handed. He mixed himself a Scotch
and water, and went into the nursery. Betsy, sitting in the
living room, began to think: she could see the pattern
emerging. Frank had been gradually spending more time with
Andy, trying to teach him elementary things, helping him
stand up against the side of the playpen, imitating him,
laughing at and with him. The change had been so gradual
she hadn't noticed it. Frank was much more involved with
Andy than she imagined. She hadn't been paying attention.

After a quarter of an hour, when Frank did not reappear,
she became curious. Silently, she let herself into the nursery and
saw Frank, drink in hand, staring fixedly into the crib. She
looked down. Andy was on his stomach, curled into a fetal
position with his backside flung high in the air. In this crouch
he was sleeping peacefully, little breath sounding in regular
rhythm.

"Dinner," Betsy whispered to Frank after awhile.

Frank gestured at Andy. "Let's wake him up and play with
him," he said.

They celebrated the birthday party alone. Even though
Andy had no friends, it was still a good evening. They had

come through. It was their celebration more than Andy's, but he fell forward facedown into the cake and came up delighted. Everyone was happy.

Several days later a letter arrived. It was from an old boyfriend of Betsy's, the man who had introduced her to Frank. He was living in New York, married, and his wife was pregnant. He had heard about Betsy and Frank's baby, and he wanted to know what the whole thing was like. Betsy was touched that he asked, but she didn't know how far to go.

"When I started telling everybody what I thought labor was like," she explained, "they were all scared to death. In retrospect, labor seems easy." Nonetheless, she felt she would have benefited from some realistic analysis of the situation, so she decided to be honest. She sat down to cover the year, but the dirt and disappointment just weren't in her heart anymore. She covered the trip back East, the flight, the resolution, all in perfunctory, helpful prose. Then she wrote this:

> Here is how it is now. I was walking Andy in the stroller, and while we waited for the light to change, he began to scream, not upset, just excited. And I couldn't figure out what was going on. There was nothing happening to excite him. Finally, I realized he was looking up, I thought at me, but he was looking up in the sky. There was a flock of birds flying in a circle overhead and Andy was going crazy. He had discovered birds. That's how it is. I think having a baby is your only chance to discover things again. When you *are* a baby, you discover everything, but you're too young, and later on you don't remember any of it. To me, birds are just birds. But when Andy discovered birds, it was like *I* had never seen birds before, never seen them that way, or never knew what I was seeing. I understood what it was to discover them. That's why, despite my better judgment, and everything that's happened, and all the garbage and exhaustion, I feel like mothering is the most gratifying thing I've ever done.

Betsy couldn't believe she had written it. It didn't sound like her; it was incessantly corny in a way she should have found nauseating. But she had really lived through it, and she didn't know how else to explain that it was worth it. Without the birds, being a mother would just be the awful slave-work she'd always heard it was, and that, in her bleaker moments, she'd found it to be.

Frank made a joke about the letter which didn't help. He wanted to use it as copy for a natural shampoo campaign that was giving him trouble. But Betsy was above criticism on this issue.

"Everyone needs to know how hard it is," she said. "But they also have to be told why anyone bothers."

Betsy Scheflin's recollections of her first year as a mother are full of unresolvable contradictions. This was not simply the best of times and the worst of times. In retrospect, some of the worst times seemed like the best. Everything is filtered through memory, and the horror stories are frequently the funniest, most popular stories of all. The first three months, unendurable period of exhaustion that it was, seemed perilously short in retrospect. The saddest part of it, looking back, was not her own misery, or Frank's withdrawal into his career, but her inability to remember it all. She could never appreciate Andy's infancy. She could not clearly recall it. Self-involvement had absorbed her concentration in those early days, and she had missed the rite of passage into parenthood.

How long she might have languished in this state is impossible to guess, but Andy put an end to it. He grew, and changed, and in pursuing his developing personality, Betsy was forced to keep alert. By the time she had come to her senses, he was crawling, then walking. Order was brought out of the Scheflins' chaos by Andy. His birth had messed things up to start with, and then, as if he understood what he had done, he righted it. In part, he accomplished this by becoming attached to his father.

There are very few constants in this book—all relationships are different—but one of them is this: fathers get interested in their children when the children become sophisticated. When babies begin to *be* someone, fathers begin to interact with them. It usually starts at about nine months. Mothers, by contrast, are able to evolve a relationship with their babies much, much earlier. We would not venture a guess as to whether this difference is a product of society's training, our mimicking of our own parents' behavior, or genetic/hormonal difference in the sexes. The difference between male and female is a controversial topic at the moment, and not one we are qualified to comment upon, but it is a difference that manifests itself throughout all our interviews. In only the most unconventional couples did we find fathers who were able to keep up with the developing relationship between mother and child.

This unequal development is the cause of frequent flare-ups, jealousies, and resentments. Mother is spending too much time with baby, father not enough. Father may feel that mother is replacing the marital relationship with the parenting relationship. Mother, if she gets angry enough about the whole thing, may do just that. Usually, father will catch up. Mother will welcome him into the relationship when the time comes and gradually things will re-tune themselves. We see this as a natural human process. It may not be admirable, but it happens. Mothers have demanded the reorganization of this system, but we are far from sure that such a thing is possible. Every couple has to make decisions on its own; it may be that a mother needs her mate *there now* for emotional or physical reasons. But, for the most part, we take this attitude: the flow of a relationship will be less strained if demands are kept to a minimum. According to our evidence fathers tend to bloom late. Unless there is a reason in your personal case to change this, why bother? A little faith in that future blooming may make the earlier months a lot less frustrating.

This does not mean that we advocate fathers ignoring their children. Unquestionably, fathers have a responsibility to mothers and newborns to be there, to nurture, and to offer physical help. We mean only to suggest that ours is a difficult era for fathers. We were brought up in a time when a woman's place was still in the home. For the most part, our own fathers did very little actual child care, and they are the only role models we have ever had. Suddenly, everything has changed. Fathers are being redefined as active parents, and we have nowhere to look for any kind of example to follow. Going back to the old way is not the answer, but the new way is uncharted ground. So fathers are confused and uncertain. Like Frank Scheflin, they have the capacity to be guilt-ridden and self-righteous at the same time, surely a common contradiction in emotions. The authors are in no position to tell any mother or father what his or her role should be—we beg only that sympathy be extended from one to another as we try to create a new kind of American parent. No one yet knows what he or she will be.

THE
SECOND
FAMILY

Doug and Casey Sterling

AND LEORA

CHOOSING PREGNANCY

CASEY STERLING knew something was changing when she found herself on her knees in the bedroom closet, applying a quick coat of wax to the linoleum beneath the winter clothes. No one had ever before seen this particular piece of the floor. Casey had no business with sponges or shoe boxes; she was a rock and roller. Nonetheless, it just seemed to need doing. Her husband, Doug, came home from Wally Heider Recording Studios at eight o'clock and found her on the floor, rubber gloves and all.

"Aha," he said. "Nesting instinct."

Casey had not recognized it. She had been off the pill for six months and was not yet, as far as she knew, pregnant. But if this sudden binge of domestic drudgery was something as definable as the human equivalent of a nesting instinct, that could be considered a step in the right direction. Aha, indeed. Doug and Casey believed Mother Nature took care of these things; they were letting her handle the pregnancy. She had been in a whimsical mood when she tossed Doug and Casey together seven years earlier in a Toronto television studio.

Casey was black; Doug was white. They could both compose, play the piano, sing, and manage the guitar, when called upon. They had celebrity looks—a tall, thin, fine-boned woman with mahogany skin and oversized eyes, and a too-tall, well-built man with black hair that curled behind his ears and enough of a mustache to signify gentleness. Clothes came to life on both of them, and all they wanted out of life was music. It seemed irrelevant to them that there was not a shred of common ground in their backgrounds. They were escaping where they had come from and had no desire to be reminded.

Casey was from Brooklyn, raised in a family of musicians and performers going back four generations. Doug was Scottish-born, raised in Toronto, the son of a Presbyterian minister who considered John Knox his spiritual ancestor. The day Doug brought Casey home to meet his parents was the last day he had seen them. The family hated show business, hated interracial love affairs, dreaded miscegenation. Doug and Casey made their own way.

They married, moved to Los Angeles (the center of the music industry), and joined the mass of young, hopeful singer-songwriter rock and rollers as a duet. Their Canadian reputation got them work in the small clubs along Sunset Strip, opening the bill for midpopular groups on the way up to the concert world, or on the way back down. It was good, hard, mainstream work, and they found it rewarding. A major record contract bought them the down payment on a canyon house away from everywhere. Suddenly they had the security of knowing what their steady diet would be; they had to compose and record twelve songs, and do nothing else. With this freedom, this unexpected sense of having entered the real world, came the idea of the baby.

For seven years (five of them in marriage), they had done just what they had wanted to do. They had done the work and reaped the benefits. They had been to the parties, to the movies, to the concerts. They had laughed a lot and slept late.

Life had been awfully sweet to them. Children were the natural next step. They had known through all the work and the pleasure-seeking that the right time would come, and that they would recognize it. Other things came first: their careers, a selfishness about their time, their freedom. They saw family expansion as a total upheaval of their lives, but they had had seven selfish years, and sometimes it felt as if they had already done everything at least once. The day they took possession of the house, Casey ran out of birth-control pills, and the prescription was not renewed. Six months went by. Casey did not panic. Her gynecologist told her to wait nine months before calling. It was shortly after she received this counsel that she registered the irresistible urge to clean everything.

She missed the next period and cautiously began predicting that someone new was growing inside her. Doug, who was playing studio piano during the day, called every noon to see if she had begun to bleed, returning ecstatic to work with each negative reply. She was pregnant. By the time the tests confirmed it, they had already accepted it as an inevitable fact. Some good Columbian grass had been sifted for the occasion of her test results; the couple got blissfully stoned and called everyone in Casey's family. There was no one in Doug's family to call, a point on which he was silent.

Doug Sterling was a minister's son and a proud emblem of the cliché that such children make the very best hell-raisers. He had been at war with his parents for so long that neither side could possibly recall the first shot. Doug had spent his early teens clawing gleefully at every hypocrisy he could dig out of his father's behavior—a reaction, perhaps, to the minister's temperamental use of the belt and hairbrush during the boy's formative years. Reverend Sterling admitted no pleasure from these frequent whippings; he believed them to be God's way. Doug saw them as a challenge to perform even more daring and rapacious feats, threatening his father's reputation in the community whenever possible. His mother, silent and powerless, grew old watching this raucous dance of antagonism.

In a sudden, and even to himself, inexplicable gesture of

conciliation, Doug married at twenty-three. The bride was ideal —a local girl, the organist at the Presbyterian church in suburban Toronto. The marriage lasted two pointless years. Doug could not stay away from the music scene. He was consumed. His wife was quietly appalled. A year after his quiet, uncontested divorce, the magnitude of his father's hypocrisy made itself suddenly, stunningly clear. Doug attended his sister's wedding, presided over by his father, and was surprised to see his ex-wife playing the organ. He was even more surprised to find her positioned next to him in the receiving line before dinner. It was a large party, with guests coming from all parts of the United States, Canada, and Scotland to attend. It did not take long to realize that none of them knew about his divorce. His father had engineered the ceremony, reception, and dinner seating so as to reunite the estranged couple for public display. He had told neither his son, nor his ex-daughter-in-law of this plan. Both were dumbfounded and went through the entire day anesthetized by the old man's effrontery.

Still, when Casey laughed on the phone to her crazy vaude-villian father in Toronto, Doug could not help but wish that he and his own family had declared a cease-fire. Too late to do anything about it now. It had been a year since the last, brief letter.

Casey's family was fragmented, but they were at peace with her. The only thing her upbringing had in common with Doug's was the frequency of violent beatings, administered, in her case, by her mother. Casey recognized the temper; it was in her as it had been in her mother and her grandmother, whose screech of fury she could still recall. Casey was capable of anything; she had grown up throwing ashtrays across the living room and working nights to pay for broken plate glass. But she was not going to beat her child. Teaching herself not to explode was part of the five years of marriage. The tantrums had not disappeared, but they were rare, one a year now. Usually they were directed at some crooked practitioner in her profession—an agent or club manager. She believed it exorcised her inborn need to have it out in full color and sound, an experience she would never inflict on her child.

Children could not be asked to deal with adult emotions. They had no equipment for it. Casey watched adults respond to the selfish demands of children as if the children were simply small, ill-behaved grown-ups, and she was horrified. These adults were missing the point of parenting. Casey's mother could rarely interact successfully with *adults*. With children she had shown no ability whatever, and simply resorted to the folded belt and the open hand. It had shattered Casey's youth and broken up her parents' marriage. Casey's father moved to Canada, a dreamworld of peace and quiet. When Casey was fifteen, she had fled Brooklyn and joined him there. Gradually, she had rebuilt a strained friendship with her mother, keeping the distance as a protective barrier.

Eight years after her flight from the United States, Casey met Doug. The assistant director at a television station placed them on opposite sides of the same microphone, and they spent fourteen hours staring at each other's lips. Both had escaped to music.

The new album took shape with almost otherworldly speed; pregnancy had unleashed an emotional tide—memories, dreams, hope and awe. These functioned as new materials and were crafted into rhyme and melody. The emotions of pregnancy became functional commodities, and the Sterlings' work reflected the day-to-day movement of their minds. They vowed to continue the pattern. The infant's upbringing would not be cordoned off, but would take place in the mainstream of their activity. The experience of parenting could be mined for inspiration, and their work would nurture the child.

As her belly grew, Casey made several tours of the bookstores, bringing home an occasional choice from the child-care shelf. She wanted to know how everyone did everything, but it was hard to get interested. Bathing and changing—people had done these things for centuries. How hard could they be to learn? She covered some child-development stuff, then put it all in a carton in the garage. The books were spoiling all the surprises for her.

Not every day was a good day. Although Casey never gained a lot of weight with the pregnancy, there were times when she felt the real old Casey had been swallowed up by her widening torso. Her reserves of high-flung energy flagged easily; she found herself seated more often than ever before. She tried to take a new kind of pleasure in her new body, her Mother Earth gait, but there was no pleasure to be had from it. She missed the old, lithe, dancer's limbs and the muscular flexibility of her waist. She missed being sexy for Doug, and she was not pleased when he seemed to mind not at all. Their sex life tapered off somewhere during the eighth month, and they satisfied themselves with long hugs. There were weekend late-morning naps; they wrapped themselves around each other to whatever extent they could and tried to get comfortable. After one pool party, Casey fell silent for several hours. It was the first time in her life she recalled staring enviously at other women's bodies. She wanted hers back.

At the couple's request, Casey's stepmother and aunt arrived in Los Angeles from Canada a week before the baby was due. They were to cook, clean, and take care, moving into the house the day Casey went to the hospital. In the meantime, they hid out, allowing the couple their last free days alone. But the phone began to ring. What kind of pacifier did Casey prefer? Should some formula be laid in, preparatory for a nursing failure? If so, what kind of bottles? What kind of diapers, talcum powder, shampoo, and lotion? Casey and Doug began to come unglued. They were showered with enough helpful concern to sink the entire parenthood, possibly the marriage. Selfishness once again became essential, and diplomacy was sacrificed.

Unhappily, Doug called his step-mother-in-law. Casey got on the phone, and together they explained, never wavering, that they had changed their minds. They needed one uninterrupted week alone with the baby to get their footing. It would have to be arranged. Reluctantly, the two women agreed. Doug and Casey had regrets about the whole thing, but there was never any choice. Politeness was a low priority.

Throughout the pregnancy, they had speculated lavishly on how their child would look. With one white and one black parent, anything was possible. Would it be a golden girl, a dark, pouting mysterious boy, or a lily-white daughter who would run from home cursing her invisible Negro blood? They laughed at these invented scenarios and invented more. Every prospective parent indulges in this game; the Sterlings had more chips to play with than most. But one night it all came to an end with Casey's dream. Casey dreamed her baby had heard its parents' endless conjecture and was good and sick of it. Casey's baby climbed from between her thighs, wearing a rag diaper and a T-shirt. It was a radiant, maple-syrup-brown baby, wide-eyed and gorgeous. The diaper obscured its sex. As Casey watched in amazement, the infant executed a wide circle of cartwheels, showing off every aspect of itself. This was followed by a short toe dance. Satisfied that everyone now knew what it looked like, it hopped up on the bed and climbed back into Casey's womb, never uttering a sound.

Doug awoke abruptly and discovered his wife laughing in her sleep.

Doug and Casey Sterling are everything one doesn't expect from a rootless biracial couple in the entertainment field. Both had had violent upbringings, neither came from a stable background, and no one approved of their marriage. They had to be perfect. Never has there been a truer indication of unpredictability in this world than the Sterling marriage. From this rebellious, unreliable past, there emerged a relationship that was as mature as it was serious. Doug and Casey protected their self-interest aggressively, and when they were ready to give themselves away, they were genuinely ready. They held off on having a baby for five years. There is no magic in the number; it was the right number for them. Some couples come to readiness in two or three years, or sooner; others take a decade or more. Knowing when to have a baby can be as tricky as you make it. Doug and Casey had a lot of things they

wanted to do, both in their career and in the ways of enter-
taining themselves. They had the wisdom to know that a child
would put an end to free living as they had become accus-
tomed to it. They also believed that the time for a baby would
make itself clear, that if they were questioning it, it hadn't
arrived yet.

Unquestionably, their faith was rewarded because it was so
strong. If a couple doesn't really believe in letting nature ring
the bells, they may never be rung at all. Still, we believe that
it is not all that difficult to decide when to have a baby. Rarely
is it a moment of perfect adjustment. Usually one mate is
ready before the other, and there can be a period of disagreement. There is nothing wrong with disagreement if it is resolved. Time and talk (the usual remedies suggested by this
book) can do the trick, but one thing is certain. If a child is
conceived even though one parent is against it, there will be
serious, lasting trouble—not necessarily divorce or disaster, but
trouble.

The Sterlings were in agreement, and it is important to em-
phasize how they got there. They lived the life they wanted to
live. They were unstintingly selfish. They *knew* when Casey
got pregnant that their free days were numbered. They fully
expected to give up everything idle as soon as the baby was
born, at least for a couple of years. They were sure they
wouldn't miss all their old activities. Never for an instant did
they think, "We'll live like before, only the baby will be in
on everything."

The Sterlings are an extraordinary couple, of course. They
worked together, and they worked at home a good deal of the
time. They had a freedom of schedule that most couples do
not enjoy. Their plans for the baby were easier for them to
make than similar plans would be for an average man and
wife. Still, Doug and Casey exemplified an attitude; their
physical movement in this book is not as important as what
their thinking represented. For modern, unconventional people working in what is possibly the most unstable profession
in the world, they remain the most old-fashioned couple in the

book. They had no advisers to seek out on the question of
children. Casey's parents had botched the job, and Doug's
weren't speaking to him. They did not read books, nor were
their friends (mainly single) much help. But for all their late
hours, dope-smoking, and irregular working conditions, Doug
and Casey saw the family as the central unit of their lives. Far
from being dead, the family to them was that thing into which
they expected to pour their life's blood and energy.

AT ONE WEEK

The Hospital Mystique

CASEY STERLING went into labor gently, in the early evening. She had some trouble recognizing her contractions, which were mild and irregular, but by ten at night she was on the phone to the doctor. They were still slow at midnight, so Casey went to bed. At noon the next day, she went to the hospital. It didn't seem real. She had expected to be awakened at 2:00 A.M. by agonizing inner pulsations threatening to destroy her, but nothing like that happened. She was sure she'd be sent home. Her own doctor was out of town; she was examined by a stranger, a young man who looked about half like a doctor. He was short-haired and had cherub cheeks, so pink and white that they looked like they must be stinging. His eyes were watery grey, hardly lighting up his face at all. His lips were soft and full, and his small delicate hands seemed to possess no more force of experience than a newborn kitten.

"Check in," he said. "You're halfway there."

Casey thought she was dreaming.

"By the way," the young obstetrician added, "as of now, I'm your doctor."

Doug and Casey went back down to the car and shared a joint. This was going to be an adventure.

"He's just a kid," Casey said. "He doesn't know if I'm in labor."

"Look," Doug replied, "you didn't have anything to do today anyhow. Let's give him a try."

The doctor met them in the labor room, unaware that they were mildly high. It was a cubicle, really, with barely enough room for the three of them, a bed, two counters, and two cabinets of medical supplies. On the wall opposite the bed was a grand photographic mural in color: the surf at Malibu in late afternoon. Nothing could have been further from Casey's mind. Aside from the artwork, the room was white and chrome, with a tiny, high-pressure compactness that meant business.

"This is great," Casey said. "I feel like I'm in the movies."

The doctor, slipping on a rubber glove, administered a stern warning. "If I feel you need drugs, anesthetic or otherwise, you're going to get them. That's going to be *my* decision. If you feel uncomfortable with that, you'll need another doctor."

Casey began to bolt up in bed. Doug took her hand and spoke before she had the chance.

"It's a little late for us to be interviewing doctors," he said.

The doctor smiled faintly.

"We want you to know," Doug said, "since we're reading the rules at the beginning, that we've been planning a drugless delivery for almost eight months now. We *want* to do it that way. We just want you to understand that before you make any decisions."

Doug's eyes gave no ground. The doctor looked at him for a long moment.

"All right," he said, finally. "Everyone understands."

The day wore on, but in a windowless labor room there is nothing but a wall clock to measure it. Casey progressed slowly, dozing between contractions, waiting. The effects of the marijuana wore off well before the serious discomfort started. Fresh air circulated through the room, in one vent, out another, the atmosphere mechanized and private. The world outside had become remote. The doctor and a labor nurse passed in and out, checking, bringing coffee to Doug, measuring Casey's vital signs with a surprising amount of enthusiasm. In the passage of time, the doctor had become an ally. He was giving Casey an internal when a hospital administrator poked her head in the door, an intrusion that made Casey jump.

"Mr. Sterling?" the administrator said. "We need you in admitting. Your wife hasn't been admitted in the records."

"I'm busy," Doug said with quiet anger.

"Well, come down as soon as you can," the lady said, backing out of the door.

"No," Doug said. "You'll have to bring the records here."

The administrator stepped into the room, ignoring a glare from the doctor. The internal exam was now in abeyance.

"We don't do that," the lady said. She was right out of "General Hospital." "It's hospital policy."

"I'm sorry," Doug said. "But Sterling family policy, going back generations, has an unswerving rule. The admitting office *always* brings the records to the labor room when a Sterling is about to be born. That's the way it is."

The admitting lady looked as if she had been physically struck. She was silent, unyielding.

"Call a cop," Doug advised. "Have us thrown out."

With that she turned and departed.

The doctor waited a moment of silence before looking at Doug. "Far out," he said. He was not about to suggest drugs.

The records arrived five minutes later, brought by an assistant. Doug signed Casey in quickly, and the assistant departed.

As the hours went by, Casey had more and more trouble. Night came. The doctor delivered two other babies; finally, he had nothing more to do than sit and wait with the Sterlings, monitoring the progress. None of them had tolerance for card-playing, but life in the labor room suggested that kind of activity. Nothing was happening. Nothing did happen until eight-fifteen, when Casey called for a bucket.

She vomited twice, but she knew that might happen. She also knew that meant the time was near. Doug took his blue, sterile scrub suit from the nurse and put it on, moving quickly, so as not to be distracted from Casey, who suddenly needed him. With all the casual slowness of the early stages of labor, the crucial moments were still cluttered, confused, and without organization. Doug was convinced there would be a drug argument amid the chaos, but the doctor remained supportive. Somehow, in the intervening hours, everyone had come to the same conclusion. Casey needed nothing.

The delivery room looked odd to Doug, like a wholesale medical supply shop with equipment just strewn around the place. The whole process seemed primitive. They had fantasized that the hospital would be a depersonalizing monster, the paranoid nightmare of some science fiction world. Instead, it seemed like a special place set aside for special acts. Doug was happy never to have seen the delivery room before. Everything was new, unexpected.

The surroundings suited the experience.

They were not there long. The pressure was on; everyone got down to business. Doug coached, and Casey pushed. The doctor was silent, waiting. There was a brief moment of panic when the machine monitoring the fetal heartbeat showed a drastic drop. The baby was caught in the vaginal canal. The nurse slapped an oxygen mask over Casey's mouth and turned it on. The heartbeat returned to normal immediately. These people are pros, Doug thought. Less than a minute later, Casey gave one concerted push with whatever was left of her abdominal muscles, and Leora Sterling eased out into the young doctor's hands. She let out an immediate howl. She was grayish tan, the color of burnished metal, and somewhat the worse for wear from the long labor. A white gooey substance covered her skin like a protective gel, and there were traces of Casey's blood in her hair. But she didn't look ugly, at least not to Doug and Casey.

Doug forgot to look at the clock, but the labor nurse recorded it. They had been at it eleven hours.

Moments later the placenta, the prenatal food supply sack, was ejected from Casey's womb.

"You've been terrific," the doctor told them. "Now I've got a job for you." He put a pressure clip on the baby's umbilical cord and handed Doug the surgical scissors.

"Right there," he said.

Doug was honored. He cut the cord that loosed Leora from the other world and lay her on Casey's belly.

Exhausted, Casey looked down at the little gray thing, comforted by its bed of flesh.

"How do you like that," she said, taking a tiny hand in her hand. "She's got the nerve to have fingernails."

Life in the labor and delivery rooms is a great mystery to most expectant couples. There is enough fear generated by the prospect of going into labor and suffering the pain of childbirth to make fearing the labor nurse, the doctor, and the hospital administration a waste of anxiety. The Sterlings had the right idea. They saw the hospital as a place created to serve them. They knew what they wanted, and they were not shy people. Having a baby was a once or twice in a lifetime experience, and it was *their* lifetimes that were involved. Labor nurses and administrators, even doctors, regard the labor and delivery processes as all part of a day's work. The only ones who saw it as magic time were the Sterlings themselves, and they were not about to be infected by the hospital's blasé attitude.

This kind of thinking really comes under the heading of consumer awareness, and consumer awareness is one of the reasons we feel that expectant parents should consider prepared childbirth classes. These courses (they include the La-maze method, the Bradley method, and others) concentrate on the act of childbirth itself, but they dispense a good deal of useful information on related topics. It seems to us that childbirth should be fraught with as few surprises as possible. It was in a prepared childbirth class that Doug Sterling learned he could talk back, make demands, and otherwise control the hospital situation. His familiarity with the procedure in the labor room made him comfortable. His knowledge of his rights made him bold. For those reasons alone, the prepared childbirth class was a worthy choice for the Sterlings, and it probably would be for any couple. The Sterlings preserved their own euphoria, and the attitude of the hospital could never have affected them.

There is no way to overemphasize the importance of this situation. The hospital doesn't care specifically about you. It provides similar services for thousands of people a year and deals equally with patients dying and patients birthing. It cannot afford to become personal. If you demand a personalized hospital, you will be disappointed every time. If the birthing experience is going to be emotionally satisfying, you will have to make it so yourself.

If you feel strongly that the hospital atmosphere is too impersonal, there may be alternative forms of childbirth that can be arranged for you. Home deliveries are once again being accepted, although only among those adhering to the most radical schools of thought. An "in-between" alternative is being presented in several major cities, where hospitals have set up birthing centers. These are simulated home environments providing parents with the comforts of a bedroom and kitchen without the risk of being any distance from medical equipment and care. In addition, there are several birthing centers which are affiliated with hospitals but not located within their walls. You may wish to ask your doctor about the possibility of using one of these three methods of birthing, so you will know, at least, what is available. All three possibilities are still quite uncommon, however, and if you are like the vast majority of American families, you will find yourself facing the prospect of giving birth in the hospital.

The hospital does not have to be a hindrance, however. This chapter is not to be taken as an attack on the country's health facilities. The hospital is there to perform certain technical functions. The staff has its work. Part of that work does not include becoming emotional about your baby or anyone else's. You must supply the emotion, but you can also keep the hospital from getting in your way, which, from time to time, it will try to do.

Aside from certain medical procedures and procedural policies, to which you agree when you are admitted, nothing about "hospital policy" is law. You do not have to eat when they want you to, sleep when they want you to, or do many other things that you will be asked to do. Nurses have busy schedules, and they would like their patients to make it easy on them. It is not your obligation to do so. You are in the hospital for the delivery, rest, and recovery. The staff is there to serve you. If you begin to serve them, resentment and timidity will prevent you from enjoying the full impact of having just become a parent. It is important to think about what you want from a hospital, and to talk it over with your doctor. Many prepared childbirth classes will give you a tour of the labor and nursery facilities, as will some hospitals on their own. This is worthwhile. It means that when you check in, possibly in the middle of the night and in a good deal of pain, the place will not be strange to you. You'll know what all the equipment is and what it will do. If your hospital does not offer a tour, you might ask your doctor if he can arrange one or speak to someone in the hospital administration about seeing where you'll be.

If you take a prepared childbirth class, you will discuss the benefits and liabilities of using various anesthetic drugs during labor and delivery. You should make some decision about what you want to do about drugs. You may change it later, but at least know what you think. Your doctor will have an opinion, but remember that your baby may not be delivered by your doctor. You may have to think and talk on your feet at the last moment to a total stranger. He (or she) will certainly have more respect for you if you speak knowledgeably and have given some thought to the situation.

There comes a moment in nearly every labor when the woman's discomfort is so great that if drug relief is offered, it will seem irresistible. If you feel strongly that you don't want drugs, and if you have spoken to your doctor about it, that moment may be one in which he takes time to encourage you through the crisis, rather than to call the anesthesiologist. A woman at the height of labor does not think clearly. If her mate is present, he can often make split-second decisions for her, but nothing can replace the preliminary thought and discussion with mate and doctor. As many things as possible should be cleared away before labor begins.

Finally, you will have to confront the process and personnel in the labor and delivery rooms as they are dealt to you. Again, this is no time for timidity. You cannot predict what the crises will be. The Sterlings had to cope with a young doctor and a balky administrator. You may have entirely different experiences. The crucial thing during the labor and delivery process is to think "me first." This is *your* labor, *your* delivery, *your* child. Aside from basic medical procedural rules, say and do what you want. There is no need to be sarcastic or vindictive. Just be serious. The hospital is at your service. The bills will be high. The food will be bad. Parking will be inadequate. But if the hospital *intimidates* you, it is no one's fault but your own. You have the power to demand and receive the best service the hospital has to offer. Think hard, say what you mean, and do not settle for less than you know can be provided.

AT ONE MONTH

Help at Home—The Relatives Move In

THE STERLINGS had Leora to themselves for a week and a half. For the first days her schedule was upside down, as Andy Scheflin's had been. Her few wakeful hours came between two and six in the morning. This was less than ideal. Dazed and half-asleep, Doug and Casey forced each other to take turns singing, cooing, and waltzing their daughter around in the dark. An occasional harsh word was spoken. There was a lot of napping during the day. They had crossed off this period anyhow and weren't expecting to get anything accomplished. On the fourth day home, Leora slept a full three hours between feedings all night. Somehow she had gotten the message. For the next seven days, the three Sterlings lived with a peace so pure that it lit the rooms of the house. Doug brought meals into bed. Casey slept and played the piano. They listened to music. There was nothing else to do but watch Leora.

Only Doug's parents were to be fretted over. At about eleven every morning, Doug would tune out of whatever was happening and wait for the mail. He had sent his folks a telegram the morning of Leora's birth. There had been no response of any kind. Doug kept this routine to himself, but Casey knew what he was feeling, and he knew she knew. Leora was short one set of grandparents.

On the eleventh day, when the daily routine of Leora's life had just gotten set, Casey's stepmother and aunt, the Croswell sisters, descended. Doug sensed that it was a bad idea, that there might be trouble, but he could put them off no longer. To some extent he resented their arrival out of pure jealousy.

It was only for a week, but a week can be a long time. The Croswell sisters had been a singing team in their earlier days. They moved as a united front, even though one of them was married to Casey's father. They took Leora from Doug and Casey's room and moved her downstairs to sleep between them —so Doug and Casey would get some rest. They had lots of ideas about child-rearing, and Doug and Casey tried to be tolerant. The Croswell sisters recommended apple juice and sugar-water. They popped a pacifier into the baby's mouth at the first sign of vocalizing. They made things warmer, cooler, brighter, dimmer, on a regular cycling basis: the room and Leora's clothing were monitored like the atmosphere of a capsule in outer space. The Sterlings tried to steer clear. They felt Leora's stability was established, that nothing could affect her.

But immediately she was constipated and a day after that she stopped sleeping. Doug became taciturn. Casey began to feel humiliated. Her aunt and stepmother corrected everything she attempted to do. Little could be said, however; these people had come a long way to help. As the Croswell sisters seemed to want complete control of Leora, Doug and Casey relinquished it. They played with their daughter, let her know they were there, but left the changing and bedding procedures to the two older women. In one stern argument Doug managed to eliminate the fruit juice, but the sugar-water stayed. Casey nursed Leora, cooing to her about the temporary interruption in their family life. Other than that one regular bonding process, she had little to do with her. It was just too difficult.

The Croswell sisters had their cheerier side. They were out

of a show business tradition, full of stories and songs, and Doug and Casey felt a kind of generation-gap kinship with them. They were yesterday's entertainers, and they understood the Sterlings' compulsion about making music. Best of all, they embraced the marriage, interracial or not, in true show business fashion. Both of them had a tendency to get slightly drunk at dinners; Doug and Casey could smoke grass in front of them without worrying. So the evenings, while Leora slept, were all right.

As the days dragged on, a more serious effect of the Croswells' presence was felt. Doug and Casey found themselves whispering to each other in bed or conducting serious conversations in quick, hushed tones because one or both of the old women might enter or return at any moment. The flow of communication was wrecked; short, intense speeches of explanation were issued instead of the normal exchange of talk. Doug and Casey found themselves imprisoned in their own home because two women were doing them a favor.

The week ended appropriately. The sisters packed while dictating a list of do's and don't's to Casey, all of which were headed directly for the fireplace. Doug waited silently for it to be over. The week had seemed like a month. The last few hours seemed like a year. In a burst of ironic justice, Leora claimed the day. Resting comfortably in her mother's arms, she stared the two Croswell sisters out to the garage and then, just as Casey waved good-bye, had a massive attack of diarrhea all over Casey's Danskin. It was her first bowel movement since the sisters had arrived, and certainly a triumph. Casey greeted it with mixed feelings.

Now things had to get going again. The album Doug and Casey had recorded during the early months of pregnancy was about to break. There was publicity to take care of and bookings. For the first time since before Leora was conceived, they would have to perform: live, on tour. This was part of their record contract. In the eight weeks left before their tour debut, they had to put together material for a second album. As soon as they came off the road, they would be slotted into the studio. There were arrangements and musicians to pick and worry about. Between them they had not one idea for a new song. And all the time they had allowed for adjustment, for Leora to dominate, was gone. The leisure days had melted away. Eight weeks seemed like a long time, once. Suddenly it hardly seemed to exist at all.

Three weeks had been set aside for recovery, but Doug and Casey had not recovered. They were physically all right. Emotionally, they had just started. The schedule kept running away with them: they would program their day around Leora's naps, but with each week her naps got shorter. They could never fully concentrate on making music while she was asleep because they knew they'd never hear her if she started to cry. Their work became half-measured, done with one eye and one ear elsewhere. It wasn't first-rate work, and they knew it.

It seemed impossible that they were not ready for the complete upheaval they thought they had prepared themselves for, but that was what had happened. "Complete upheaval" was just a phrase before Leora was born. Now, it was a reality. They didn't know what it could be like until those last eight weeks started bearing down on them. They didn't know quite what to do, so they just went on living, a half-life in a half-world. They did what they could about the record, and they did everything for Leora.

"We were saved by the six years before," Doug said later. "We had those six years to ourselves. Now we knew we'd never have that kind of time again, not while we were young anyhow. And despite everything else we tried to do to make things work, we never tried to recapture that feeling of being only a couple. We were ready to leave that behind, which was lucky, because holding the fort with everything else was all we could do. If we'd had second thoughts about leaving our private days behind, that would have brought the walls down."

Those six private years began to loom larger and larger in their minds as they ate one meal standing over the kitchen sink with a paper towel in one hand and a dripping wedge of pizza in another.

"Those first weeks after my aunt and stepmother left," Casey recalled, "they were like running through a swamp in a rainstorm. You just can't stop 'cause you'll fall behind, but even when you go, you never get anywhere."

Still, the only serious issue was Doug's parents. Leora's needs were met; the songs, for better or worse, got written; the tour was arranged. As they came into the stretch of the first month, Leora began to produce a cockeyed smile, which they took to be recognition, devotion, and appreciation. It was hardly a controlled grin, just a spring upward of the lips and a thrust of toothless little gums, but it kept them going. A few days after the smile appeared, they discovered her rocking more or less in time to the music as they rehearsed numbers from the old album. From then on they kept her with them; she seemed to like every song, and she could sleep through the loudest drum and piano duets if she was tired.

In October, just before the tour began, Doug's uncle sent a postcard. It read:

> Stopped by house to pick up
> mail. Got your cable. Reverend S.
> and your mother are in Europe now
> and didn't see it. Congratulations
> from me anyhow.

Doug read it over and over, and threw it out.

"That ought to make you feel better," Casey said.

Doug nodded.

"But it doesn't," she added, looking over.

"No," he said. "When I get a piece of mail like that, I want to settle everything. This doesn't answer a single question."

"Like what?"

"Like what would they have done if they *had* gotten word?"

When your baby is born you will be offered help and advice from all quarters. You'll need some of it, and you'll suffer with the rest.

Baby nurses have been explored in chapter 2. Having relatives move in for a week or two is a second option, and, in some cases, not a happy one. Relatives are a personal responsibility. Whatever inadequacies a nurse may display, she is an employee, and you are not prevented from taking her to task, keeping her in line, even dismissing her from service. That's the risk she runs by going into the baby-nursing business. With a family member, it's tougher. You're being done a favor, and it's hard to complain. This is not a cut-and-dried situation. One of the authors had a near-perfect first week of parenthood with the aid of a mother-in-law. The other happily did without help.

It's a safe bet that you will have more trouble with a relative whom you know only marginally well. Chances are you will not have discussed philosophies of childbearing in any depth with her (or them). No matter how many times your aunt or cousin says, "Just tell me what you want to do," it's very hard to be blunt about it and assign her certain tasks, keeping others for yourself, exactly as you wish. Surely she will say, "Oh, I *love* giving babies a bath," and you will succumb, even if that's your favorite part of the day.

Ask yourself this question: Would I go on a two-week vacation with this person? If the answer is no, you can bet you won't want her around for a two-week rest and recovery period. If the answer is yes, you *might* want to consider her. In general, we reiterate, the couples in our sample who had the least trouble were those who were stubborn and kept all the child care to themselves for the first weeks or months of the first baby's life. (In all fairness, this changes with a second child, when demands on your time will be severe, and you will have a good deal more confidence in your ability as parents. Our "do it yourself" urging applies specifically to first children.)

Getting to know how to raise children takes time and practice, and it requires a listening to your own inner rhythms. A lot of things you believe in as theories and plan to put into practice may seem wrong, or silly, or inappropriate when your child arrives. You need the privacy and the room to establish your own techniques, to make the most of your own character as a parent, and to change your mind without embarrassment. With the intrusion of a relative who is part-helper, part-houseguest, it's almost impossible for things to run smoothly.

The houseguest aspect of having these people around should not be played down. If Betsy Scheflin felt hemmed in emotionally by a hired nurse, that can be called neurosis; but when you have relatives living in your house, the lack of freedom will be real and unalterable. The breakdown in communication between husband and wife during this period is common enough as it is. With additional people in the house, it is almost unavoidable. Becoming a parent is a daring act, and daring requires privacy the first time around.

Get all the help you need. Maids, heavy cleaners, cooks, and drivers. If you want help with your baby, you should have that, too. But relatives, to an even greater extent than nurses, present potential problems. *If* you have one you know and love, *and* your mate knows and loves her, too, *and* you feel you can be blunt and honest with her without bruising feelings all around, it may be the greatest thing that ever happened to have her move in.

In the case of Doug and Casey, the Croswell sisters took over to an outrageous extent, but the Sterlings let them do it. This shows a certain bravery. It is important to remember that your baby is quite resilient. The relatives may be doing everything wrong from your point of view, but it may be easier to let them do it than to fight every point. Chances are they will do no harm to the baby. In other words, if you've already got the relatives there, and you find yourself in conflict, consider taking the passive position. A week of fruit juice isn't going to kill anyone, and then it will be over. Obviously, if your baby is being hung out on the line to dry after a bath, something must be done. But minor transgressions are just that—minor—and nothing is sacred about each and every detail of child-rearing.

AT THREE MONTHS

Faith and the Crisis—What Breastfeeding Means to Husbands

THE TOUR kicked off at an arena in Sacramento, and right from the beginning something was wrong. Casey didn't feel right, couldn't concentrate. Banks of lights blinded her on stage, making the crowd of 15,000 an invisible mob. They had all come to see Elton John. Doug and Casey were opening the show. The music was so loud that both of them had to wear earplugs. It was like performing underwater.

About halfway through the set Casey had a premonition that she would not get back to the hotel room where Leora was waiting with a regular sitter, who was hired for the tour. Casey didn't know why, but there was a churning in her stomach; something was wrong. It wasn't stage fright.

She thought it was a kind of silly mother-panic. She felt she was cheating Leora in a way, bathing her own ego in front of a crowd while her daughter stayed home with a sitter. She didn't want to bother Doug with it, especially on stage, so she finished the set.

In the confusion backstage as they came off, no one saw her pass out. Doug was following the band down the stairs, technicians were beginning to wheel equipment off and on, setting up for Elton John.

Casey set a tambourine down on a passing amplifier and collapsed. She lay in the dark for several seconds before the Sterlings' road manager tried to roll an electric piano over the space she was occupying and found her.

Rock concert promoters keep ambulances on hand. Casey and Doug made it to the emergency entrance of a hospital they had never seen before in under twenty minutes. Casey had regained consciousness and was asking for Leora.

The pressure had probably forced the faint, but Casey's illness was not the result of worry over Leora. The diagnosis was appendicitis, and within moments of her arrival at the hospital, she was in surgery. Doug breathed easier when he found out what it was, and that it wasn't serious. He called the hotel and gave the news to the sitter. He didn't know when he'd be back. Casey's milk had been stored in a portable refrigerator, and there was enough to last until morning. Leora was asleep.

The operation was routine and without incident. It was not until morning, when Casey rested fretfully in a bright-orange room with sliding windows overlooking the parking lot, that the trouble developed. Leora would not be allowed in. Casey would not see her for three days. They protested, argued heatedly, and ultimately took their case to the chief of the hospital, but to no avail. There were no hospitals in Sacramento that would let the infant in. Casey wanted to check out, stitches and all, but her body betrayed her. She was just too weak.

The inhumanity of "policy" got to her, though. She and Doug conferred and formulated a plan. She would not take any medication. Doug brought her an empty, sterile milk bottle every few hours, and she would pump it full of her milk, giving it to him to take home to Leora. Leora never knew the taste of formula.

Casey couldn't say why she was so fanatical on this point. She had once looked at a can of formula and saw that it had a shelf life of almost two years. What must they put in it, she wondered. It had an awful smell, tinny and chemical. She wasn't going to subject Leora to that kind of food. For three days, she continued to supply milk by messenger. No one at the hospital knew.

Doug had a hard moment before the first milk run. He was furious at the hospital, at the fates, at life in general, and he wasn't thinking any too straight about things until Casey hatched her plan. The plan just seemed to make things more complicated. Now, on top of everything else, he had to bear a conspiracy. It took a lot of self-control to remain passive. Doug didn't know what was wrong with formula. It wasn't his preference, certainly, but it wasn't something he was willing to make a federal case out of. He didn't think Casey cared either. Her attraction to nursing was not feminist-inspired, nor was she a health-food type. He didn't know exactly why she was so suddenly militant as to become a guerilla in the cause of nursing. He wanted to tell her to go to hell about the whole thing, and he hated himself for feeling that way. But he managed to keep silent. This is her war, he figured. She was his wife, and she had her reasons. He took a deep breath, made up his mind, and spent three days sneaking down the hospital corridors with milk bottles in his sweater.

After three days, Doug picked Casey up at the hospital, and the two of them met Leora and the baby-sitter at the airport. Casey cried a fair amount on the way home, holding her baby in her arms, and Doug left her alone. This was private time in a public place. Leora, of course, had no idea what was happening, which made it all the more poignant. The miscarriage of their first promotional tour was complete and done with, Doug thought. They were like ragged troops in retreat.

But the crisis was far from over. When they got home, Doug left Casey in the bedroom with Leora and brought up the luggage. The instruments had to be moved, and the music room had to be reorganized. Black plywood boxes, with a white stenciled STERLING BAND diagonally painted across them, awaited Doug's supervision in the driveway. Some had to be transferred to storage in Hollywood, others packed off to the attic. Coming off a tour was a lot of work. Coming off no tour seemed even harder.

The baby-sitter interrupted things as Doug was checking the contents of one big crate.

"She wants you," she said. "Upstairs."

Doug was troubled. He locked the crate back up and went into the bedroom to see Casey.

"She won't nurse."

Casey was sitting by the window in a rocker. Leora was in her arms, wailing. Casey would present her breast, gently guide Leora's mouth up to it, and try.

The baby pulled her head away and cried out in fury. She would not take the breast. The cry cut through Casey's flesh. She had nothing left to give. Doug watched and tried to make the situation his own, but it wasn't. Whatever it meant— the nursing process—he could only comprehend its importance, not its reasons. It was something for Casey and Leora. He was left out.

"What can I do?" he asked.

Casey sighed. "Just stay here," she said. The room was darkened by the late-afternoon sun. Doug closed the door quietly. He sat on the bed in silence, looking at Casey and Leora, the baby whimpering in her arms. The nursing and wailing process repeated itself twice in a half-hour. Hungry and discontent, Leora finally dozed off in Casey's arms, shallow short breaths coming in quick succession. Casey was drained. She looked down at her baby and there was something like resentment in her eyes. But the operation and the trip had knocked her out. In a few minutes her head lolled backward and she, too, was asleep. In the darkness Doug separated the two and put Leora down in her bassinet. Then he let himself out of the room and quickly dispatched all the equipment from the tour. In forty-five minutes, he was back in the bedroom, watching his wife and daughter sleep.

Leora awoke finally with a little cry of hunger that had

become her trademark, and Casey stirred instinctively in her sleep. Doug picked up the baby and deposited her in Casey's lap. The process began again. The offering, the wailing, the waiting. Doug took it all in, like a foreign movie without subtitles. Some primal battle was going on here, one to which he had no clue, but its very central importance was never in doubt. This was something that had to be done.

Its resolution was unknown.

Again Leora slept without sustenance. Casey tried to explain, but all she could say was "I'm not going to lose her."

Doug didn't understand what she meant.

"Nursing her is what I have with her. It's part of my loving; it's part of what makes up who we are to each other. I'm not going to lose it. I don't care how long it takes."

It took all night. As the sun was just beginning to warm the darkened bedroom with a diffused amber light, Leora changed her mind. She awoke with a howl and went right to the breast. For a moment, it didn't seem to be happening. It was so different than what had been going on during the long night. She made no protest. She was not tentative. Casey looked up at Doug, her dark skin bathed with sweat, her eyes loaded with exhaustion. She shook her head back and forth in rhythm as Doug watched. It was like the end of a nightmare.

"That's a good girl," Casey said, smoothly swinging Leora up onto her shoulder for a burp.

They didn't talk about it until much later. First they slept, and then as Casey lay dazed in bed, thinking about it all, Doug came in with a postcard in his hands.

"Your folks?" Casey asked hopefully.

Doug nodded.

"They're coming in three weeks," he said.

One of the hardest things to accept, especially after six years of marriage, is that you are not your mate. Your mate is an independent soul. One of the things that keeps marriages together is a firm understanding of this point. One of the things that makes so many marital arguments blow out of proportion is one mate's disbelief that the other can hold a different position at all, on anything. The problem becomes augmented as it relates to parenting because, no matter what anyone may tell you, being a mother and being a father are not the same thing.

At the moment of crisis (not every family has a major one during the first year), patterns of behavior are called up out of the past. Strange things may not happen, but they can, and a mother separated from her child can be expected to have certain deep, almost primitive reactions.

Casey Sterling's behavior after her appendectomy emanated from a gut level. She had trouble explaining it later, although she vowed she would do it again. We might look at it in this way: she refused to stop mothering. Nursing was the deepest symbol of her role as a mother, and she would not let it be blotted out. She was undergoing some anxiety over her role shift anyhow because she had begun to work again and had left her child for the first time; so she was in a vulnerable position to begin with. When she lost the important link to Leora, she fought with everything she had to get it back.

Crucial to the success of this subliminal campaign was Doug. He could have done any number of things to help or hinder. What he did was stay out of it. He recognized the crucial fact that he could not understand what Casey was going through. Not that he didn't understand it, or hadn't yet understood it, but that he *never would* understand it. Having accepted that, he simply made himself available as a soldier. He insisted on no explanation, knowing that none would ever make things clear. He just pitched in. This takes a remarkable, flexible ego, and that is what this chapter is about.

Because you can never be your mate, and because you are bound to find certain behavior by your mate incomprehensible, you have two possible reactions. You can say, in effect, "What the hell is going on here? Stop this nonsense at once," or you can let whatever is happening happen, at least to a point. Judgment is called for, and this is one spot where we do not think communication is necessarily the best thing. There are some reactions that are private, that need to be tolerated, or encouraged, without a full explanation. If Doug Sterling had said to his wife, "I'm going to let this bizarre situation continue, but tell me what you're doing first," the entire thing might have fallen to bits. Casey's behavior needed to operate at an instinctive level. It wasn't going to be helped by reason.

These are judgment calls. When do you intrude, and when do you hang back? We can't say. The important thing is to ask yourself the question before you act. Consider the possibility that something you don't understand may have value even without your understanding it. Judgment does not mean endless indulgence, however. There are patterns of behavior that are neurotic and do need curbing. We are not suggesting that anything a mother or father wants to do is fine, but tolerance is urged. The crucial question you must ask yourself is this: Why do I want to interrupt this situation? Is it because I think it is unhealthy, or is it because I don't understand it, I'm left out of it, and my ego is bruised?

The situation tends to apply to fathers more than mothers because fathers tend to be left out of more during the first year. (They also tend to do less direct parenting and have fewer direct responsibilities, this being a two-way street.) It can happen the other way as well, and often it is harder. Mothers expect to have a private life with their children, but they do not expect fathers to have the same kind of privacy. Whenever it happens, to whichever parent, a display of faith should come first. Believe in what your mate is doing for as long as you can. If it has to be stopped, understand why and prepare to face the consequences of having interrupted serious business. Presumably, if Leora Sterling had refused to nurse for two days, Doug would have felt that her health was more important than Casey's need to have a nursing relationship with her. He would have taken action if it had come to that. He was willing to wait, however, and, in refusing to erode her position, he strenghtened his relationship with her and his stature as a father.

AT SIX MONTHS

Grandparents

CASEY had written the letter before the tour, before the trouble, and she hadn't really expected it to work. It was an impulsive act. One Sunday morning she woke up, thought about both elder Sterlings in church, pious, on bended knee, and it burned her up; so she wrote them a letter. An excerpt follows:

> I don't think God smiles upon racial prejudice, and I think you know this, but it is not my reason for writing. Because, frankly, I don't want you for myself. If you don't like me, or don't want to talk to me, that's something I can live with. I don't have any choice, do I? But this child is your flesh and blood. She's only two-and-a-half-months old, so you can bet she has not done anything sinful, and there is no reason to punish her. Yet she is being punished because she has only one set of grandparents. That's not something she deserves. You are punishing her for something you hold against me, or Doug, and I think it's unfair.

Casey was no fool. She enclosed a picture of her golden girl in the letter and posted it. The picture was her secret weapon. She told Doug about it, but he didn't have anything to do with it.

"I just woke up angry," she said later. "If not, I might never have written it. I think I could see what it was doing to Doug, even though we never mentioned it, but I don't know where it came from really. It just happened. I woke up, I thought about it, and I said, 'This is it.'"

She had hoped for some kind of response—a beginning of negotiations, at best. Instead, there came a postcard. They were arriving. Their first time in the United States in fourteen years. It was terrifying.

Doug was especially confused about what he should do. He hadn't seen them in six years, had gotten formal, if not hostile, communications from them on holidays, and had grown to think of them as strangers. Now the protective wall he had built up was to be tossed away. He didn't know if he could do it. He went to the airport not knowing what he would say, what he would and would not discuss. It was like the beginning of a sporting event. He really didn't know what would happen. When would be the moment to rehash everything? Certainly not at the beginning. But the issues were so plain and so galling, how could anything else be discussed? How could you talk about the weather when the hills were on fire?

Doug learned how from his parents. They came off the plane like grandparents, nice people, too well dressed for Southern California, all smiles and decorous embraces. He shook his father's hand, and received his congratulations. It was the same hand that had terrified him in youth, pointed the way to the door in adolescence, and blessed a thousand parishoners on the same afternoon. Doug looked: it was an old hand now, white and soft. It was not a hand with power. These were tired travelers.

The ride home was through the dark. Doug talked about the baby, about being present at delivery. His mother talked in a

sheltered way about her own delivery experiences with Doug.
The Reverend Sterling looked out the window and held his
tongue. It was a ride imbued with the color of darkness, buoyed
up by trivialities. As they began to climb the canyon leading
to the house, the three parties fell into silence for an extended
moment. Finally, Doug's mother broke it.

"How's Casey?" she asked. It was if she had just single-
handedly pushed over the Empire State Building.

"She's looking forward to seeing you," Doug said. That
was all. The barrier had been crossed, at least once.

It was a week-long visit, and throughout that time Doug and
Casey kept thinking, how can this be happening? There was
never any mention of previous hostility, of the threats and
ultimatums that had brought the curtain down on Doug's
previous relationship with his parents. The Reverend Sterling
wanted to see San Francisco. They all drove up in the car. The
grandparents took Leora on their lap, bouncing her, poking
her, doing anything in their sedate repertoire to get a laugh
out of her. And there was nothing said.

They were no more than polite to Casey, but they *were*
polite. They were barely more than that toward their own son.
There had never been a scene of demonstrative affection in the
Reverend Sterling's house, to anyone's knowledge, and this
was what all Doug's life had been like. More than once, his
mouth half-opened with confrontation on the tip of his tongue,
an opening phrase kept repeating itself in his head. He never
said it.

They walked along Fisherman's Wharf and ate crab cocktail out of little paper cups. Casey and Mrs. Sterling went into
boutiques and browsed through the jade collection at Gump's,
leaving the men alone, but the men took no opportunity for
private conversation.

"She's awfully sweet, that child of yours," Father would say.

"We're glad you could see her," Son would reply. That
was the beginning and the end of it.

On the way home Casey opened a corner of the conversation, quite innocently.

"I want you to know," she said, "that it means a lot to us that you came to see us, and Leora. We're glad you changed your mind."

It must have been the last sentence that did it. There was a fifteen-minute silence after she said it.

Every step was tiny, made on quiet, nearly invisible ground; yet there were steps. As the week approached its end, both parents and children knew the ice had melted, although no one would say just how soft it had become.

"Ten years ago," Doug told Casey when the house was quiet at night, "I would have busted them on it. I would have taken him on every point. I don't have to beat him anymore."

"You already beat him," Casey said. "They're here. You don't have to make 'em go and feel bad about it."

Still, Doug was amazed, not at his father, but at himself. His restraint was something new to him. He didn't even want to take his father to the mat anymore. His father was an old, sad man who had missed a lot and was afraid of a lot. He didn't pity him, but he was willing to let him alone. The feeling seemed to be mutual. Doug was an adult now, out of his father's reach, and the Reverend Sterling seemed to know it. He treated Doug like a parishoner he did not exactly approve of, but who was one of God's children nonetheless.

As for mother, Doug knew she was aching somewhere inside. He suspected, although could never confirm, that his mother was the moving force in this reconciliation, that his mother had mourned through the months that Casey was pregnant, because she could not be a part of it. Mrs. Sterling had cast her lot with the minister, and she would be faithful to his wishes, but hers was a lost life from which she had lately recouped a little. She cried when they said good-bye at the airport and held her granddaughter one last time. It would be beyond her ability now to tell Doug that she loved him. She could not bring herself to kiss Casey. There were too many years of ingrained aversion. It was a sad good-bye because it set the limits of the harmony ever to be achieved by these four people. There were still improvements to be made, there was still some warmth that could be kindled, but only so many and only so much.

There were stiff handshakes all around. Only Leora was kissed, and only by her grandmother. Then they were gone.

Casey's letter was impulsive, an act of momentary rage and honesty. But the roots of that impulse run as deep as the tradition of the family. Casey wanted grandparents for her child because grandparents have a natural and important part in the general scheme of things. They provide a sense of place, a background, and a location in time. That solid, simple foundation from which the self grows has been swirling away from us in the dust of progress. Especially for the Sterlings, biracial, multi-cultural people living in the hybrid city of Los Angeles, the sense of primary location was nonexistent. Leora might grow up thinking of herself as living on the edge of the world, having come from nowhere. It's a hard way to grow up, and Casey was going to fight it.

The meaning of grandparents has changed. In turn-of-the-century America, they lived nearby, helped with the sitting, gave advice, and chronicled family history to their growing grandchildren. That America has been wiped away, and now grandparents tend to live in far-off places. When they visit, they come as guests, no matter how hard they may argue to the contrary. Also, because many women are waiting longer to have first children, first-time grandparents are probably older, as a group, than ever before. Often they cannot take on the physical burden of sitting and caring for their grandchildren. Although it sounds cruel, it is fair to say that grandparents are simply not as serviceable as they used to be. Nonetheless, they may be the cornerstones of a successful family because their last function, to bear family tradition, has never been more important that it is now.

We are all lost. Beginning with the 1960s, the United States cut its moorings to its own moral and political history. "God Is Dead" and "The Family Is Dead" were phrases intoned not with solemn propriety, but with a kind of malicious

satisfaction. The 1970s have brought back the physical ac-
coutrements of family life, but do we know anything about
our own home? Do we feel at home there? In a semihomog-
enized, multicultural society, we need the pride of our own
identity, and although we may have cast it away, it is ours
still. If we did not get along with them as parents (a large
percentage of us did not), the moment when we, ourselves,
become parents may be the last good opportunity for a peace
treaty. We are not suggesting that the country should go backward and embrace a way of life that has been left behind. It
seems important, however, to recognize and keep with us the
place from which we come, and grandparents are from that
place.

There is no point in making any peace treaty with our own
parents a big event. It is best that it be unspoken, like Doug
Sterling's reconciliation with his family. By the time we have
children, the battles with our own parents, whatever the damage, should be over. The formal exchange of swords will only
hurt feelings and reopen closed wounds.

Remember that, like our children, our parents are not our
contemporaries. Not all grandparents are aged codgers, of
course, but they may not be as quick, as flexible, or as
strong as we want them to be. If you are, say, thirty, you
may find yourself in a trying spot. Your baby will be irrational, and your parents may not be all they once were. (We
are not talking about senility here, merely the physical limitations that begin to set in as early as the sixties.) You must
be the balance. Like it or not, you are the strong one in this
situation. You must practice tolerance in two directions at
once. If grandparents are coming for a visit, be prepared for
it. If you dream of the approaching time as one when you
can hand the baby over and forget your cares, you are bound
to be rudely awakened. Nonetheless, the value of grandparents
is enormous and unquestionable. Any child can take pride in
his or her heritage, no matter how simple. That pride develops
into a strong and constant foundation that will support a child's
sense of who he is and where he has come from.

From your own point of view, you may find a new understanding of your parents by becoming one yourself. This often is a time when grandparent and parent become friends, because when you have been a child *and* a parent, there is a sudden flow of understanding that can make over a lame, strained relationship. You may have always considered them narrow and intolerant, and they may be both of those things; but they have experience beyond yours. You may be able to take advantage of it. When they were parents, you judged them only by how well they supplied your needs. Now that they are grandparents, you may begin to see them as people and find what you never cared to look for when the risk of looking was greater. You will be seen by *your* children as you once saw your parents. By remembering back to that time when you were a child, and by having your parents to consult, you may be able to learn what you are in for.

AT NINE MONTHS

Nine Is a Hard Month

CASEY knew her moment would come. For nine months she had been steady-on—firm, logical, patient, in control. She had handled the appendectomy and that crisis with resolve and Doug's parents with an easy honesty. She had taken on the mantle of motherhood without any noticeable change in character. Casey was strong, but she knew there was a neurotic side to her that must by now be climbing the walls to get out. One good, short breakdown was out there somewhere, waiting for her.

The tour had been a bust. Its cancellation had given them time to get the album in shape, but they were hurting for money. They had certain projections for their financial needs and expectations, and now, for the first time since Leora's birth, they were hustling. They went back into the studio.

Nine months is a hard age. Leora had become a clinger. She wanted her mommy all the time and had developed an infuriating whine with which to make clear her demands. The studio gig, which lasted from late morning until well into the night, seemed like the right thing for Casey; it would get her back to work and away from the baby. It would be temporary, give her distance, and make her time with Leora pure and free of resentment. By leaving her milk in bottles in the freezer, Casey could begin a natural weaning process, nursing Leora only in the morning. It was a great theory.

But the first day was a disaster. Work was lost because of Casey's inability to concentrate. She missed entrances, fluffed lyrics she had written herself, and generally drew attention to herself by incompetence. Finally, she went home, leaving Doug and the musicians to lay down some instrumental tracks for the next day's work. She had never had such an unprofessional day.

The next day a new plan was implemented. Casey took Leora to the studio with her. Now her concentration was really ripped apart. Leora had to be restrained from tearing the guts out of a control panel, and Casey could see the commotion in the control room through the plate-glass panel that separated her from her daughter. Still, she was not about to waste two days of expensive studio time, and she put in a better performance than on the first day. Toward evening, when one song had been finalized, Casey and Doug sat in the control room listening to a playback. Leora was on her mother's lap, unpacking her purse in search of chewables. Everything was fine until the Sterlings' voices began to come through the broad, loud monitors in the room. Leora looked up at the speakers, looked around at her parents sitting quietly in the room, and a wild panic of confusion seized her. She began to shriek as if stung; her head spun and she began to hyperventilate. It was a totally unexpected reaction. Casey took her out immediately, but she was inconsolable. The scare kept her crying for almost twenty minutes, longer than she had ever cried before. Casey was a wreck.

They were facing a weekend, and time for recovery. Casey knew this was it, the great neurotic collapse she had been dreaming about. They always came at the most inconvenient times.

There was not much to do about it. Doug was not having

the same kinds of worries, and his sympathy wasn't much help. Casey spent the two free days keeping Leora at her side, taking her to the market and to dinner, refusing to be separated from her. On Monday she knew she would have to have this thing licked. Monday came, however, and Casey felt terrible. She dropped Leora with the sitter, and she and Doug rode to the studio in silence.

"This is for her," he said. "You're doing this for her."

This was true. Most of the songs on the album had been written during Leora's infancy, a few during the pregnancy. The album was very much a product of that time; it was a sunny album, a little out of step with the darkening mood of rock and roll, but it was all theirs. Casey tried to concentrate on that; it was Leora's album, so it had to be good. It got her through the day. When they went to pick up Leora that night, Casey burst into tears in front of everybody. Leora hadn't missed her in the slightest, but she was disturbed to see her mother crying. The result was that Doug took the baby while Casey put herself back together.

"I was going through fruitcake time," Casey recalled. "So many things were operating inside me at once that all I *could* do was cry. Part of it was that I *wanted* to be away from her. I *wanted* that freedom, and I didn't want to want it. It made me sick to think I could need my own, old life back. Like I was some kind of a failure as a mother."

There were bad days and entire bad weeks. Sometimes it was reassuring to know that Leora didn't miss her, other times it was depressing.

"The one thing I hate to think about," said Casey, "is that I might need her more than she needs me."

Casey could produce any side of herself without warning. There were days when she felt that the rock-and-roll world had passed her by, that she had become an old woman overnight, left behind by sexier, bolder women with more time to devote to themselves. There were days when the music industry looked like a sick monster, eating away at her family life. Casey felt everything at once and nothing with any certainty.

"It just happened," she said. "This bad wave of depression. It came and, eventually, it went. I started fretting about my body, about whether I was attractive anymore, about whether anything could ever be sexy again after you spent the day with a lot of vomiting and dirty diapers and drooling all over everything. I really got to wondering, I tell you."

She never stopped loving Leora, but the resentment knotted her up inside.

"I just couldn't handle any negative feelings toward her. Any time any downbeat emotion would come to me about her, it would short-circuit my system. I couldn't react to it. I couldn't *believe* it. And I felt guilty in front of her, like she knew."

It receded as the weeks went by. A balance was struck between career and motherhood. Physical adjustments were made to accommodate new needs. The Sterlings couldn't be in the studio as many hours a day as their record company wanted them to be. That adjustment was made. They had to stay home one day of the weekend with Leora. That adjustment was made. It was an annoyance to have to make rules and regulations about their emotional life, but they did it. The object was to move Casey away from her bad feelings. They attacked each one separately, until there were no more left. Certain inadequacies remained because they were unchangeable. But at least they had been acknowledged, confronted, and dismissed.

"I kept waiting for post-partum depression," Casey recalled later. "And I waited and waited, and finally I forgot about it. Wouldn't you know it was just standing in the shadows till I forgot. I just had too much on my mind."

The ninth month is a tough month. It's tough partly because the sixth month is so terrific. One mistake people make with babies is that they keep thinking they're over the hump. Babies get tough, then easy, then tough again. At nine months they tend to be clingy, fussy, demanding, and active. They get into trouble, and they aren't above annoying you on purpose. For this reason, the ninth month is a big month for guilt and a big month for second thoughts. Just to deepen the problem, it is around this time that parents start feeling like their old selves again. The parenting adventure has stopped being an adventure, they're just about over the shock of childbirth (it takes this long), and they're ready to move on. To where?

A lot of arguments take place during this period about whether the couple was "ready" to have a baby yet. This is, of course, beside the point by now and rather like asking if you are "ready" to have a headache or "ready" to turn forty. The Sterlings were as ready for parenthood as anyone ever gets, but being ready doesn't mean you have to enthusiastically embrace the trying parts of parenting as well as the blissful parts. There are some painful moments due here, and you're entitled to complain. They'll go away if you're like most couples. Following is a brief summary of why the ninth month can be so bad:

1. Your baby is at his most demanding and troublesome.
2. If you are a wife, you may be just starting back to work and going through all the guilt associated with leaving your child for the first time. If you're *not* working, you still will want to get out, relax, have some recreational time to yourself, and that makes the guilt even worse.
3. If you are a husband, you can bet you'll be called on for extraordinary support because of the above two items, and just when you thought you could work late without worrying.
4. You will actually be pretty tired of being around your baby all the time. This makes a lot of people feel guilty, but it makes sense. At nine months, you've done it all. You'll want to be a couple again, at least part of the time.
5. If you are a nursing mother, you may be starting to get your period for the first time in eighteen months. This can make things seem pretty bleak.

6. If you are the husband of a nursing mother with reduced sex drive, you may start to feel you've been a
pretty good sport for an awfully long time.

Usually there is no one huge emotional catastrophe that
strikes you, but rather the endless nagging of a hundred minor
problems. If you untangle each from the other, you will be
better off than if you try to lift all the weight at once. Make
sure you have time alone together as a couple. Make sure
you have some leisure/entertainment time reserved. Be patient
with the wife-returning-to-work situation—it usually cures itself. Unfortunately, there are no more encouraging words than
these to be said: wait this one out. Nine is a hard month.

AT ONE YEAR

Instinct Takes Over

LEORA's first birthday was a big event. A lot of people were coming over; there was going to be a party. Leora was only included in the first part; the rest was supposed to be for grown-ups. Doug mysteriously disappeared in mid-morning, however, and returned with the evening's prime attraction, a borrowed movie projector and four Looney Tunes—a Bugs Bunny, a Daffy Duck, and two Roadrunners. This was a party where no one had to be too grown up.

A year had gone by since Leora's birth, and no one was going to forget that that's what they were celebrating. Party hats and noisemakers were too corny, and Casey was afraid all the guests would feel like idiots. So there was only one other kid's thing: an enormous square cake with little rock-and-roll bands made out of icing. The baker who designed it was famous, but it was evident from his work that the last time he had seen anything to do with rock and roll was the 1950s. The cake looked like a frieze of a sock hop. There were little forty-five records flying through the air, and fragments of the musical staff were made from ropes of red icing. By the time the first guests arrived, Doug and Casey had been laughing quite a lot.

Leora got far too many presents. People brought toys, clothes, a plastic fire engine to ride in, and even a lone savings bond. Leora, having no idea what the meaning of it all could be, was nonetheless hysterical with delight. She had a paper crumpling contest with herself in the corner while everyone else drank wine and smoked grass, then she cut the cake with a plastic knife, or at least took a good poke at it. Everyone cheered and Leora began to cry. She was frightened. She was tired. Casey carried her off to bed, and the party got going in earnest.

Casey didn't drink often, but when she had two glasses of wine, the world seemed an immensely satisfying place. While Elmer Fudd chased Bugs Bunny across a bright-green carrot patch, Casey looked out across fifteen friends and thought about the year, her introduction to motherhood. She had changed, and it had everything and nothing to do with the baby. She didn't care what people thought anymore: about her, about Doug and her, about their life or their child. These were good friends in the room, and she was glad to see them enjoying themselves, laughing and drinking, but she didn't care the way she used to care. There were too many important things inside herself to take up her concern.

Casey had a kid who was doing fine. She didn't take all the credit, but she didn't care about much else. That was what her year had been for—to have a child who was a year old and doing fine. Casey felt they had done it all right, or as right as you can do anything you've never done before. That assurance had been affecting her lately: it carried into every aspect of her life. She could speak with more assurance. She didn't feel lazy anymore, and she knew Doug wasn't carrying her. She was more than keeping up. She had a feeling she had never had before, a feeling that even though life was dangerous, especially life with a baby, nothing could touch her anymore. Her softness hadn't disappeared, but her vulnerability had melted away. She had never known before that she was all right, not even after two glasses of wine. On the night of Leora's party, she knew.

Everyone got drunk. There was some nude swimming and loud music. Casey found she could dance and still be a mother. She could take her clothes off and still be a mother, and she could even drink, smoke dope, get hysterical, and still be a mother. It hadn't hurt her, and it hadn't made her anyone else. She was still Casey.

There were terrible headaches the next morning. It was gray and wet outside, and Leora was hard to keep amused. Doug and Casey bundled her into the car and took her out for a ride up the coast, past a flat, threatening ocean reflecting the cold gray of the sky. The beach was damp and empty. The air was cold, moving abruptly against them as they walked the waterline. Leora, sitting in a backpack on Doug's shoulders, played at dodging the gusts and grabbing at the gulls hundreds of feet above her. She laughed at the impossibility of the game. Doug and Casey didn't talk. They were feeling just a little smug and awfully proud of themselves to have this beach—this life. Another couple jogging past them with a seven-year-old in tow brought them back to reality. They weren't the only couple in the world with a one-year-old baby.

As the light began to desert the sky, Leora dozed off on Doug's back, and Casey placed a blanket around her. They made their way back to the car and put on some music. Leora slept all the way home in Casey's arms.

The house was still a mess. Doug collected a ton of paper cups and dirty ashtrays and began stuffing garbage into trash bags. They ran two loads of dishes through the dishwasher, and Casey began to vacuum. As she made the narrow turn from dining room to living room, she backed one step too far and gave a sharp elbow jab to the TV set that someone had thoughtfully perched on the edge of the dining-room table the night before. Her grab was too late. The shattering of plastic and electrical parts against the tile floor brought

Doug in from the kitchen. He surveyed the wreckage and looked at Casey.

"Whole big TV set," she said. "Gone."

Then she began to giggle. It was months before they bothered to replace it.

"We just threw it out," Doug recalled, looking back on the whole year. "We thought we'd just let Leora entertain us. She's a howler compared to TV anyhow."

It was a bright day some eight months later when we talked over the year. Leora was walking and talking a stream-of-consciousness nonsense. The television had just been replaced, but was not on. Doug and Casey were pondering their first year, why it had been so emotionally easy and what they did that was different.

"Of course, we have an advantage," Casey said. "We're always together. But I think even if Doug went to work every day and came home at night he'd be the same. Because he doesn't *think* of Leora as "my" job. We both have two jobs. Her and music. We obligated ourselves to those two jobs."

"That makes it sound very unromantic," Doug added, "calling her a job, but what it comes down to is—those two jobs are just about all we do, and we do them all the time. We never cut off little pieces of time and said, 'this is child-rearing time' or 'this is music-making time.' Leora has been raised right in the middle of our time."

They went on to talk about other subjects—discipline, their own parents, their unconventional life-style—and then, as the tape began to run out, Doug attempted to sum up the way they attacked the problem of raising a child.

"We were ready," he said. "That was point one. We knew we'd have to change completely—but what we didn't count on was the way Leora would cement our relationship. I think if that's why we had wanted her, she never could have done it; but because we were all right, because we were looking on our marriage as a kind of construction—something we were building—she just became a piece of the architecture."

He thought about the statement for a moment, looking off into space. Then he spoke.

"That sounds like such a load of crap," he said. "The amazing thing is that it's true."

The Sterlings had close to a model first year. Few are so fortunate, but there is certainly more to the Sterlings than luck. Coming from a broken and a rebellious home respectively, Casey and Doug maintained a remarkable degree of faith in the family unit. Their upbringings were rocky, and each of them emerged tough and resilient. They are self-sufficient people, who believe in nothing so much as their own way of doing things. They have complete trust in their instincts and are not above bruising a few feelings in the process of following them.

This brings up the subject of instinct, something that is usually discussed in relation to hibernating bears and raccoons, who wash all their food. People have been arguing for decades about whether humans possess instincts. We aren't scientists, and we wouldn't know how to go about testing such a proposition, but the fact is there was a time before child-care books. There was a time (there must have been) when women gave birth and raised children without any professional help, and enough of them survived to lead to overpopulation, smog, and war. What we're calling instinct may not be instinct, in the strictest scientific terms. But it's something—intuition, soul, whatever—that is being buried beneath a barrage of professional advice. Professional advice has a habit of making you think that you can't do without it. What started out to be a specialized field for people in trouble has become a multimillion-dollar machine bent on destroying your faith in your innate ability. The trouble with the advice-givers (this book is, sadly, part of the syndrome) is that they thrive on your confusion and cannot help encouraging it, because the more you need them, the healthier their industry becomes.

So instinct has become an impoverished quality in human beings today, if indeed it exists at all. Listen to any group of mothers gathered at a children's party, and you will hear theory and countertheory, arguments pro and con about everything from discipline to toilet training. If you could eavesdrop on the various conversations between the husbands and wives, after the party was over, you would hear each mother explaining to her husband what was crazy about the way every other mother was raising her kids. This seems to be a universal kind of gossip. Both the authors plead guilty to it, and we can't think of anyone who shouldn't.

The conversation grows out of a lot of partly digested reading matter from various sources—magazines, books, doctor's pamphlets. No one knows, of course, what any particular kind of upbringing will do to (or for) any particular child. We're all guessing and then promoting our guesses to the sky. This is really a nasty game of gossip masquerading as a stimulating exchange of ideas. In fact, people bring up their children however they see fit. They probably try to improve on what their own parents did, while using many of the same methods. Beyond that, there's not much to say on the subject.

Not that mothers shouldn't talk: there are helpful hints to be passed back and forth. But we have yet to meet a mother who radically changed her philosophy of child-rearing after talking to another mother. Parents can be parents without constantly craning their heads to see what everyone else is doing.

The Sterlings believed in themselves, and they were right. Most of us *can* bring up children if we pay attention. Listening to our own inner voice is something we have gotten bad at, and we need to reintroduce it as a way of life. In most of us, it's there and reachable. That does not mean the conflicts will be erased, or that the process will suddenly become as simple as sleeping through the winter. It only means that, as Dr. Spock says in the beginning of his famous book: "You know more than you think you do." This extends beyond child-rearing. You probably know why your mate is behaving the way he or she is behaving, why you are furious, tired, cranky, or depressed, and many other things if you will only look. We've all been trained to consider ourselves incompetent in self-investigation. We need to retrain ourselves.

The Sterlings, having been on their own for a long period in a marital situation that no one approved of or understood, had to make the rules themselves. In doing so, they created a self-sufficient universe.

One of the best things about this place was that child care was a part of everything. Casey never separated mothering from anything else. She was able to work around her child, and raise her child around her work. In this respect, she is unique among the mothers in this book, *but she need not have been*. More and more mothers are demanding and receiving the right to bring infants to work, or to work at home. One reason Casey had so little trouble adjusting to the career/baby dilemma is that she made her own rules. This is, of course, a special family; husband and wife share a career and work at home much of the time. Few people have this kind of opportunity for togetherness—and Doug embraced fathering in a way that few men do. Still, the reason for the Sterlings' success can be traced not to their physical circumstances, but to attitude. They saw Leora as a second, full-time career, and they were ready to take her on.

They had negative credentials all down the line—racially mixed, raised in bad homes, victims of violent beatings, practically candidates for psychopathia—but they had one positive credential that made all the others theoretical. They had been together seven years, and they knew each other as totally as two people can. They knew there would be surprises from their baby, but they knew there would be none from each other. That, combined with a willingness to give up a lot of life's trivial pleasures for a long time, made them golden. The baby couldn't threaten them. Someone once said that the time to have a baby is when you can't figure out why you haven't got one already. That's an instinctive moment, and when it came, Casey and Doug knew what to do.

THE
THIRD
FAMILY

David and Ellen Welles

AND EDWARD

THE
CONTESTED DECISION

*Having a Baby
with an Unwilling Partner*

DAVID WELLES had an inspiration during the slow movement of Mozart's Piano Concerto no. 26. It is a child's theme, with graceful, childlike variations, and it put David in mind of children. He was sitting in his den, in apparent silence. Earphones communicated the music directly to his ears, which was how he liked it. Now, quite suddenly, an inspirational solution to the problem of having a baby seemed to shape itself between him and the earphones. Physicists almost never receive these things out of the air; generally, they move ploddingly, point to point. David was proud of his luck. The inspiration was simple: adoption. It had never occurred to him because he and Ellen were perfectly capable, as far as anyone knew, of conceiving a child. He just didn't want to.

The debate was as old as their marriage. David had hated being a child. He had hated being on the butt end of the disasters his parents rained down upon each other. At least he had never felt responsible for chewing up anyone's life, the way his parents had chewed up his. With a baby in the house, he might have to be responsible for just that—a baby. God only knew what a baby was or would be. There were certain people, David said, who were not meant to deal with babies.

That was the argument. Ellen had married this man, loved him, and needed him, but she was a woman who had to be a mother. No simpler impasse had ever existed. And no simpler compromise could be found, David thought, than adoption of an older child. An older child would fulfill so many things for him—a sense of philanthropy, a sense of intellectual commitment. He really was not at all displeased by the idea.

Broaching it to Ellen might prove a problem. He watched her in the spare room at her loom, her delicate hands working with multi-colored strands of yarn. He was fully aware of the power there. Ellen, he explained to his friends, was Greek. That implied olive skin, deep, bottomless brown eyes, and reserves of emotional fireworks that he could only admire and fear. To a neurotic Jewish scientist, Ellen was a wondrous and unpredictable thing. She watched him with the fierce jealousy that he had only seen before in the movies. She allowed him his peculiarities and extracted a price in possessiveness. She called his office four times a day and would appear from nowhere at a party if he was engaged in conversation with another woman of any description whatever. All this was highly flattering and only occasionally frustrating. David did not speak harshly to her, either in public or in private, but he couldn't help noticing that a tote board was running in his head. Grudge was too strong a word, but David never seemed to forget his wife's actions, positive or negative.

He decided, as always, to bring up the adoption question as a postulate of debate. These were the advantages to adoption:

1.) There would be no pregnancy, and none of the emotional imbalance that might result from one.

2.) There would be no infant—the unknowable little thing he feared, sucking and squalling, a mystery living right in their house.

3.) Ellen would be able to continue her work.

4.) Life could go on the way it always had. This was a high priority. An adopted child would come into their life, not commandeer it.

David wrote these down in black felt-tip pen on a yellow legal pad, leaving Mozart and the earphones alone for a moment. There was a fifth point about Ellen's body—he didn't know if he could handle the transformation. He was a big fan of thin women. On consideration, however, he crossed these lines out; they seemed insulting. He ran his fingers through the brown curls on his head, as he always did before tackling a problem, and tugged at the sleeves of his bulky sweater. In the spare room, Ellen had finished with the loom and was packing up for the night. David went in to see her.

Ellen had already been looking at adoptable kids on television for a week. She wanted every one of them—mixed races, Vietnamese orphans, kids whose lives were heading for catastrophe. She had the almighty power to intervene, but she wanted her own child more. She felt, despite all David's points of debate, that he did, too. Coping with the complexity of her husband's character was a point of pride with her, a mark of devotion. She could be a subtle negotiator as well, and was not about to set off unnecessary explosions in the relationship. It had rocked this way and that since its inception. She had sea legs. Every marriage, she reasoned, operates on its own unique set of bylaws, has its own emotional language. Her husband had extraordinary strengths and weaknesses. He had boundless energy and curiosity about everything; he was brilliant, ambitious, and emotionally scarred from childhood. Shaping herself to these peaks and valleys was not to be accomplished without friction. Unlike David, Ellen had no aversion to friction.

Adoption counseling was a compromise step Ellen was willing to take. She thought maybe an adopted child would mellow David, and he might then want a natural child as well. Or, she figured, they might end up with a natural child once the complications of the adoption process had begun to set in. At times, she wasn't sure what she thought. Adoption counseling seemed like some kind of forward motion on the baby issue; it was a great relief.

Neither David nor Ellen was prepared for the reception they got at the adoption center, however. They were, according to their counselor, dubious candidates. This was outrageous. They had never been dubious candidates for anything before in their lives. They were bright, financially sensible people with a well-established marriage. David felt they were offering the adoption agency a quality of material not often seen. How frequently did a couple capable of having children come in because they *preferred* to adopt? David's voice was defiant.

That, explained their counselor, was exactly the point. How close were the Welleses to their own true feelings about having babies? Their logical rationale seemed to be that an adopted child was somehow easier, less disruptive, less demanding than a natural child. This was certainly not so. Most adopting parents were unable to have babies; they felt blessed by the entrance of an adopted infant into their house. Did David and Ellen feel the potential of this blessing, or did they feel they would be doing the child a favor by taking it in?

These questions proved a setback. David tried to explain. What he was frightened of was not the time involved, or the commitment, but the unknowability of a fetus. The thing would be growing inside Ellen, right in front of him, but totally out of reach. He could not control or even influence the development in there. At least with an adopted child he would know what he was getting.

Ellen watched her husband's eyes when he spoke. All she could see was garden-variety panic—an anxiety attack that wouldn't come out. She knew what was happening inside David, and it was eerie. His own childhood, so long buried, was being exhumed by the idea of becoming a father. Control was the operative word in David's plea against childbirth. Control was what he could never give up.

His mother had lost control of everything, slowly at the beginning, then with horrifying acceleration. For the first eleven years of his life, she had been perfect, an object of devotion and total trust. Then there was drink and wheezing afternoon naps on the living-room couch in a housedress. There was an ugly divorce. Toward the end, she began baring her breasts to her teenage children, shouting, "This is nothing to be ashamed of!" Shortly after that, she was gone. In the years of his mother's decline, David's father had become a hero, suffering but glamorous. As an art critic of national note, he had seemed to uphold the finer things in cultural life, but David's maturity had shattered that image, too. He now saw his father's egomania as a primary source of his mother's collapsed self-esteem. Parents were nothing to cling to. Adoption seemed a fair middleground—nothing pressed too hard, nothing stirred too vigorously.

David dreamed of his macrocephalic cousin, and an aunt, born with an enlarged heart, who died at thirty-four. He found these dreams prophetic and refused to be comforted by the information that everyone had such dreams. The adoption counseling progressed, and the Welleses made strides. David talked more and more: a sudden tirade about the commerciality of baby clothes, a scientist's argument against husbands being permitted in the delivery room. As Ellen's ear became more acute, she began to understand one thing she had never understood before. Her husband's fear, as complex and neurotic as its source might be, was a fear of simple things. It was a six-year-old's terror upon entering a carnival laugh-in-the-dark. For David, dirty diapers and breast-feeding were like poisonous snakes and ghosts. He was just plain scared of babies, and everything they did and meant. When Ellen recognized how many of his objections were based on this simple, childlike panic, the prospect of adoption suddenly became ludicrous. A six-year-old's dread was not about to keep her from having her baby just because it was emanating from a grown man.

The last thing David had always done when he moved out of an apartment was disconnect the stereo system. The first thing he had always done when he moved into a new place was connect it again. Music—the mathematics of Bach, the dignity of Mozart—nourished and pacified him. For a time, when Ellen's belly was just beginning to show, the crashing symphonies became a kind of armor; he surrounded himself with them. He did not tell anyone about this, but Ellen knew. She had been married to him for eight years, and she could read his emotions by the volume knob on the receiver. There was nothing she could do about it either; his alarm grew in proportion to her body.

He had agreed to the pregnancy by acknowledging the defeat of his arguments. Adoption simply did not make sense. He had already admitted that the marriage deserved some kind of a child. This implied syllogism defeated him. David lived by the resolution of arguments. He tried to have no feeling about winning or losing them, but beneath the rationality, there was a deep core of emotion. That core was a sore loser. As a result, Ellen, who was a natural expert at expressing *her* feelings, learned to bottle them up while his moods were running their peculiar courses. She sat for hours at her loom, now moved to the garage, turning out a series of wall hangings.

David's experience with his mother had convinced him that *all* women should have an occupation; weaving was Ellen's solution, although she never pictured it as a career. Mothering would be her career, but that was a fight for later.

Her own parents, like David's, were divorced. She knew divorce, and she knew that it had to be avoided. She was willing to do whatever had to be done to preserve the peace. Books on child care began to mount up on the workbench. The lump in her belly became a major research project. There would be no question of David's that she could not answer. His mind would be at rest.

On a rare, rain-soaked Saturday afternoon, Ellen sat at the loom reading Dr. Spock. The grim, melancholy third movement of Mahler's First Symphony began to drum through the floorboards of the living room above her. She had tried to be tolerant. This was too much. She marched upstairs. David was staring out the window at a flat of battered geraniums left in the garden. Mahler was tolling at such a volume that she had to shout.

"Goddamnit," she said. "Stop celebrating the death of this marriage and your meaningful life! You are going to have a baby."

David looked around and turned down the volume.

"You are not going to put all your problems on my kid's head," she said more softly. "I don't want my kid to turn out like you."

She turned and went back to the loom without waiting for a reply. None was forthcoming.

But the music did not go back on. This was late in the afternoon. Around dinnertime Ellen put the loom in order and made herself some eggs and English muffins. In the living room David had begun to play the guitar. She recognized Vivaldi, only because he had told her a million times. She could still hear him at ten when she drifted off to sleep.

He was thinking of his own parents, of his behavior toward his wife, of his next few years. Pieces of a concerto modulated through his fingers on the fretboard of the guitar. He didn't know what he was playing. Something had to be done. There would be a baby. The baby would grow up, and David would be father to this process. He would *have* to do a better job than his own father had done. He had already become his father in other ways, tormenting his mate with his insularity and his ego. He saw himself now in his father's emotional pose: the silent tantrum. All he wanted tonight was the strength to throw his father out of himself. That, as he perceived it, was what needed doing.

He went into the bedroom and got undressed. Standing over the bed, he apologized to his dazed, half-awake wife—for today, for the preceding seven months of the silent tantrum, and for all the difficulties of his character. It was an emotional scene, and it was bound to turn into a sexual one. His reach encountered a different woman than his wife, however. A wide, heavy, graceless woman was in bed next to him, with Ellen's voice, Ellen's attitude, and Ellen's emotional needs. No amount of positive thinking could endear him to the size and shape of that body, and Ellen knew it. But she refused to express it. To hell with him; let him fantasize if he has to. David did the best he could.

"Marry the man today and change his ways tomorrow!"* sing the two heroines of *Guys and Dolls,* and never was a piece of bad advice so sweetly put. It might be instructive to pay heed to a few more lines from this comic anthem of misguided plans:

> Carefully expose him to domestic life.
> And if he ever tries to stray from you . . .
> Have a pot roast,
> Have a headache,
> Have a baby,
> Have two!

The above lyrics were intended as a joke, and we were all supposed to see just how crazy some women are to get married (this was in 1950). Although the philosophy is rather overstated, it nonetheless prevails in a surprising number of relationships even today. Women try to change men, men try to mold women, and the results tend to be disastrous.

Not that there's anything to be done about it. Two people fall in love and get married. Normally, they have done some exploring into each other's character, they have found some disagreeable things, but they have decided to live with them, or change them. That's the pattern. No two people are ever totally satisfied in a relationship, nor should they expect to be. The tension arises when the "changing" process slows down, or comes to a dead halt. And this always happens. People don't change, at least not often and not much. They grow, on their own. They shift concerns, they alter their taste, they mature.

---

* MARRY THE MAN TODAY by Frank Loesser. © 1950 FRANK MUSIC CORP. © Renewed 1978 FRANK MUSIC CORP. International Copyright Secured. All rights Reserved. Used by Permission.

But they don't stop being who they are, and it is crucial to understand the difference in your mate between what is changeable and what is not.

David Welles didn't want children. His reasons, as expressed, may seem foolish or immature or crazy, but they *were* his reasons, and they were real. Ellen thought that because they seemed foolish, immature, and crazy, they could be disposed of in time, by logically answering each point, which wouldn't be hard to do. What she did not reckon with was that David's character was all tied up with not wanting children. His fear, abhorrence, whatever you want to call it, was a part of him. It was driven into him throughout his traumatic childhood, and those things are hard to exorcise. In getting him to agree to the pregnancy, she had not won him over to her side, but simply defeated him. As a parent, he saw himself as the vanquished. He was going to make the best of captivity, but he was not going to call it freedom. This is a worrisome way for a family to begin.

Solutions to this problem do not exist. If one mate in a relationship does not want a baby, and the other does, family life will likely have its problems. Before any child is conceived in such a marriage, serious talks ought to be opened as to who will do what, and who won't. If it is the husband who is ambivalent or opposed to parenthood, the wife had better be prepared to do nearly all the parenting and nurturing for at least the first year or two. By parenting, we mean the dirty work as well as the clean. Maids, housekeepers, nurses, and other paid employees may make the difference here, since the home is going to need more than two hands to stay afloat.

If it is the wife who does not want the responsibility of being a full-time parent, the trouble will probably be worse. Here we can only recommend a full-time mother's helper who will live in, or an extreme form of day care, which should be arranged well in advance. Mothers who are eager to get on with a career will not be ideally equipped to handle the time-consuming (all-consuming) role that has been thrust upon them by parenthood. The exception is, of course, a "reverse"

family situation, where the father stays home for a few months
or a year to take care of the child while the mother pursues a
career. These situations are still quite rare. We applaud the
few that exist as a step toward the end of sex discrimination.
But more often than not, these arrangements are halfhearted,
with two mates pursuing two half-careers, a baby being ignored
in the middle, and the whole thing going to hell at the speed
of lightning.

The Welleses made no specific plans about what would happen to their baby. Ellen said she'd take care of it, but she
didn't really expect to do it all. David said he'd help if it
wasn't too painful. Their inner attitude was simple and unex-
pressed: we'll cross that bridge when we come to it. For
most families it's not a bad attitude, but the Welleses were
an exception. They were starting parenthood with one strike
against them, and they needed all the breaks. The breaks, however, cannot be bought or rented.

AT ONE WEEK

"I Feel . . . Weird"

WHEN Ellen Welles went into labor, a sense of precision and cool descended upon the household. It was four o'clock in the morning, and immediately Ellen moved to the living-room couch to let David get his sleep. She timed her contractions, checked all her belongings for the hospital, washed the last cup and spoon in the sink, and lay back to listen to the radio. She watched the dawning of what she assumed would be her first day on earth as a mother, and it seemed like a nice day. She made a thermos of coffee. She emptied the garbage. At six-fifteen, her water broke, and she noticed a small bloody discharge. Her contractions were irregular, only a few an hour and of varying lengths, but she had waited long enough and called the doctor.

When David awoke at seven-thirty, he found his wife missing. Too sleepy to put two and two together, he stumbled into the kitchen, dreading the worst.

"You're going to be a father today," Ellen told him.

He scratched his head and reached for a mug of coffee.
"Should I go to the office?" he asked. He was a slow riser.

"I don't think so," Ellen said. "You're taking me to the
hospital."

These words brought forth in David the same call to efficiency that Ellen had been experiencing since 4:00 A.M. He
took his coffee into the bathroom and emerged eighteen minutes later, showered, shaved, and dressed. There was no excitement. They were feeling very professional.

Labor was long, but without complication. At eight in the
evening, David and Ellen entered the delivery room, and
David faced up to the moment of truth. That thing he hadn't
wanted was battling to get out in the world, to disrupt his life
and make its demands. But watching in the mirror, he was
unable to relate the furry little dome of head, pushing through
his wife's vagina, to anything in himself. Who knew what it
meant? It was a piece of nature as ineffable as the Rockies or the
coral reefs. It never occurred to him that he had caused it. All
the efficiency, both his and Ellen's, had been directed at the
easy passage of this moment. Now that it had come, he felt isolated from it. He watched it as one watches the sunset: awed
by the forces of the world. When it was over, David knew that
whatever might happen next, or for the next eighteen years, he
could never wholly regret having become a parent; it had
afforded him this moment.

By midnight, he knew that he had been wrong about everything. Having a baby was the best thing that could happen
to a man. Edward Mark Welles, six pounds, fourteen ounces,
was his: his creation, his charge, his to influence and mold and
teach and learn from. When they brought the baby into
Ellen's room, shortly before sunrise, David held him and
looked back on a lost day in which everything he believed and
feared had mysteriously disappeared. He realized he was deliri-
ous, that the change couldn't be that total, that everything
would come back into alignment. Ups, downs, he didn't care
at all. He had a wife and a son. All the images, the horrors
that had dogged him for most of his adult life, seemed like

misreadings. They were products of his own bad family luck. This was different. He was surprised and delighted with himself. He was a new man.

He was such a new man, in fact, that for twenty-four hours he did not notice Ellen's distance, her quiet. She was in bed the whole time, and she slept most of the day, but even when she was awake, there was no excitement in her voice. She sighed when she saw her baby and took him to the breast in reverential silence, but there was not even a smile. By the evening, when Edward was one full day old, David began to watch her, wondering what was wrong.

"Did you want a girl?" he asked finally, when the baby had been taken back to the nursery.

"No," she said. "I always wanted a boy. You know that."

David shrugged. "Sometimes you change at the last minute. You seem disappointed, that's all."

Ellen looked at him oddly, wondering if that was what she was feeling. Disappointment didn't exactly cover it. It was more amorphous than disappointment; she couldn't put her finger on it. There had been so much expectation, so much tension built up over the months, and so much pain and excitement in the delivery that the baby seemed an anticlimax. He was so small and so simple. When she held him to her, he seemed only marginally alive, partly there. It wasn't disappointment she felt when she looked down at him, it was bewilderment. She was used to being pregnant, and motherhood was supposed to be an extension of pregnancy, she thought, but this was all different, a new and unrelated state. She felt serious and dignified to have been so bestowed, but she didn't exactly feel happy.

The hospital stay was torturous. David could not sleep in the room, and each night when he left she cried. Her sleep was profound: when the nurses would wake her to feed the baby, she would emerge from such depths that she didn't recognize her surroundings. She was given pain-killers for her stitches, and these made her groggy when she was awake. Nothing was clear to her. She felt that a proper attitude would make things better. If she could only be happy and enthusiastic, all of this leadenness would be shaken off. As it was, she felt dwarfed by what had happened to her, and sorry for herself, although she could not imagine why.

David was handing out cigars to everyone he knew. He readied the house for Ellen's return by having a cleaning service in and buying a dozen long-stemmed roses. It was the first sentimental gesture he had made in years. He wanted to do more, but could not think of what. Champagne gave both of them headaches, and it would be pointless to have friends in. He wanted to cheer her up and decided that this simple, elegant homecoming would have a sobering effect instead. Nonetheless, it was all he could come up with, and he did it.

Ellen was touched. This brought more tears.

"It's post-partum," David explained. "It's very common."

"I'm not depressed!" Ellen insisted. "I'm just . . . weird."

Seeing the baby asleep in his own bassinet, in his own room that they had made for him, Ellen felt stronger. She was no longer part of the labor and delivery machine at the hospital, and her baby was individualized. In the nursery, where he was lined up with dozens of other infants in identical Lucite baskets, she had thought more than once of a visit to the candy factory, where rows upon rows of Mars Bars traveled a conveyer belt to the chocolate-dip process. Here, in his own house, Edward seemed like a small person, not just another Mars Bar. It was a relief.

"There," she said after a sip of white wine, when the baby was asleep down the hall and the house was quiet. "How are you?"

"I'm spinning around," David said. "I don't know what got into me all these years. I just want to wake him up and hold him and hold him, and I don't think I ever want to go back to work."

Beware the immediate reaction. It can be relished or wallowed in to whatever extent you wish, but it should not be trusted for an instant. The delivery of Edward Welles marked one of the high-tension moments in the lives of both his parents. Both were facing up to the consequences of a life decision that had been made without agreement. Each was watching the other to see how events were taking effect. Each was overconcerned with the other and unable to concentrate on or organize his or her own reactions. What we have here are two people whose emotional balance is being seriously overtaxed. The results don't necessarily imply anything.

Post-partum depression is such a common phrase that we all assume we understand what it is. By its title, it should be a simple depression, brought on by a happy event rather than a sad one. These things are common. People often become depressed by watching parades, going to the circus, or witnessing any relatively innocent, supposedly joyful event. The suicide rate around Christmas is phenomenal. The reason is probably that all the exterior signs of joy only remind us of how far from joyful we are at the time.

For some people, post-partum depression is just like that, or so we are told. Personally, we have not spoken to anyone who experienced anything of that description. For this reason, we would favor dropping the expression from the parenting vocabulary and substituting the phrase "post-partum reaction." Post-partum reaction might be defined as any illogical or inexplicable emotional reaction to having a baby. It might include depression, but it would also include pathological euphoria, hyper-energy, and any number of other things. The important thing to remember is that all these reactions are, to some extent, a product of physiology. They come from being victimized by your hormones; they come from being too tired to act out your joy or your anxiety. They are, in other words, not products that the normal, healthy "you" would or could produce. That's why they can't be trusted.

They are, in part, psychological as well. The pressure specifically affecting the Welleses was the pressure that comes from ambivalence about children in general. It took its toll at the time of delivery, and it did not affect any other couple in this book in quite the same way. Until delivery, the question seemed to remain theoretical. Even though the time for abortion was long past, the Welleses didn't yet have a baby, and somehow, it seemed that anything could happen. The future was just uncertain enough to make the baby unreal. Upon delivery, there was no more uncertainty. The baby was there, flesh and blood. Time had run out.

Why did the two parents react the way they did? It's not a question that has an answer. You can say that David's relief at finding the baby so attractive and healthy made him go crazy with delight. You can say that Ellen felt the need for the moment to be proclaimed with solemnity; or that she was simply trying to make up for David's high spirits by anchoring her own; or that the profundity of childbirth had hit home for the first time, and she felt it was too important to take lightly. You can say all these things, but you'd just be guessing.

One thing that *may* have happened to Ellen (it happens to a lot of new parents) is that her baby was not exactly whom she was expecting. Most of us think that we will *know* our newborns instantly, that they will reflect us both physically and emotionally; but a newborn baby is quite neutral of character and frequently does not resemble anyone for quite some time. He is unfamiliar, you don't *know* him or necessarily even recognize him until you take some time to be with him. So your first expectation is immediately undercut. That's one reason for one kind of post-partum reaction, but it's only one and an easy one to pinpoint. There must be a thousand others, more vague and elusive. People do all kinds of things under physical and mental pressure. It's pointless to ask why. What explanation would be satisfactory? Post-partum reaction is what it is. To question its logic will only lead you down a twisted road that has no end.

The nice thing about it is that it's usually short. We are not talking here about depression that can set in months after parenting has begun, or serious reactions that are caused by a collapsing relationship between parents. We are dealing only with the first emotional tumble that can come immediately after delivery.

It can affect the healthy and the frail, the neurotic and the well-adjusted. It may have more to do with the difficulty of your labor and delivery than it does with your emotional or physical state during pregnancy. Your key responsibility during this reaction period is to recognize how temporary it is. Ride it if it's high, and weather it if it's low.

AT ONE MONTH

Should Fathers Learn to Mother?

RUMMAGING through the garage in search of an old pair of Ping-Pong paddles one night, David Welles came across the sight of Ellen's loom gathering dust in the dark. He began to worry. David was set off by little things like this. He thought about what an active person Ellen had been before Edward was born—all the pieces of weaving she had turned out, and how proud she had been. Then he thought about his mother, who had lived only for her children, had gone mad when they began to grow up, and died when she could no longer mother them. Ellen had better get back to work, he thought. These emotional dependencies were surreptitious, forming in the dark, tightening their links with each passing moment.

"What about your work?" he asked Ellen with far too casual an air later in the evening. "Wouldn't you like to go back to the loom?"

Ellen looked at him as if he was crazy.

"When?" she asked. "When do I have time?"

"I don't know. What do you do all day?"

Ellen laughed, but she couldn't exactly say what she did. It took her about three hours to get dressed, as far as she could remember, but she wasn't sure why. Something about the baby made everything take forever, even when the baby was sleeping. It was hard to explain.

David pressed his point: "I really want to know what you do."

"Well," Ellen said, "I have a terrific way for you to find out."

David looked up at her.

"You stay home one day and do it. Then you tell me."

David thought for a moment before he spoke.

"There would have to be conditions," he said.

"Such as . . ."

"Such as: you have to show me where everything is, write down everything that needs to be done, give me a feeding schedule or whatever. In other words, you can't leave me out in the cold."

"Done," Ellen said.

David sighed. He was going to be mother for a day.

Ellen rolled over in bed when Edward awoke at six-fifteen in the morning. It took a moment of muffled whining to rouse David, who sat up bleary-eyed and looked around the room as if he had never been there before. There was a bottle of Ellen's milk in the refrigerator and a pot on the stove. These facts wandered into his head a moment later. Gingerly he swept Edward up from his bassinet, blankets and all, and padded into the kitchen on a cold tile floor. It was already a dreadful morning. Edward was fed and changed and back in the bassinet in twenty minutes, and David settled back down beside Ellen for a few minutes of rest. Songbirds and a brightening sky precluded any possibility of sleep. Also, there was worry: he was in charge here. Even though Edward was sleeping, causing no trouble, David could not rest properly. He was already beginning to resent this bargain he had made with

Ellen, especially since she was snoring comfortably beside him, evidently enjoying a deep sleep.

At eight-thirty, he heard Edward awaken, and once again, he got him up. While he was walking him, Ellen rose and showered, taking her time, giving her hair a proper double-shampoo and taking care with the conditioner. In forty-five minutes she was dressed and ready to go out.

"Are you all right?" she asked David, who seemed to be in a sweat. Edward was still twenty minutes away from a scheduled feeding, and he had started whining ten minutes ago.

"I'm fine," David said, although the words barely came out at all. "Enjoy yourself."

When Ellen was gone, David quickly fed Edward. There was a whole school that believed in demand feeding, and David had just been converted. The bottle seemed to comfort the infant. David laid him back down again and picked up a report that had to be gone over before a morning meeting the next day. He was not dressed yet, and his one day of beard made him feel like a bum. His feet were cold; a breeze was attacking his chest, where the buttons of his pajamas caused stretch gaps. The pajamas had shrunk, he noticed with far too much anger.

Getting up off the bed, he checked on Edward, who was awake but silent, looking up at him with glazed, barely focussed eyes. David checked his list. The bed needed making, and the coffee cups had to be cleaned, but first he had to shower and shave. Then he could read.

Reconstructing the day some time later, this is what David came up with:

8:45 A.M. Got up from bed to shower. Edward quiet.

8:55 In shower. Edward crying. Got out of shower.

9:10 Edward quiet again. Why? Who knows. Back to shower.

10:00 Blessed! Edward sleeping, me showered and shaved and dressed. Elapsed time for shower & dress: one hour fifteen minutes.

10:30 Bed made/dishes done. Amazingly easy. Sit down to read report.

11:00 Report difficult—fifteen pages read when Edward awakens.

11-11:30 Ellen has marked down this hour for play. How do you play with Edward? Too young to bounce. Put Vivaldi on stereo and waltzed him. Hard to know what he makes of it. He stares at speakers.

11:45 Mystery solved. Edward needed bowel movement; hence, the concentrated stare. Bowel movement fouls

    a) his diaper and stretchy suit

    b) my shirt sleeve

    c) living-room carpet.

12:15 Diaper, suit, and my shirt changed. Carpet scrubbed. Edward wailing for bottle. Very healthy cry, which I rarely hear. Does he miss mommy? The rat!

12:40 Edward fed and sleeping. Me reading.

1:55 I wake up. I do not know when I fell asleep or why. Checking watch, it appears I have about thirty–forty minutes before the baby gets up and needs food again. I need food, too.

2:15 Half-grilled cheese sandwich comes out of oven prematurely when Edward cries. Cheese still cold in middle. Eaten in four gulps as Edward becomes desperate. Milk (for me, already poured) will have to wait.

2:55 Edward is inconsolable. I *can't* feed him again yet. First of all, the remaining milk is frozen. Secondly, it isn't time yet. What to do?

3:05 Defrosting milk in pan of water. Edward wailing. Blood pressure going through roof. Every minute counts. Ellen gets back at three-thirty. Can I make it?

3:10 Ultimate catastrophe. Edward wants a second bottle, and it's frozen. The cry has become wild. He's not used to waiting. Breast milk is always ready. Come on, stove!

3:30 Where is that bitch? Who does she think I am?

When Ellen came home at three forty-five, she was met by a snarling husband and wailing baby at the door.

"Goddamnit," David told her, "don't you ever be late again, not for anything!"

He thrust Edward into her arms and stormed out the door, slamming it behind him. Ellen looked around bewildered and took Edward to her breast. In a minute he was asleep.

"What happened?" she asked the sleeping infant. "What did you do to your daddy?"

David raced the traffic lights to the office and threw himself into his swivel chair. He touched the desk in front of him as if it were the last symbol of freedom in the world. He was still shaking inside, although his secretary had not seemed to notice. His head shook involuntarily, back and forth, back and forth. It was the crying, he decided. The crying made it unbearable. The work was easy—constant, but easy. If it weren't for the crying, the accusatory little voice, the perpetual critic, it wouldn't have been a bad day. As David calmed down, however, a single thought was running in his brain. It sang to him from inside with disgraceful abandon. It wasn't a very nice thought, but it was boosting itself shamelessly, and it didn't care who heard it. Over and over it went: never again, never again.

Two couples in this book tried reversing roles for a day. In one case (the Bradfords, still to come), the switch was forced by an angry wife walking out of the house. In the other (the Welleses, above), the switch was carefully planned and executed. In both cases, the results were disastrous. We now have to do a difficult thing. We have to recommend something which has proved disastrous.

Why do we recommend it? Because we feel that the results are worth the agony. It is true that David Welles was a wreck after spending nine hours with his infant son, but it's important for a father to find these things out, even if it makes him a wreck. Most fathers have no idea what their wives are doing at home all day with a one-month-old baby. It could be argued that most wives don't understand what their husbands are doing at work and so what difference does it make? It makes a difference. (Life would probably be easier for couples if wives had a full understanding of their husband's workday, too, but that's not a subject for this book.) The major failing in most of the relationships we've watched comes from a lack of communication. This is a big cliché, but that doesn't make it a lie or an unimportant point. Husbands don't know what their wives are going through, and they can't understand the constant exhaustion, the sour moods, the exasperations of an average day. Wives don't really know why their husbands are so dense, and that makes matters worse. The reason husbands are so dense is that it is hard to picture what is going on at home if you're not there. If you've already had a baby, think back to your pregnancy. Remember how wrong *you* were about what life with a baby would be like, and you'll have some idea of what most husbands are thinking while they are at work.

Reversing the process, even for a day, is as instructive as it is dangerous. In letting a husband find out just what an average day entails, you make a lot of things clear that simply can't be communicated in words. You may also cause a lot of anger and hostility and frustration to come bubbling to the surface, and you may find yourself in the middle of a scene. However, this anger and hostility and frustration, if it exists, is far more lethal when it is buried and causing spiteful behavior than when it is out in the open, causing a tantrum. On balance, if the scene clears the air, there is reason enough to try reversing roles.

Some husbands and wives do try to split the child-care chores in a more equitable fashion than the Welleses. The husband participates in all the gritty work—changing, bathing, feeding—from the beginning. If he is pursuing a career, he may take a turn on weekends, in the evening, and/or in the early morning. This, we feel, is ideal, but it still isn't the same thing as staying home with the baby five days a week, getting up with him at dawn, and being alone with him for eleven or twelve hours, week in and week out. Husbands' child-care participation is well and good: we recommend it, and we think it's only fair. To get a true taste of mother's work, however, you have to do it for extended periods, and without relief. Even a single full day delivers only a hint, but it's better than nothing, and it's all most men can spare.

It may only happen once, but the men who do it end up with a worthy understanding of what their women are doing at home all day with an infant. Their women are busy: they're harried, they're often frustrated, and they're to be applauded for surviving. It is impossible to appreciate their problems without putting yourself in their place, and impossible to misunderstand those problems once you have done so.

AT THREE MONTHS

The Eleven-Pound Catalyst: The Baby as a Wedge

IT BEGAN slowly, almost unnoticeably at first. The pattern of living had reestablished itself, and life was running smoothly for David and Ellen. Ellen was home with the baby; David was entrenched at the office. This was what life was like for young couples with a baby: industrious, difficult, tiring.

By the time Edward was two months old, Ellen felt that she would never again be fully rested. More and more often, her days ended in a black mood. Communication with David was brief, never dipping below the surface. Often, David would come home and have Edward thrust into his arms as he shut the front door.

"Gotta go to the bathroom," Ellen would explain.

David would wait, make himself a drink, try to keep Edward amused. Sometimes Ellen remained in the bathroom for an hour. Sometimes longer. David understood that something was driving her away from the baby, and he thought back to the day he had spent with Edward and tried to multiply it by sixty, the number of days since Edward had been born. He could see all too clearly the reasons for Ellen's distress, but he didn't see that anything could be done about it. When he got good and sick of Edward, he would stand by the bathroom door, letting the infant cry penetrate into Ellen's inner sanctum. Eventually she would emerge.

Strangely, nothing was ever said about these incidents. To begin exploring the bleak presence that had entered the house was felt to be dangerous by both David and Ellen. It was impossible to judge what might be found if one dug deep enough.

Edward was still not sleeping through the night. He might give Ellen as much as five hours rest at a time, but that was on a rare night. Usually she was satisfied if he slept from midnight to three-thirty in the morning, and again from four to six-fifteen. It was a debilitating schedule with no relief in sight. Edward grew, he ate, and he seemed happy most of the day, but he would not sleep. The house was perceived through a fog of exhaustion by Ellen, and shied away from by David, who found more and more work to keep him at the office. For three nights he ate dinner in the office basement: a hamburger dispensed cold from a vending machine and warmed in a microwave oven with an automatic timer. He found time at the office to read the paper, chat on the phone with friends, even indulge in an occasional game of solitaire. It was peaceful at the office.

At home he rarely relaxed. Edward was either awake, just going to sleep, or just waking up. At any moment the crying might begin. At any moment Ellen might thrust his son at him and disappear. Home was a constant round of surprises, none of them pleasant. Time he had always reserved for himself—time to read or watch television, most especially time to listen to music—was no longer his.

Ellen didn't see it quite that way. She had stood by him in all his neurotic confusion about the baby; she had weathered his professional hard knocks; she had been there always and forever. Now that she was in trouble, she felt deserted. Then, on a Monday evening, after a particularly noisy weekend, she *was* deserted.

David called around dinnertime. She had not heard from him all day.

"I can't come home," he said.

"What's wrong?" she asked.

"I don't know."

"I mean, are you working or what?"

There was a pause.

"I'm not working," he answered her at last.

"What are you doing?"

"I don't know. I'm not doing anything. I'm just sitting here, and I don't want to come home. I don't want to *be* home. I don't want to go to my house."

Ellen didn't know what to say. She was silent. The phone was clutched so firmly in her hand that a muscle cramp began to seize her left forearm.

"I'll call you," David said. "I still love you."

Ellen hung up. "To hell with that," she said to herself. Edward was sleeping. She didn't know what to do, who to call, what would happen next. She was alone for how long? Overnight? For a week? Forever? The whole thing took her by surprise. She didn't really feel it. It was an hour before she sat down and began to cry, not because she missed David, but because the center had fallen out of the pattern she lived by. She didn't know what to do.

She slept in the baby's room that night, on a couch that had never been used. The irony of the situation was clear to her: she had heard countless stories of children crawling into bed with their parents for comfort during a crisis. Here she was trying to get in bed with her child. For the first time in a month, she was glad when he wakened her to nurse. She was glad someone was still in the house with her, someone with whom she could have some human contact.

David turned up the next day during his lunch hour. He didn't call. He just let himself in and appeared in the living room. His suit looked tired, and he was wearing a shirt Ellen had never seen before. He looked around the room as if he was seeing it for the first time. He had lived here for five years, but it all seemed unrecognizable, not his home. Ellen came in from the kitchen with Edward on her chest in a front-pack.

"Hi," she said.

"Are you all right?" David asked.

Ellen shrugged. There was nothing to tell him. She had become a character in a mystery play, and she didn't have a clue about the mystery.

"Need anything?" David wanted to know.

"Are you staying away?"

"I came to get clothes," David said. "I won't stay away long. I just . . . need to be away for a while, that's all. I know it isn't fair."

"I don't give a damn about fair," Ellen said. "I'd like to know what is going on."

"I need a little time, that's all," David said. "I can't call it by a name. I don't feel I can function properly and live in this house just now."

Ellen nodded at him. He got his clothes and kissed her good-bye, an ambivalent kiss she did not think to resist. And he was gone again. She knew, as his car pulled out of the driveway, that the second night would be easier.

On the second day, he visited again, this time for longer. He talked about the office for a few minutes and she talked about Edward, who was sleeping less well than ever. In the evening, he called and said he missed her, but he didn't offer to come home. He was staying at a motel near the office, working late, breakfasting in a coffee shop, listening to music on the radio at night. He assured Ellen that there were no other women, and she knew he was telling the truth, for his distress sounded so genuine that she almost felt sorry for him instead of herself.

The third and fourth days were much the same. On the fifth day, he called three times, and she knew he was coming back. He didn't say so, but there was a longing in his voice, and she could sense the nagging dissatisfaction that had begun to envelop him. He had spent two nights at the motel and three with a friend. He was prowling the borrowed living room until after midnight, arriving at work before seven-thirty, and an ebbing energy told him that it could not go on. He would hardly tell all this to her if he were not planning a return. So she waited. She had gotten used to his absence, and, physically, life was easier. She didn't have to worry about dinner, his clothes, his cigarette ashes, or a host of other things. If his walkout had proved anything to her, it had proved how many things she did for him without noticing. Free of him, her life had become quite manageable. Still, she wanted him back, and when he called in the late afternoon of the sixth day, she knew what he was going to say.

"I gotta come home" was how he put it. It wasn't especially attractive, but she was willing to settle. She ran to the market and bought some veal scallops, some mushrooms, a pound of broccoli, and the real butter she needed for hollandaise. Why am I doing this? she wondered. Just because he hasn't eaten a decent meal in a week? It's not my fault. I've been here, ready to cook. Perhaps it was her guilt over feeling the ease of having him absent. Perhaps it was a way to make *him* feel guilty by feeding him a welcome-home meal. Whatever the reasons, they were far from healthy. She didn't know what anything would lead to, but she cooked.

He returned, and they barely spoke of it. He was sheepish, apologetic in his movements and his attitude, but unready to explain. His vague, general answers were all Ellen could get, and finally, she fell silent. When he got up the next morning to go to work, she asked:

"Are you coming home?"

"Of course I'm coming home," he said.

There didn't seem to be anything obvious about it to her, but the conversation wasn't worth pursuing. She could see that once again she was pressing in on the dark places in David's being, the places no one ever went. She was not about to gain admission. She wasn't sure she *wanted* to gain admission. Quietly, over the next two weeks, the events that had no explanation began to recede in her memory. They seemed to be altogether removed from David's. He was playing with Edward more, changing him more, being a little more tolerant. And Ellen was more careful not to use him the way she had done before. She hesitated before hauling the screaming baby over to him if he had just come home or just awakened. For reasons that were not entirely rational, she did not want him to go away again.

This is how we learn, she thought. Not by conversation, not by request or confession, but by action. He leaves, I sulk. When he comes back, certain things have been changed. We treat each other differently, but nothing is said.

Ellen had to admit she was involved in a very strange marriage. As three weeks passed from the date of David's return, however, there was a minimum of tension, and some warmth was beginning to return. Like an old car, which you dare not have tuned up for fear of finding out how bad things are under the hood, the Welles marriage was being driven with a light foot, a lick, and a prayer.

Becoming a parent reorganizes a marriage in many ways, and some of them are hard to grasp. One of the things a baby does, through no active behavior of its own, is to bring into sharp focus whatever the strains on a relationship have been. This is the reason that having a baby "to save the marriage" is such a poor idea. Babies don't save marriages. They do, occasionally, destroy them. Babies bring pressure.

In many marriages, leisure time functions as a kind of glue; it keeps everything together, giving husband and wife enough privacy or private thinking room to ward off whatever major disagreements may be lurking in the darkest corners of their character. Leisure time all but vanishes when a baby is introduced into a marriage, and when the glue dries up, things can begin to fall apart. The baby is not, per se, the "cause" of the trouble. The trouble, whatever it is, is there already. The baby acts as a catalyst by clearing out all the niceties that disguised the trouble, such as sex, free time, and a sense of freedom. When two people who are not, perhaps, made for each other face the stark realities of character and situation, the results can be combustive.

Why did David Welles leave home? At the risk of being accused of amateur psychology, we would suggest that it has to do with his own childhood. David revealed—in fact, talked compulsively about—his unhappy childhood. His home had been a constant battlefield; his family was held together only by the thinnest possible threads, and eventually by nothing. His concept of family was one of enormous tension, ill will, and unhappiness. As he became a father, the emotions of his youth began to haunt him, not in any identifiable way, but subliminally. Being "in the home" with a wife and infant son brought on a kind of panic which was, in a sense, a replay of his past. No doubt the situation was made worse by Ellen, who was close-mouthed about her resentments and acted them out by thrusting the child at him (making it seem an unwanted child, a psychologist might say) instead of talking about them. She was married to a neurotic man, but she didn't care to hear his side of things all that often. She kept quiet, didn't invite communication, and tried to *will* things into working. Between the lack of communication with his wife, and the ghosts of his past, David felt little choice but to flee.

The confusing thing about it all is that he loved Edward. He handled him well, played with him happily, and thought about him constantly. He just couldn't live with him in that family situation. Only when it became obvious that living separate lives was a hopeless situation did he come home, feeling very much like a man without a country.

The possibility of neurotic behavior when one mate has come from a very unhappy homelife is worth some consideration. These things are not always controllable; the sweetest man or woman in the world may have a vicious reaction if properly provoked. We cannot control our neuroses at all times. David's feelings about home were as hard to correct as a bone defect or a case of the common cold. They were real fears, not something that could be knocked out of him with a stern talking-to. His return home was a signal for some serious soul-searching, possible counseling, psychiatric help, or some kind of professional assistance. The Welleses were tempting the fates by burying the experience and whitewashing their feelings in an attempt to "be normal."

AT SIX MONTHS

The Mother as Emerging Woman

DAVID had come back, but he was not entirely there. On some mornings he would wake up with his teeth clenched and his hands in a fist. On others, everything seemed fine and serene, and Edward's cry filled his heart with warmth. He was perplexed much of the time. For a man who valued control, logic, and order, things were quite out of hand. And, like a reformed alcoholic who knows that somewhere out there, a long way away, there's a drink with his name on it, David knew that he was secretly, blindly, planning an escape. He didn't know when it would be necessary, or even why it was necessary, but he could feel the necessity of it at certain moments of the day. The contradictions within his emotions grew deep and complex as time went on. There were days when he could not predict his reactions to things more than two minutes in advance. His work remained reliable. Everything else was in turmoil.

A month after his return, the Welleses began going to a marriage counselor, joining another couple with similar problems. In these sessions of five, anything could be said and no statement was belittled. It was an invitation to mawkishness, accusation, self-pity, or whatever anyone was feeling. Everyone spilled fountains of inner emotional stress on the floor except David. David didn't know what to say at these appointments. He was given to the occasional outburst, usually directed at Ellen. But he rarely spoke of himself, however, except to admit hurriedly, in an almost inaudible tone of voice, to whatever Ellen accused him of.

"That's right," he would murmur, nodding at the floor. "You're right." She was right. She wasn't getting anywhere, but she was right. As his tacit admissions produced no results at home, Ellen began to dig deeper and deeper. She began to say what she meant, to push David's moods aside, to look underneath them to find out what was going on. The results were odd. All the little fights, the nagging, and the nit-picking disappeared. The big fights became apocalyptic.

It was Ellen who had changed. There was a time when a harsh word, a good scowl, and a sudden burst of loud, morose classical music would send her scurrying. David hated to scare her that way, but at least it worked. It gave him solitude, and it allowed his moods to pass in peace. Ellen had begun standing her ground, however, and while David had to admire her for it, it also drove him crazy. When he came home from the office, he was closely questioned about his anxiety if any was showing; if Ellen was the cause, she wanted to know how and why. She was tired of making life comfortable for him. She wanted some comfort in return, and he never seemed to have any to offer.

Concurrently, her intense jealousy over him had all but vanished. He would have been pleased by some lessening of her possessiveness. Instead, near indifference had set in. Ellen really cared about Edward to the exclusion of everything else, including David's fidelity, at least according to David. He was hurt and he was angry a lot of the time. The things he had feared would happen if a third party was introduced into the marriage were all happening. The delicate balance that had taken years to establish was being sent sprawling. When a couple had a baby, a three-part equation was supposed to replace the old one, but David couldn't see himself fitting in. He had liked it the way it was, and he knew before they began that the new way was not for him. Ellen hadn't listened. Now it was her problem.

The baby was forever. And he loved the baby. This was hopelessly confusing, for David was in love with the very child who was destroying his marriage. It wasn't the baby's fault; it was Ellen's. *She* was the one who wanted more of him, who suddenly expressed needs for sharing and communication that he had never been asked to acknowledge before. He was not built to communicate that much, to give that much that openly.

"I married a Greek," he would tell her, pretending no racial slur. "Life and love and arguments—moussaka and laughter and tears: How can you ask any neurotic Jewish boy to tolerate all that?"

"This isn't Greek," Ellen would say, smoldering, "this is human life the way people live it: talking to each other, sharing the good and the bad, *knowing* each other! Go up and down the block and ask people! You don't have to be Greek to talk about things—you just have to be a whole person."

"Well, that's my problem, then. I'm not a whole person. I'm damaged goods, I suppose that's what you think."

That was just what Ellen thought. He was damaged, and it wasn't his fault. He was brought up wrong, he was put through more childhood trauma than anyone ought to be asked to tolerate, and it all left its scars. But he *had* grown up. He *had* gotten married, and he *had* gotten through graduate school, established a prestigious position, and fathered a child. He had all the exterior markings of a human being, and he ought to take responsibility for who he was. She had married him knowing there were problems, but she thought he would pull through, that he would grow and mature like any normal man. For the first years she so admired his brilliant, neurotic mind that all she wanted to do was make life better for him, give

him the emotional and physical sustenance that his parents
had neglected to provide. But time was up. He had had five
years of it, and she was tired. She wanted a husband and a
father for her son. She was ready for him to rise to the challenge as she had done. She felt as though she had become an
adult in the past six months and David was regressing to infancy. It kept her furious most of the time.

David became furtive in his ways. He would be unreachable
in the office, taking long lunch hours and unexplained breaks.
He would nap on his couch in the afternoons after getting a
perfectly good night's sleep at home. One afternoon, after an
uncharacteristically expensive and leisurely lunch, David began
the long walk back to his office when his eye was caught by a
sign on a new apartment house that had just been completed
several blocks from his building. The sign read: "All luxury
singles and one and two bedrooms: sauna, pool, Jacuzzi, recreation room. Now Renting."

He had been thinking about it for some time. Now he was
pressed by curiosity: What did one of these places cost? How
did they look? What were they really like? With no serious
intentions admitted, he buzzed the manager's office and walked
in the double glass doors. The place was sterile looking, dotted
with plastic plants in pots. There was a loud blue stripe
painted on a white pasteboard wall, interrupted by two eleva-
tors. Through a sliding glass door he could see the small pool
and an even smaller Jacuzzi set in a barren courtyard.

The manager, a middle-aged woman with bleached blond hair,
double-knit slacks, and a print blouse, met him in the lobby.
She showed him two singles, one facing the street, the other
the pool. There was a wet bar in each and a fireplace that
could be turned on and off at will. The swimming-pool view
cost an extra twenty-five dollars a month. David pretended to
ponder. Madness was coming over him.

He excused himself and walked around the block. He felt a
tightness in his chest and his palms were sweating. His subconscious was to be blamed, he decided, because the apartment seemed to him to be the fulfillment of a desire he did

not know he had. As much as he wanted to concentrate on the personal ramifications of what he was contemplating, he found himself instead calculating the difference in price of the two places. The larger issues would not stay locked in his mind; it seemed to him that the larger issues were too great to be considered. Or perhaps there were no larger issues. Perhaps they had all been decided months ago, and he had never told himself. They no longer bore thinking about at all, he decided, and he buzzed the manager's office again, just as she was preparing to leave for her own lunch. With the panic of a boy trying to enter a bar with a forged identification card, David walked into her office and took the cheaper apartment.

It seems a great mistake that people spend much of their lives searching for an inert living situation. Any man who, like David Welles, expends his energy trying to make his marriage stand still is chasing a shooting star. Marriages are dynamic. All kinds of things make them change—but nothing changes them like children. To understand why, it is important to understand that we are not always honest in our dealings with other people, and this includes our mates.

It would be nice to think that all any man wants from his mate is someone strong, humble, lacking in ego, and self-sufficient. The trouble with this is that if it were so, men and women wouldn't need each other very much. The facts are less ideal, but easier to live with. Men and women want to need each other; they want to feel incomplete without their mates. This may not be "healthy," but, after untold centuries, it appears to be the common order of things. The intricacies of a marital relationship are frequently bound up in the needs each mate has for the other. A wife may see a man who is ego-centered in public as really being frightened of inadequacy in private, and part of their relationship may consist of the confidence she alone is able to give him. A woman who is frightened of working in the "real" world because she was brought up to be only a housewife may take on strength from her husband's urging. In each case, the "stronger" mate derives some ego satisfaction from helping the "weaker." In some cases, the weak/strong quotient is lopsided, even if the couple refuses to admit it.

David Welles took great pains to make sure Ellen was active in something other than housework—this made him feel that she was earning her self-respect. However, Ellen's "work," weaving, was hardly a career, and as long as that was all she did, David was allowed to feel superior to her. He saw himself as a difficult, special man who needed a woman to care for him and keep him. He didn't think of this view as chauvinistic: he didn't mind doing the dishes or making an occasional bed. David's view was, if anything, beyond sexism. It was not men who were superior, it was David specifically. Ellen, for her part, guarded him like a precious stone. She was possessive and jealous, and that suited David because he wasn't about to run away, and it was soothing to the ego to know that he meant so much to her. This, at the time of Edward's birth, was the essential nature of the Welles relationship.

Edward himself did nothing. His arrival was innocent enough and much less traumatic than his father had expected. It was not until several months went by that the dynamics in the Welles relationship began to shift. They shifted because Edward taught Ellen how little she had been getting. Taking care of Edward was hard work, and Ellen found she was good at it. It was full-time work, and Ellen had never done full-time work. It was exhausting, and Ellen had never trusted herself to do anything that might exhaust her before. Now, by sheer dint of experience, Ellen Welles had discovered she was as good as anyone else, perhaps better. She didn't feel guilty about not doing paid work, and the thought of returning to her loom as anything other than a hobby was preposterous to her. As the months went by, it became clear to her just how much of a charade her "career" had been. David needed her to be everything for him. He needed to tell his friends how creative she was, so he encouraged her weaving. More important, he needed her to be available all the time to absorb his hard knocks, so he never pushed her out into the cold, cruel world of earning and spending. She was an emotionally kept woman, and she hadn't even recognized it. Her success as a mother made her intolerant of the nonsensical part of her marriage. She pushed David for better terms, better understanding, and a stronger identity for herself. When she pushed, he escaped.

For almost six years David had held a grip on Ellen's self-esteem. When Edward came along, he lost the grip. It is sad to report that a greater number of marriages than anyone admits are based on the same balance: a poor sense of self-worth in the female and a subconscious sense of manipulation in the male.

Having a child almost always shines a light on this dark area of the marital relationship. Mothers find their views of themselves changing radically after three or four months of mothering. In this book, at least three of the women found that their sense of self-esteem rose so precipitously that they began to see themselves as different, more successful people. This has nothing to do with the success of their child-rearing techniques. It is a result of the simple survival of hard work, which many women have never before faced. (As indicated, the results are hardly unanimous. One woman, Betsy Scheflin, reported substantial guilt and *lower* self-esteem after becoming a mother because she really wanted to go back to work.)

This higher self-esteem will certainly affect a marriage. The only question is, how seriously? The Welleses were prone to do battle, and Ellen had almost no sympathy left for David when she realized she had been used. In other couples, the reactions can range from temporary jealousy to positive pride, although this last is somewhat rarer than we might wish or hope.

In the future, if women win the many battles they are currently fighting for self-worth and equal treatment, the problem may be minimalized. Most feelings of self-esteem are drawn from childhood, however, and a sadly small number of adult women today are equipped with the sense of worthiness they deserve. As they go through the weeks and months of mothering, and their own picture of themselves improves, their mates will have to face the consequences. Human pride is such that the adjustment may not be simple. No man likes admitting that his wife's new-found inner resources make him uneasy or jealous.

Only a few dynamic shifts in the course of a marriage are as difficult or as delicate as the redistribution of self-esteem. One partner's strength does not imply the other's weakness, but it may take time, effort, and sympathy before this truth sinks in and a new balance is constructed.

AT NINE MONTHS

You Can Never Not Have Been Married Again—The Male Urge to Be Single

ELLEN WELLES had suffered so many surprises at the hands of her husband that his impulsive move to take an apartment had little exterior effect. He had not, of course, come home and announced that he had rented a place. He told her he was leaving, that he needed to relieve the pressure in his life, that he could not see why they were living under one roof anymore with nothing to say to each other. It was only as the evening dragged on, like some uncut scene from an old movie, that she discovered he had already rented the apartment. It was a cruel piece of information, a loaded gesture that told her she meant nothing to him, that his decisions were entirely his own. She could not handle it. Suddenly she was exhausted by the whole thing. She looked at her watch and saw that there were still hours left before they would fall into separate beds. What would fill those hours she knew only too well. It was a hollow feeling knowing that all the words, the tears, the angry stingers had been spoken a thousand times by other couples, in movies and in real life, and especially on television in the afternoon. Ellen listened to herself, and her husband, and noted the following thought: a writer could cover this ground in five minutes. Why does it take real people five hours? She was tired of the whole thing.

David only wanted it to go smoothly. Inside him was a monstrously cold, calculating self that had spent the afternoon considering the options—how to break the news, how to handle the tantrum, how to wait out the evening. For both Welleses there was a dreadful sense of the cliché about their breakup. The truth was that the scene was played out of obligation; they had already drifted so far apart that nothing they said to each other that night was news.

A month passed in making minor adjustments. A baby-sitting schedule was worked out. It seemed that David and Ellen saw each other almost daily for one reason or another. They were civil, and not always cool. Ellen's life was simpler than it had been in some months. She had herself and the baby to look after and the house to keep clean: all reliable elements. There was very little heat in her emotions. She missed David at certain points, but at just as many, she was thankful for his absence.

For David, things began to go downhill after a month. The initial burst of freedom from the family had given him a giddy feeling of ecstasy, but living the single life was not something he was either used to or designed for. The apartment was tacky. The people were mostly losers and deadbeats. The friends who had once been casual with him were now so concerned with his well-being that they were smothering him. None of them knew whether to encourage a reconciliation or fix him up with a girl. His evenings were often lonely, and he found himself overstaying his welcome at the homes of the people he knew. Still, like Ellen, he found life a model of simplicity. For all his dissatisfaction, he remained unharried, and he felt he was growing closer, not more distant, from his son.

He had Edward on Tuesday and Thursday evenings, and

Sundays all day. These were times when he planned to do nothing but play, and he began to find that what he had planned as a sacrifice had become a bright spot in his week. He would play whatever Edward wanted to play. If Edward crawled around the room, David would crawl around behind him, occasionally lying down lightly on top of him, invariably causing squeals of laughter. Edward was a natural music lover, and David had him staring wide-eyed into the speaker system of his stereo, listening to Vivaldi and Mozart. Edward reacted so violently to anything written after 1900 that David began to believe he had taste.

The trick to these thrice-weekly play sessions was that they came to an end. David arrived at seven-thirty at night, or ten-thirty on Sunday morning, and he knew absolutely that he could leave as soon as his hours were up. Nothing further would be asked from him until next time. The severe circumscription of his obligation made it pleasant, free from resentment or anxiety. These hours were for Edward; there were only a certain number of them, and, except on rare occasions, they were a pleasure for father and son alike.

Only once did a fight take place, and it had nothing to do with Edward. David arrived on a Thursday night and discovered that Ellen was planning to spend the evening going to dinner and the movies with a man she had met while swimming at the Y.M.C.A.

"Are you kidding?" David asked. "I'm not baby-sitting while you go out on a date!"

Ellen was stunned.

"You've gone out on dates," she told him.

"What does that have to do with anything?"

"Well," she said, "what do you think I'm doing while you're out on dates?"

"How the hell do I know what you're doing?"

"I'm home baby-sitting!" she screamed. "I'm home taking care of your goddamn son!"

David steamed in silence for a moment. Finally, he spoke.

"What am I supposed to do, meet this creep at the door, tell him you'll be right down? Tell you not to be in too late?"

"He's not coming here," Ellen assured him. "I'm going out."

"I can't believe this is happening," said David, as Edward began to cry in his room. He had been playing happily by himself until the noise of loud voices interrupted him.

"You will *never* do this to me again," David told Ellen. There was an undertone of menace in the corner of his voice. Ellen ignored it.

"I won't tell you next time," she said, and quickly went out the door.

David stood silent for a moment, listening to Edward howl, and then went in to pick him up.

"This isn't your fault," he told him, "but I'm not in the mood for you." Something was getting through to the baby. David's attempts to comfort him were superficial. He didn't care if Edward cried. He wanted trouble. He wanted misery. Life, as far as he could see, was playing him false again. True to form, Edward stayed awake until almost midnight, fretful and on the verge of tears until his mother came home and put him down. While she was nursing him and tucking him in, David slipped out the door and went back to the apartment.

He hoped her date was lousy. He'd been on two himself, and each seemed worse than the other. He had never enjoyed dating; he hadn't had to do it for the past eight years. Ellen had always been there. As much as he sometimes longed for freedom, he'd never once thought happily about the years of dating, of sending his ego out to do battle on a Saturday night. But even dating had changed. It had once been painful and threatening, but now it was worse: it was silly. On each of his two dates he had gone to ridiculous restaurants, with deep-brown walls of slanted redwood slats and bad California wine recommended effusively by a headwaiter who introduced himself by his first name. The crowd was young and noisy, and David's own small talk rang with such a clattering foolishness that he could barely force the words from his mouth into the air. What he got back was not much better. Through it all, he was possessed by a single thought: I'm too old for this. He was not single, not free, not unconcerned about the world around him as all these others seemed to be. He was a man with a child and a job to do, and a wife who would not leave his consciousness.

The ultimate failing of these dates was symbolic; he had re-created the circumstances of his long-past, free young years. And the old truth had come rushing to greet him: you can't go back. You can't be that person whom time and age have obliterated. The David Welles he was trying to recapture was as dead as a vacation preserved on color slides. If he was unhappy in his marriage, with his son, with his life as he alone had made it, there might be some possibilities open to him; yet the one thing he wanted—to go back and try again—was not possible. And when Ellen went out on her date, his jealousy was mixed with a much more important fear—a fear that, having lost his youth and his freedom, he would now lose Ellen and be left with not a single piece of life to call his own.

"The trouble with getting married," a famous bachelor once said, "is that even if you get divorced, you can never not have been married again." Whether the effects of marriage can ever be shaken off is an open question, but one thing is certain. If the effects of marriage are hard to dislodge, the effects of parenthood are doubly so. Marriage is only forever in a theoretical way. If you get divorced, it's up to you to decide whether you want to forget you were ever married. Parenthood, on the other hand, leaves evidence: the child. It is the step off the cliff, so to speak. It is impossible not to be a parent once you have become one. This may seem simple beyond all telling, but the implications are far-reaching and can be complex.

One of the dangers of a book like this is that it may be seen as an attempt to discourage people from having children. That is by no means its intent. On the one hand, we don't want parenthood to sound like an uninterrupted nightmare, for it is surely not that; on the other hand, people have been glossing over the difficulties of becoming a parent for far too many years, and those difficulties deserve to be examined. One of them is that parenthood takes everything that went on before you were a parent and puts it in a glass box. You can see it, sometimes you can even smell it, but you can't have it. You can't have the freedom and the sense of carefree abandon, and the *youth* that goes with being childless. If, like David Welles, you try to outfox the system by leaving your wife and child, you only become aware of how strong the system is. You can buy a uniform and a bat and a ball and a glove, but you can't be on the team. Because being a parent changes everything inside you forever.

So, while we do not wish to discourage people from becoming parents, we do state strongly that, to whatever extent possible, you try to know what you are doing before you do it. This is Catch-22 time again. On the one hand, we're telling you that no one knows what it is to be a parent except parents. On the other hand, we're telling you to find out what it is before you try it. It really isn't fair, it's not nice, and it can't be done. But it can be attempted. You will never know what it is like having the demands of a child on your time, your emotions, and your physical stamina until you try it. You must recognize, however, that those demands are more concentrated, more continuous than anything you have yet experienced. More importantly, there is no way to escape them, short of having someone else bring up your child. Your desire for children has to be strong, or you won't put up with the difficulties. David Welles didn't want children, except in the most superficial way. He also was not especially adept at doing things he didn't want to do. The combination proved devastating to him, and to the marriage.

Should the Welleses have remained childless? It's an impossible question to answer. Ellen wanted a baby from the moment she met David, and she spent eight years talking him into it. If he had won the argument, and there had been no baby, she probably would have been as miserable as he was *with* the baby. The mistake, if you can call it that, is that a woman who saw her purpose in life as child-rearer married a man who didn't want children, hoping to work it out. These things can't be prevented, or even really discouraged. People marry who they marry, and we are certainly not going to advocate the reinstatement of matchmaking, but the nature of a marriage establishes certain ground rules. If mates are in serious disagreement about the question of children, the decision will be difficult, and the results, whatever they are, will probably cause resentment and strain. Those are the facts. We don't expect them to alter the pattern of marriage, divorce, childbearing, or anything else, but they should be recognized as unalterable in most cases. They really shouldn't surprise anyone; the world is hardly a perfect place. It would be nice, however, if couples learned that problems like these can't be wished or pretended or laughed out of existence.

There is an added point. In the current trend of self-oriented pop psychology, the tendency is to ignore the plight of unborn children. Get yourself in shape, you are told, and the children will follow suit. Look out for yourself first and always. The children will get along somehow. Unborn children cannot think for themselves, however, and they do need *some* looking after, even as regards their conception. It is not fair to bring a child into the world unwanted, or half-wanted, or as the reward of some negotiation to which he or she could not be a party. If the family is to retain any credibility in this day and age, children have to be nurtured, and to be nurtured they have to be wanted. Experience has taught us that children who are left to "get along" in a hostile family situation suffer extraordinary damage. To say that this situation is irrelevant to the parents who created it is to say, in essence, that nothing matters. The existentialists not withstanding, we hope it hasn't come to that.

AT ONE YEAR

The Gender Gap—Old Habits, New Rules

THERE was no lease on David's apartment. Notice of cancellation could be filed in writing by either the tenant or landlord with thirty-days' notice. This sense of impermanency had begun to bleed into every aspect of David's life, and when he had been gone five months, it became intolerable. He had told himself that decisions would have to be made, that he would put things in order as soon as his mind and his life-style had settled themselves. The time never came, however. He saw Ellen four or five times a week and Edward at least three. Consequently, he was free of nothing. It had seemed that the separation would make certain things come clear, and for a month, he believed that his life was actually de-fogging. But, as time passed, life clouded up again. His emotions about everything were mixed.

As he looked back, he could see that his emotions had always been mixed, that he was never wholeheartedly content with anything. All his life he had been searching for simple perfection in any one thing. He would wed himself to that purity. He tried to remember the last perfect thing that had happened, the last time he hadn't been disappointed by a flaw in anyone or anything. He couldn't go back far enough to find it. He was able to remember many happy things that had taken place when he was eleven years old, but none of them was perfect. Each was tinged with some sour color somewhere. At eight, things had been simpler, but not without problems. His memories of being six were dim, and as he went back further and further, he was more often confronted with disappointment, confusion, and fear. At his youngest, he remembered only trauma. There had never, as far as he could tell, been one sweet, perfect event in his life. When Edward was born, he thought that might have been it, but the past twelve months had made a mockery of his delivery-room experience. Looking forward, he could only see more of the same. In what direction could he logically turn?

For Ellen, things were no less confused, but somehow less bleak.

"The great revelation for me," she recalled later, "was that I wouldn't die. David was gone, and life went on. Once I realized that I was all right, that I could get along, things just started happening."

She took herself to counseling. She took hold of some of her hostility and tried to understand some of the things David wanted from her, but she didn't ask him back. She never felt single, or even that she was headed toward being single. She just saw the neecssity of making her life, and Edward's life, as smooth as possible. Within a month, she had taken a job teaching rug-making in an extension program of Los Angeles City College. She arranged for a baby-sitter one night a week, and David sat the other two. The sitter was a big step, something she had never wanted to do, something that David had always pushed her to do. Teaching, too, seemed to please him. It was the cozy, little kind of job he had always wanted for her. Nothing too ambitious. It brought in some income, and it gave her some contact with the outside world. As time passed, she seemed to be pleasing him without intending to, doing the things that she would never do as long as he kept after her to do them.

She was freer, too, because she did not have to take care of her husband. She tried to explain that the job, the commitment, was a direct result of David's departure, but it didn't quite wash. There was a stubborn streak in Ellen, and she knew that she had only taken the job when she felt it would no longer give David any satisfaction.

As the months dragged on, it became clear to Ellen, too, that no progress was being made. She knew that her marriage had not ended when David walked out, and that if it hadn't ended then, it probably wouldn't end. They had plunged themselves into this life together, and neither had enough desire for escape to make the enormous amount of work it demanded worthwhile. That hardly seemed a valid reason for staying married, but it was the only one they had. During the fifth month of the separation, David began to come to her counseling sessions, to try to talk. He was disturbed and often lonely. Aside from his colleagues, he had no one to talk to or see socially. His independence wasn't worth much.

"The high point of my week," he told the counselor in one session, "is taking my laundry over to the house to do it. At least I don't have to explain anything to Ellen. She knows me, and she knows my laundry. It's not the high point of *every* week. But an awful lot of weeks it is."

On a Thursday night when Ellen was teaching, she returned to find David asleep in the den on a pulled-out hide-a-bed. His laundry was done, and his clean pajamas were occupied. She said nothing. She went to bed, and for the first time in six months, she and her husband spent the night under one roof. It was, she thought, a shy and endearing way of asking to come back. She felt no desire to probe it or point out its obvious meaning to him the next morning, for which he seemed grateful. The following week, he stayed both nights, and on the Tuesday following that, when Edward awoke at three-thirty in the morning, David went in and gave him a bottle. He had moved back in.

The arrangement was never formalized. David had moved

back the same way he moved out: embarrassed, unable to express, or even fully comprehend, what he was feeling. Six months earlier, he had seen a sign on the wall of a new building, and it had caused him to leave his wife. Now he had washed a pair of pajamas, and it had caused him to come back. He never proclaimed himself right or wrong in either of these moves; he had done what he felt he had to do in both cases.

Ellen saw it as pure David Welles—he was the man she had married. She *did* want him back, despite everything. She supposed he was in love with her still, and she knew he loved Edward more than anything he had ever loved, herself included. She was willing to accept the situation, because, unlike David, Ellen had never expected anything to be perfect. She wanted a reasonable life, and with David back in the house, there was a promise of rationality in the air. They continued the counseling. She continued work. The baby-sitter came and went. A week after David's return their sex life resumed, following two nights of tentative affection. They were chastened: the Welles marriage was not a dream. But things weren't bad. In confronting the question of why this had all happened, both denied Edward's influence. The problems were always there, they insisted, and would have eventually exploded, baby or no baby.

The problems had to do with a difficult man and a stubborn woman, a neurotic combination of willfullness and unpredictable emotions. It was not until well after Edward's first birthday that his influence finally became clear to his parents.

"He made us know who we are," Ellen recalled. "And when we knew, like we had never known before, we looked at each other in a clearer way, and there were a lot of things we couldn't live with. They'd always been there; Edward didn't create them. He just blew the dust away."

"Pressure does that," David added. "Men in battle, people facing death in a hospital, surgeons with people's lives in their hands: you show your true colors in that life-and-death situation. That's what a baby does: he put us on the battlefield.

And there was a time there when we didn't know what to do
about it, except to run like hell."

The Welleses began parenthood in what must be the second
hardest position. The hardest would be with neither parent
wanting the child. The Welleses were better than that by
exactly half. The complications were enormous. David not
only didn't want a baby, he didn't want Ellen to want one
either, and the intricacies of his resentment were many. In
some sense, David didn't want Ellen to be anything by herself.
It was almost as if his delicate emotional balance couldn't
tolerate another complete human being in his midst. As odd
as this sounds, it is so common that it necessitated the women's
movement. So many men interviewed for this book resented
the full flowering of their mates that we can only accept the
situation as being the norm, and issue a word of caution.
It is easy to be submissive if you are brought up to be that way,
as most women in our society have been. We learn to let men
handle things, and then, when our babies are born, we begin
to handle things ourselves, using our own methods, our own
imaginations, our own rules. As a result, a dichotomy is created
for many women; they are ruling their children, but being
ruled by their husbands. They are, in other words, in two
positions at once. It can't last. As their new strength flourishes,
women begin to let it take over other aspects of their lives.
Men, who have been brought up to rule and to dominate,
don't like it.

We wish to be very clear about politics here and make our
usual disclaimer. We are not selling an ideology in this discussion, merely reporting what we have found to be the case.
Men and women are probably further apart, both emotionally
and ideologically, than at any time in recent history. The
dichotomy between the generations that dominated the 1960s
has been replaced by a new, even more problematic one, which
we might dub the gender gap. Men can't control the way they
were raised any more than women can. We are all, to one

extent or another, products of our parents' age. We are locked into certain patterns of thought and behavior, and when our new ideas clash with our ingrained characters, friction is bound to develop. It is directed within the self as well as toward our mates.

When David Welles moved out, it was in part because he could no longer understand his own reactions to things. He had become such a mass of self-contradiction that the whole world stopped making sense. Ellen, who had always done his bidding, because he was a complex, difficult, fascinating man (but mostly just because he was a man), got tired of him, and without him her life actually became simpler. But tired of him as she was, she wanted him back. Their reconciliation was hardly a case of "seeing the light." They found marriage more fulfilling than single life, especially with a child in the picture. Even at the end of a year, Ellen and David saw themselves as making the best of a no-win situation. Their fate was probably sealed from the beginning, when they chose to let the argument over parenthood lie dormant for a few years and get married anyhow. These disagreements rarely go away, and by sweeping them under the carpet, the Welleses were setting up an insoluble conflict. They refused to get to know each other deeply, and they paid the price of ignorance eight years later.

If the above smacks of superiority, or suggests a detailed testing process be instituted before courting couples are allowed to tie the knot, nothing of the kind is meant. People will court, get married, and have children with or without this or any other book. The problems *are* visible, however. That the Welleses could have solved their differences regarding children and worked everything out to the mutual satisfaction of husband and wife is an outlandish pipe dream. They walked into the dark together, and while they walked back out, sadder, arguably wiser, their agreements, now and forever, resulted and will continue to result only from arduous negotiation and compromise.

THE FOURTH FAMILY

Alan Sheinman and
Nina Degarmo

AND LAUREN

PREGNANT BODIES

NINA DEGARMO was standing naked in a back-lit mother-of-pearl waterfall when she felt the first twinge of nausea. Immediately she thought of dinner—*mahi-mahi*, the Hawaiian fish specialty—and food poisoning. It never crossed her mind that she might be pregnant. She made it through the number, the finale of the show called "Waikiki Nights," but missed the encore walkaround, the final bows, and the exit music. She was in the ladies room. The next morning she tried to explain to a young Hawaiian doctor why she could not be pregnant.

When Nina Degarmo was fourteen, well before it had occurred to her that she might make a professional living by taking off her clothes, her chief interest was romance. Romance, for her, encompassed everything from the grandiose to the tawdry, even to the slightly dangerous. She was lonely, privately awed and vaguely excited by the religious rituals of her Catholic upbringing, a dreamy, lost girl with a woman's body. In one particularly lofty flight of expectant fantasy, she copied a lurid passage from a paperback novel into her diary. The passage was written in the first person.

Nina's mother, bewildered by her daughter's sudden retreat into dreams, broke into the diary, desperate for insight. She was treated to a vividly worded scene of orgiastic deflowering. The passage so shocked her that she was unable to confront her daughter with it. Instead, she made what she supposed was the most progressive move possible; she put her daughter on birth-control pills.

Nina was a virgin at the time, but the pills made her feel sophisticated. She took one a day for six years.

When she was twenty, a doctor in Las Vegas told her she could stop taking the pills forever. Their early use, he said, had stunted her organ development. He was quite certain she could never conceive a child.

Now, four years after that doctor's appointment, Nina was getting different information. The link between early use of pills and reproductive organ development was shady at best. Nina was confused. She was not used to getting contradictory information from doctors. Her other doctor had seemed so sure. However, there was no doubt that Nina's uterus was capable of nurturing a fetus; there was a fetus growing there as she and the doctor spoke. After four years of reckless unconcern about the possibility of pregnancy, childbirth, or motherhood, it came as quite a shock.

Alan Sheinman was in the Texas panhandle, working with a reclusive screenwriter on a story about a religious cult. He had left town with the last of his money when Nina got the Hawaii job. For Alan, this was typical behavior. A tall, wiry, intense young man, he owned exactly three pairs of blue jeans, eight plaid shirts (four of them flannel), and a dark suit. He had single-handedly produced and directed two low-budget movies. At thirty, he was scrambling for any unoccupied piece of ledge to stand on in the film industry, and he carried with him a sense of chaotic activity, almost frenzy. Nina believed he could succeed by the sheer force of energy that seemed to radiate from within him. Although she did not know it at the time, she was not part of Alan Sheinman's plan; she was simply the most beautiful girl he had ever spoken to.

Like Nina, Alan was a loner from childhood. In early adolescence he had seen his grasping, lower-middle-class parents as the enemy. They were the kind of people, he would say, who brought out the anti-Semitism hidden in even the most progressive hearts. Later in life, after their marriage had torn itself apart, he came to see that he had been cruel in his assessment. His parents were not so much wicked as insane. His mother took to calling him long distance from the Bronx, claiming that she had seen him on this or that TV quiz show. What was he going to do with the prizes? His father drove a cab in Pittsburgh and wrote only once a year, only to remind Alan what an untrustworthy terror his mother was. It had been a long time since Alan had responded to either parent.

They met in Vegas; Nina had been stripping for four years there. She worked a series of clubs just outside the city limits, driving the few hundred yards between each joint. Men followed her. Every girl had a small group of faceless, rumpled fans, who would make the rounds a few minutes behind their favorite girl. Nina could spot her faithfuls from the stage. Most of them stood at the bar, staring and dreaming. From nine at night until three in the morning, Nina's dusty gray Plymouth station wagon would prowl the furthest reaches of the strip. Four shows a night in each club, trailed by this secret, anonymous society of men. It brought $12,000 a year.

For Nina, it was an expressive act of the body. Her body, she felt, was all she had to communicate. Its movement, the tuning of its flesh, the meaning implicit in its turns and stretches, these kept her alive and sane. She was not a talker. She did not think these thoughts out. She only knew that when she didn't dance, she got depressed.

Alan Sheinman was susceptible to this woman. He had never been to Las Vegas, but a hungry Nevada backer paid his way there to see if a film story could be concocted. Alan's interest was not in big-money Las Vegas. He gravitated naturally toward the back of town, toward the haunted faces of men whose only hope was to get back on the strip some day, to the sunblasted stucco tracts and the chipped Formica bars in cool, blue and silver dives. The grifters and the drifters were his people. Nina was dancing for them.

Their affair was casual, athletic. Nina got off work at three in the morning, the perfect time for a romance out of *Guys and Dolls*. Neither one expected development. They slept beneath a thin sheet in a blind-darkened room on blistering afternoons, and never wondered if this was *it*. When Alan exhausted the film possibilities, he went home to Los Angeles and Nina stayed in Las Vegas. They visited when either one could get free, and talked on the phone. Neither was a letter writer.

Four months into the relationship, the Hawaiian job came up. It was a big, all-nude review, with a substantial pay hike and travel allowance. Nina felt lucky to get it, but once there, she realized how attached to Alan she had become. She began to call him in Texas almost daily, running up fabulous, unpayable phone bills. On the days when she would resolve to be good, he would get nervous and call her to find out why she hadn't called. They talked more during those two weeks than they had ever talked before. It was three days before "Waikiki Nights" closed that Nina had to make the difficult phone call to tell Alan she was pregnant. He reacted slowly and without open emotion. They would meet in L.A. in three days.

These were hard decisions for people who hadn't been thinking. This was not a long-term love affair; it wasn't even really a short-term love affair. It was dating, with a certain amount of caring. Neither partner expected marriage. Alan had vowed earlier that the next pregnancy he caused (there had been one previously) would be carried to term. He had not considered the specificity of dealing with a particular woman who might have thoughts of her own on the subject; Nina had many. The logical arguments were all for abortion. Her possibly damaged reproductive system, her career, the casualness of the relationship, Alan's economic instability, and the generally uncertain future. She lined up her points and fired one after another.

One of Alan's particular talents as an artist was his ability to perceive subtext—the emotion behind the words. It's a hard talent to trust. What he thought he heard was Nina, begging to be dissuaded from her own arguments. So he asked two simple questions.

"Would you love this child, or would you mistreat it?"

Nina admitted that, in some inexplicable way, she already loved the child. The second question:

"If you abort the child, will you feel that something has gone out of your life forever?"

Tears began to run from the corners of Nina's eyes, and Alan's own sobs joined hers. Twenty minutes later, they were crowding each other on the one twin bed in Alan's Hollywood single, surrounded by wadded Kleenex. Nina was explaining a fantasy about her daughter, a three-year-old with sausage curls, a dimple, and a bonnet. It was Easter, and there was a smear of chocolate on the little girl's cheek.

"Who wipes it off?" Alan wanted to know.

"In this fantasy," Nina explained, "there's a governess." Nina moved into Alan's apartment, but things did not fall into place naturally. In trying to jam courtship, simulated marriage, and expectant parenthood into an eight-month period, the couple came to appreciate the rituals society has set up for such events. Rites of passage have a natural flow. They often require time; they always require intention. There had been no intention in Alan and Nina's relationship, and now there was not enough time. When Nina's condition began to show, and she could no longer work, there was not enough money. She took a job waitressing at a health-food restaurant; Alan had made her promise to stop smoking and become a vegetarian if she was going to keep the baby.

Soon, nothing was the same. She was eating strange food, working in a strange place at a strange job, living in a strange town. Then her body, old trusty friend that it was, began to explode. With the only instrument of expression she possessed suddenly out of order, depression set in; she had no place to dance and couldn't even exercise properly. She had never realized how wrapped up in her body she had been. Its altered shape scuttled her self-esteem. Somehow, in a different body she became a different person, a fat, lazy frustrated, aching bitch.

None of this was physically rooted. She was not, in fact, fat, and her inability to exercise was not brought on by the limitations of her body. (Pregnant women often enjoy heavy gym workouts well into their ninth month.) For Nina, it was something different. Her body was the only friend she had at the time, and it had deserted her. She didn't know the new one and felt betrayed by it.

Alan didn't know what to do with her. She would go to work and come home, silent, bulky, exhausted. Only in bed could she be rekindled. Alan was thankful that her pregnant body, which he had feared before he saw it, appealed to him in its wide, graceful curves. At least one of them still loved that body. But Alan had problems beyond Nina.

His career was at a standstill, and, for the first time, he found himself unable to generate work out of his own energy. He was, in fact, unable to generate much energy. His own self-image had collapsed. He found himself an unexpected family man, with a dog, a cat, a briefcase, and a pregnant woman at home. It nearly killed him. Nina did not understand. She saw his frequent black moods as simple rejections of her own problems, never sensing that she was no more than a symbol. It was the whole, inevitable future that Alan felt swirling around him as he sat on his bed in the dark.

For four weeks Alan bought groceries on Thursday after three, reasoning that the check he gave the grocer would not reach his bank until Monday. There was no money in the bank. He would spend the weekend getting up cash to cover the check and be at the bank on Monday morning at ten. The debt to friends grew. Alan recognized the quiet desperation within him as the weeks went by. It seemed a short leap from here to insanity. He began to think of his mother and the fantasy quiz show prizes she kept expecting from United Parcel. Did it run in the family?

He confessed all this to friends in Berkeley, people who were revolutionary and used to poverty. They had no money to give him, but sent, instead, an envelope of food stamps. For two weeks the stamps languished in a drawer. Neither Alan nor Nina knew how to use them. Was it possible to be arrested for using someone else's food stamps? Were they given to the cashier at the check-out counter or exchanged elsewhere? Poverty was new to them, and mysterious. How did the poor manage it?

The last loans were taken out, the last favors called in. There was no more money. Nina and Alan took the stamps to the market, careful not to put in their cart anything that the check-out girl might deem frivolous or unworthy. They waited in a long line, the longest they could find. They felt like kids setting off a cherry bomb in the boy's washroom, but there was no fun attached to the act, only tightness around the throat muscles and perspiration. That they were genuinely poor in the same way that the average sharecropper is poor had never occurred to them. Their poverty seemed different, more like a sudden disease than an economic status. When the check-out girl bagged their groceries, took the stamps, and rang up a receipt, a great weight was lifted from them.

They spent the next week seeking federal and state assistance. Neither one of them had ever worked on a payroll with deductions, so they were not eligible for unemployment benefits. They did receive food-stamp aid, and aid to parents of dependent children was arranged for after the baby's delivery. There would be day care and medical benefits.

The very gathering of help information lightened their mood. It gave them a mission, and it was an adventure onto uncharted turf. They began to remember what had once been attractive in the relationship. Their days were spent generating new hope out of federal money. When life seemed feasible again, Alan began to work and recognized it as a good sign.

Seven weeks before the baby's due date, Alan and Nina treated themselves to one simple vegetarian dinner out. They apologized to each other, held hands, walked home, and kissed under a convenient streetlamp, because they lived in Hollywood. In Hollywood, Alan explained, you had to kiss under a convenient light so the camera could catch you.

A little after midnight, Nina felt a rush of liquid between her legs. She woke Alan, and the two of them examined the wet bedsheets. They would not acknowledge the obvious, however, until contractions began at 1:20 A.M. Nina was in labor with a baby seven weeks premature.

With Alan Sheinman and Nina Degarmo we enter the realm of constant conflict. As a couple they are unusual, to say the least, and their experiences may not appear to be a useful model for more conventional people. They bear close examination, however. Degarmo and Sheinman represent the impulses all of us have, but some of us try to suppress. They live at the edge of their lives, making decisions according to the emotional strength of the moment. They are admirably free of the shackles of convention. Their experience demonstrates their bravery, their selfishness, and a naïveté that is both honorable and infuriating. At no point do they care to peer ahead so as to predict the implications of their decisions.

They begin in a rough spot, uncommitted to each other or their child. Their only commitment was not to abort, at a time when it would have been easy to do so. In allowing this baby to be born, they felt obligated to raise it, to make their lives around this seeming turn of fate. They considered themselves no less prepared for this than for anything else.

It's one thing to decide such a thing, another to accomplish it. Alan and Nina moved too quickly for assimilation; they went from being single to being double to being triple in exactly eight months. Each piece of evidence that the change was occurring was greeted with great distress. For Nina, and for a lot of women, the loss of her body was the most severe blow of the pregnancy.

Nina's body was her work, of course, as well as her pride and, therefore, her identity; but most women, for better or worse, prize their bodies. When they lose them, even temporarily, the results can be a regular, serious depression. This is unfortunate because many men (including Alan) find that the pregnant bodies of their wives stimulate a deeper, more serious sexuality than they ever knew was possible. After all, the creation of babies is a sexual act not by coincidence or convenience. Our society has put a premium on the slender figure, on youth, and on a sexual liberation that precludes pregnancy. There is something unnatural about these preoccupations, and the life-style they lead to seems unsatisfying as well. Pregnant women are sexual in the most basic sense of the word, and the emotional quality of the expectant couple's sex life can be extraordinary.

The catch is *can be*. No one can predict what will or will not appeal. Not all men respond to the form of the pregnant female. Perhaps men who are unready for fatherhood transfer their fear to the pregnant body. Perhaps it is a question of pure aesthetics. More than anything, we suspect it has to do with advertising, high fashion, movies, and television. But this possibility of male disgust and rejection has hypnotized many women, and it is common to find expectant mothers frightened of what their bodies will do in the early months of pregnancy and depressed by them later on.

Husbands are a part of this whole business. Luckily, Alan found Nina's body admirable and exciting as it took on its inevitable increases in bulk. Mates who do not share this feeling can do little to help a woman's self-confidence. Thinking about the sexual implications of pregnancy can help. In extreme cases, we are not opposed to a little dishonesty. A woman who is worried about her body needs reassurance and affection. It's your baby, too. On the whole, we cannot endorse phony gestures of affection, especially when they come during times of emotional disagreement. However, making love to a pregnant woman is worth exploring no matter what your predisposition, even if you see it as an effortful obligation. You never know what you might find out.

AT ONE WEEK

Paternal Post-Partum Reaction

EVERYTHING focuses. A little after midnight, Alan and Nina piled into the old Volvo with two pillows and a blanket and began the two-mile downhill run to the hospital. The city was crawling. It was Saturday night; the bumper-to-bumper promenade on Sunset Strip was in full swing. Shafts of light beamed into a dark sky and disappeared.

In the Volvo, Alan and Nina were alone. They were on an isolated plateau where nothing lived but themselves and their labor. Alan was quiet, reveling in the height of his own emotion. He looked at the sky, at the stars, and felt his own place in the shifting cosmos. The very meaning of life seemed within his grasp. These emotions would cause him some embarrassment at a later date, but they were real at the moment.

In the backseat, Nina was lying down, concentrating. She and Alan had been taking their prepared childbirth course, but they had barely begun. She didn't know anything about what to do next, or who would show her. Alan assumed she was wafting in silent reverie back there, as he was in front. Actually, she was making a mental shopping list of things to panic about.

She had learned one breathing technique of the four that are taught in the Lamaze course. She knew nothing of hospital procedure. She was seven weeks early. This was about to be the worst night of her life.

Once she was settled in the labor room, with a labor nurse and her doctor in attendance, things seemed slightly improved. Everyone volunteered heartily to help her through, and Alan became team captain, a man at the height of his powers. He announced officially that there were to be no drugs used in this delivery. No one fought with him. He had decided to save the one breathing exercise they knew, but, almost immediately, Nina needed it. Her contractions were becoming unmanageable, and there was still a long way to go.

Nina stared at the ceiling, breathing a shallow, metered breath, concentrating on a crack in the labor-room plaster, trying to do it right.

"This isn't going to work," she announced between contractions.

The nurse cooed encouragement, and Alan gave her a pep talk like a football coach.

"Goddamnit! she screamed. "This isn't going to work!"

With her last word a contraction seized her, and she began to breathe again, her eyes locked angrily on the plaster crack.

"I'll be right back," Alan said when she was between contractions. He turned and marched out of the room to the lobby. Begging a dime from the guard, he called his Lamaze instructor. It was one-thirty in the morning.

Forty-five minutes later, she arrived. What she discovered was a sort of emotional chaos—well earned—hidden beneath the immaculate organization of the labor-room procedure. Nina's doctor had gone off call. She was being looked in upon— sporadically—by one of his partners. All her self-confidence, which was slight to begin with, had filtered away with the departure of her doctor. Contractions were coming at three-minute intervals; Alan and the nurse were talking her through them with some difficulty and a mounting sense of panic. The breathing exercise had long since been discarded, its usefulness exhausted.

What followed was a whirlwind seminar on the Lamaze method, with practice sessions held between contractions. No sooner was a technique learned than it was thrown into action by this raw recruit. It was an improvised battle, and the speed with which Nina had to absorb each exercise held her focus. The contractions, once dreaded, became challenges. There was no letup. When all the exercises had been learned, there were constant dry runs, rehearsals for delivery, and improvements. No one cared to mention that Nina's contractions were now a minute apart. The gray light of predawn was breaking outside, but in the labor room, where there were no windows, time had stopped. Nothing jarred it forward until the nurse peered methodically between Nina's legs and saw the crown of an infant head, the size of a quarter. The doctor was delivering another baby. The nurse made the decision, and, cornered by Alan and the Lamaze instructor, Nina's bed was wheeled down the corridor to the delivery room.

By now, no amount of learned technique could comfort Nina. She gasped her way through contractions that backstopped one another like the waves of a riptide. Secured in the delivery room, still with no doctor, the helplessness returned, the fear and anger that marked Nina's entrance into the hospital. No doctor.

"Somebody get down there," Nina gasped. "I'm having this baby."

The doctor entered nonchalantly less than a minute later. This was his fourth delivery of the night. Everybody has problems. The doctor was, of necessity, unflappable. Nina was inconsolable, bristling with hostility and discomfort. The doctor positioned himself, examining first a tray of instruments, then his patient.

"Okay," he said. "Push."

No one remembers the next thirty seconds or so. Alan thinks

Nina screamed as the baby came out, but no one is sure. It is a crucial moment, lost in time as if it had never taken place at all. No one managed to look in the mirror—there is no visual impression left—but inside of a minute the doctor held a little, bluish baby girl up for Alan and Nina to see. Incoherent with relief and exhaustion, Nina looked at her daughter and uttered a remark she will regret to the grave.

"Have I got my figure back?" she asked.

Lauren Eugenia Sheinman weighed four pounds, seven ounces. She was taken immediately from her mother and placed in an incubator in the intensive care unit of the infant stabilization nursery. The magic act was over. Reality returned with a thumping uncertainty, and the most harrowing ten days in the lives of Alan Sheinman and Nina Degarmo had begun.

There was immediate disagreement. Alan's innate suspicion of the medical profession went into overdrive when he saw his daughter lying inside what looked like a modified microwave oven, with a needle in her arm. She was wrinkled and helpless, attended only by meters and recording devices. She seemed to be the victim of some inhuman torture scheme. Leaving her there was next to impossible, but when Nina was better, there were no other options. Walking off the maternity floor, they felt a physical pull, as if actual ligaments of human tissue were being torn free, breaking the link between their child and them.

From the balcony of their Hollywood apartment, they could look down on the hospital's towers, where Lauren was. Alan paced incessantly out there, a caged father. Lauren developed jaundice after three days (a common occurrence) and was blindfolded and placed under fluorescent lights to correct the condition.

"Why fluorescent lights?" Alan plagued Nina with questions she could not answer. "Why not daylight? Fluorescent light causes cancer. And why are they feeding her sugar-water? What's wrong with honey-water?"

The stress seemed to be breaking him. He was unconcerned about his daughter's natural condition; he thought the doctors would kill her. Still, he knew little enough about medicine to argue with them, so he directed his attacks at Nina.

Nina didn't know how to react. She didnt' know if he was right or wrong, she only wished he'd shut up. The doctors were doctors. For better or worse, they were in charge. She wanted Lauren to get better and come home. She absorbed Alan's outbursts and his tension into herself. It entered her and disrupted her equilibrium, making her literally dizzy. She did not speak to him except to react. She was afraid to initiate a conversation on her own, frightened of where it would lead.

Four times a day, sometimes six, she went to the hospital to deliver breast milk to Lauren. The nursery was an artificial world to her, and Lauren, blindfolded and victimized by her own littleness, seemed far away. Nina drew all the strangeness and the fear —Alan's lunacy, the baby's tragedy, her own bewilderment—inside herself until she felt she would burst. On the outside nothing showed but the fatigue, but there was a ringing craziness beneath the surface, an unspoken acknowledgment that she could not last forever.

The simplicity of her tasks kept her going. Nurses did everything; Nina's only responsibility was to bring milk. She checked in with the doctor twice a day. Lauren was in no danger. It was a matter of a few days. Nina reported this to Alan regularly, but it only served to infuriate him.

"I know she's all right!" he would say with quiet intensity. "She belongs home *now*, in the sunshine, in the family environment."

Every report of her improvement seemed to goad him. He was impossible. Upon close questioning, Nina discovered his suspicion that Lauren had been premature because of Nina's smoking habit. On this news she retired to bed. She wanted to tell him to get out, that she would raise Lauren alone, but it was too complicated. She was too tired. She turned on the television and watched him from bed, pacing the balcony and staring off down the hill toward his nemesis—the hospital.

At the age of ten days, Lauren came home. She fit like a missing piece between Nina and Alan. There was no apology or discussion. Lauren became the focus of their activity. She was where Alan wanted her, apparently none the worse for her misspent first ten days. He regarded her almost as a spoil of the victory against the hospital. He considered her rescued. She had smoothed out and pinked up. She was tiny still, but quiet and confident as she nuzzled into Nina's breast. Within days she began to gain some serious weight.

Emergencies in childbirth are rare, but even the trivial ones take their toll. Lauren Sheinman was never in any real danger. Premature births *can* have severe consequences; more often they require nothing more than incubator treatment. The shining of fluorescent light on jaundiced babies (all babies have some degree of jaundice) is also a standard procedure. The destruction wreaked on the Sheinman/Degarmo relationship had nothing, in fact, to do with Lauren's condition. This was just panic, misdirected and misunderstood: its causes can only be guessed at.

Becoming a father for the first time can bring many intimations of danger. One of them is that your life is out of control forever. Your good years are gone: your self-image is hopelessly becalmed. We would guess that Alan Sheinman's panic had less to do with Lauren than with his own, suddenly diminished size.

This ego blow is so common among new fathers that it bears some thinking about. There will be times when you seem to have become nothing—when your life is in everyone else's hands and no one pays the slightest attention to you. As much as fathers share in the *idea* of childbirth, in the coaxing, the coaching, and the caring, ultimately there comes a time when they are left out. If they have been playing "the rock" in a difficult labor and delivery situation, the letdown can be enormous. A father so suffering should be wary of making his wife the culprit. No one is to blame for this phenomenon, except possibly society at large, and they're a hard bunch to yell at. Taking it out on a new mother is futile and brings no satisfaction. The post-partum depression affects fathers as much as it does mothers, sometimes more. Men are used to being in the limelight, used to making the big decisions, used to coming to the rescue. When they find themselves cast as supporting players in the world's biggest drama, some of them rebel. Often they do not see the rebellion coming and do not recognize it when it arrives.

The new mother has plenty to cope with and may feel it is unfair that she be burdened with the peacock ego of her formerly loving mate, but if it happens, it happens. It is important to understand that these emotional upheavals are *real*. They cannot be reversed by saying, "Oh, come *on* now. Stop being silly." They need tending and sympathy. A father *is* important, more important than the well-wishers and hospital nurses tend to make him feel. Part of a new mother's task is to keep an instinctive gauge on the balance of family attention. This is an inexact science at best, performed by an unwilling volunteer. But it's an important task. During the earliest days of family realignment, every relationship is in flux. Fathers and mothers have each other's emotional comfort at stake. The unexpected emotion will invariably bubble to the top and demand to be dealt with. Flexibility is crucial.

There is a certain amount of play-acting to every romance at the courtship stage—not dishonesty, but grand gesticulation. If it returns now, when once again the terms of a relationship are being created, it is not a bad thing. The big gesture—flowers, ice cream, jewelry—has a place in this creative process, as does elaborate concern for feelings and for kindness. Usually by the time a couple has children, they are beyond the courtly stage. Perhaps it should be brought back for an encore. You may find that it is followed by the deep discussion and the ardor of earlier times—or whatever the pleasures of your courtship may have been. Your nerves will be exposed, and all the romantic trappings provide cushioning. A little private courtship (minus sexual intercourse, which you won't be in the mood for anyhow) can take you through the early weeks in style.

AT ONE MONTH

Alternative Fathering

NINA DEGARMO fully expected to be the world's worst mother. She considered it luck that Lauren seemed to like her all right. She didn't know what a mother was supposed to do. From a magazine article in the obstetrician's office she copied down a selected reading list on first-time mothering, and Alan went in search of the books.

Alan was at home, doing no business. He had severed off all contacts with the film-making world for forty days in order that he might get to know his daughter and reacquaint himself with his lover. It was a great forty days. Alan took the midnight feeding (Nina expressed her milk into a bottle), and they alternated the earliest of the morning feedings. Nina could nap when she wanted, and Alan became as familiar with the stretch garments, the diapers, and the ointments and powders of baby care as any nurse. Nina's strength came back at a rapid rate; she was rested and healthy. She also considered herself the luckiest mother in Christendom. No one else she knew had a man who took such care.

There was, of course, no money. Alan didn't care. Some things were more important than money.

"The first forty days are the formative days," he explained, quoting a theory that had come to him full-blown from an unknown source. "I felt that if Lauren had me for forty days, she'd be golden. I could drop dead after that and she'd still be secure without me. What kind of money could I earn that would be worth that? It's all in the first forty days."

Nina didn't know if that was true or not. Truth to tell, Nina wasn't sure she knew anything, and she was comforted by Alan's self-assurance in such matters, even if his reasoning was strange, or, in this case, invisible. All his transgressions during the first week were put aside, if not forgotten. The same energy that had thrown his anxiety into overdrive was now directed at creating comfort and security.

"Of course, the family in this country is dead," Alan intoned philosophically, "but having this baby I can understand for the first time the appeal of that unit. It's comfortable, and it's helpful. I can see it, where it came from."

He brought home the books, and Nina began to read.

"I'm doing everything wrong," she announced. "I never even checked to see if I have enough milk."

For a couple of days, she was absorbed in the material. Lauren began to be treated differently. Strict timing was enforced on her nursing. She was allowed to cry for longer periods of time. Nina's nerves began to fray, but the book recommended it. Lauren didn't like it either. Alan tried to be gentle about this new approach of Nina's, but it was hard to make himself heard.

"She must be crying to get rid of her excess energy," Nina would explain after reading a passage.

"I think she wants to be held," Alan would say in quiet disagreement. He would not take any action, however. Nina had her own pace.

It took a week of attention to the science of child care before Nina weighed the results.

"I'm not used to using my head," she admitted in a later

interview. "I'm used to using other people's heads. See, what I always used was my body. My body was the moneymaker, the meaningful part of my life. I was actually surprised to find out I could take care of Lauren with my body—that my mind and my body were working together. All the reading was throwing the balance off. It was good to do it because I learned I don't need it. I lost my curiosity and my fear. Those books were screwing me up."

At the end of the week, the books were still in immaculate condition.

"Take these back," Nina said to Alan. "Tell them I had a miscarriage or something. They won't dare not give you a refund."

Alan Sheinman's forty-day work hiatus can be considered to be genuinely radical fathering. Few fathers have the liberty to make such a step, but even those who could take substantial time off rarely do. A day or two is expected; a week is considered a major sacrifice. Fathering isn't a sacrifice, however, and Alan's approach seems to us as healthy as it is unconventional. Although his "forty-days" theory may have no biological or psychological evidence to support it, his presence for that period of time had an enormous impact on the stability of this particularly shaky home. His willingness to take over the middle-of-the-night feeding probably had as much psychological effect as physical on Nina; not only could she rest, she could see, right in front of her, how devoted he was to his new role and her health. Feeding an infant at midnight may not seem much like a gesture in the grand romantic tradition, but it can mean a lot. Of course, there are feedings and feedings. One wife reported the following:

Bob insisted on taking the midnight and three A.M. feedings himself so that I could get my rest. He had this wonderful thing he did: when the baby would cry he would wake up and drag himself over my exhausted body to get out of bed. Then he always forgot his glasses, which were on the night table, so he'd drag himself back across two more times to get them, and by then I'd be totally awake and ready for breakfast. He claimed it was subconscious, but I'm not so sure. After a week I told him it was very sweet of him to want to feed the baby, but it was just tiring me out too much to watch him do it.

Alan was as good as his intentions. He knew everything about his daughter and felt proud of himself for knowing. He could handle anything that came up and was confident that he could raise her alone, if necessary. The rewards of this confidence were a substantial boost in ego satisfaction and Nina's seemingly undying devotion—she saw him (quite properly, we suppose) as one man in a thousand.

Pediatricians often recommend to new parents that the father get involved in the feeding process so that the child will come to know both parents. We would go substantially further than this: fathers, in an ideal world, should do a little of everything. The more a father hangs back, the more isolated he will become from the child-care process that develops as a way of life for his woman and baby. The isolation is unhealthy. It breeds fear of the unknown, jealousy, and impatience with tasks that are plainly necessary. Most fathers cannot afford to do what Alan Sheinman did, but they can do more than they think. The first weeks are crucial. As we have said over and over, the relationship is up for grabs when it first becomes a threesome. This is no time to be absent. It would be wiser to take the time at the very beginning than to wait until the mother and child have established their routine. You may not be a part of it.

Nina's bout with books is typical of an older breed of woman. The idiot child/bride who knows nothing of child-rearing and refuses to trust her instincts is less common in our society than it once was. Nina was a career woman, but her career involved single people and an "adults only" atmosphere. She had no regard for her brain or for her understanding of any family function, which is why she couldn't believe she was doing a good job with Lauren. She was, of course, and the books and guides only confused her and headed off her natural instinct. This is not to disparage all the child-care literature on the market; a lot of it is good and helpful. But only if you need it.

For Nina Degarmo, motherhood was the most startling event of her life. She was really good at something that had nothing to do with sex appeal. She was excellent at performing a task other people failed at. This discovery began an odyssey for her that surprised no one more than herself, except possibly her lover, Alan Sheinman.

AT THREE MONTHS

The Power Structure Shifts

THE FORTY days were gone. As Lauren grew older, she grew troublesome. She wanted to be held all day long. This was, theoretically, the time of returning to normalcy, but it never happened. The number of days drifted well past forty, but Alan could not go back to work. With no one expecting him at an office, no one handing him a deadline, he just could not make the work process begin. Lauren, who was supposed to have been made secure by constant handling during the first forty days, instead had grown addicted to it. She refused to curb herself to Alan's theories. Her constant whimpering cry immobilized Alan, and Nina could not stand the pressure of seeing him idle. There was still no money. Fragments of half-finished scripts lay around the house, untouched since before Lauren's birth. The atmosphere was thick with a forced torpor, undisturbed except for Lauren's wail. Nina and Alan were rarely out of each other's sight.

Nina took the initiative.

"I'm going to Vegas," she announced. Her friends, strippers she had worked with, sent her a plane ticket. She cashed it in, bought a car seat for Lauren, and drove. Alan was left in Los Angeles with a story idea and no way to get around town for a week. He was supposed to work.

Vegas seemed changed. The surge of excitement she had always felt when she hit the strip did not materialize this time. She showed the neon lights and the crowds to Lauren as if they were a part of someone else's past, not her own. Lauren was all that really interested her this time.

She arrived in the evening—top business hours for Vegas—and drove down the strip past the city limits. Just beyond was one of her old clubs. She entered like a customer, and despite the two-and-a-half-month-old baby in her arms, no one stopped her. The management had changed, but the men were still there. She thought she recognized some of them as her men, but none turned as she passed by. She was unrecognizable. On stage, an old friend, a dazzling blonde named Leslie, was naked and moving athletically to the rhythm pounding out of two speakers behind her. Nina knew what that felt like, to be lost in sound and your own body beat, working on an inner coil of energy. Now, looking at it from the outside, it seemed different, silly. She watched Leslie dance and looked down at Lauren who was lost in a healthy sleep on her breast, undisturbed by the uproar of rock and roll.

Nina had a beer. The bartender had moved over from another club and remembered her. He ignored Lauren. The place seemed broken-down, but Nina could remember each warped section of paper-thin wood paneling, every gap of darkness around the stage where a colored light bulb had blown. It had always looked like this, but it had never bothered her before. When Leslie retreated to the dressing room, Nina did not wait for the hooting or the applause to die down. She left the bar and went around the outside, through the dark, to the stage door.

Leslie was wearing a pink robe with a long vertical rip in the skirt. She did not turn until Nina tapped on the open door.

"Nina!" she shrieked.

Lauren awoke with a wail, squinted up at the hard, fluorescent light, and began to cry.

It had been almost a year since Nina had danced in front of a crowd, and everything about dance had left her. She listened to Leslie and the others talk—all the shoptalk she had gloried in—and none of it made any difference.

"It sounds like the corniest thing in the world," she recalled later, "but I listened to all of it, and we ate, and we laughed, and I just kept thinking, none of this matters, nothing matters but Lauren. It was like I'd found something in myself that I never could have told you existed. I started to think of this old-hat phrase, like something a grandfather would say: 'There's nothing lonelier than a stripper on Thanksgiving.'

"I looked around at everybody, all my friends, and I started to think about family, about my families—the one I'm from, and the one I'm making. And I wanted to get married."

In Los Angeles it was quiet. Alan was working well. He slept and ate regularly, and pages rolled out of his typewriter with relative ease—six a day. A treatment for a movie was pouring out of him. Nothing earth-shattering, just a good, routine, commercial film with action and a love story. The success of his work-in-progress nearly kept him from confronting the inevitable implication of his situation: he was glad to have Nina gone. He was at peace, undisturbed for the whole workday. His needs were few. He didn't want this week to end.

At night he went out with friends to a health bar down Sunset Boulevard. Yellow and orange Formica tables set the tone there, and the gleaming stainless-steel juicers and blenders were never silent. Although like a Paris bistro in no other respect, the management allowed customers to sit forever. The talk was about film and sex and money, and how the struggle would one day pay off. For Alan, this was the old days. He liked talking, dreaming aloud, then strolling home for a last forty-five minutes of work. At the end of the week he would be finished. Of course, he would have to be if the work was going to be of any value, because Nina and Lauren were coming home, and then God alone knew when he would ever get to work again.

No doubt about it: guilt took him to the florist. The treatment was done—pristine in a clear plastic binder—and Alan still didn't want Nina home, so he went to the florist and bought a fourteen-dollar bouquet. He had been telling her half-truths all week over the telephone. Now it was time for the big lie. None of this was quite as clear at the time as it seemed in retrospect:

"She looked beautiful to me," he said. "Lovely and fulfilled, sexy, too, like she'd made a decision as to who she was going to be. I have to admit it, she looked beautiful. I just didn't want to see her."

Things were all right at the start. Alan had to go out and peddle his treatment, so he was gone. Nina had the house to herself. Her man was off working, and although Lauren continued to cry a lot, it seemed like a normal life, the life she wanted, right out of "Father Knows Best."

Alan's treatment was evidently good work; a week after Nina's return he walked into the house with a check for five hundred dollars. Nina was amazed. He had earned five hundred dollars with just his brain and a typewriter, in a week. Far from overjoyed, however, Alan was distracted, remote. Nina didn't disrupt him. She told him his work was terrific, congratulated him, and let it go.

He was supposed to begin developing the treatment into a script. Each morning he would take his papers, a spiral notebook, and a pocketful of sharpened pencils to the park and sit on a bench, undisturbed. There was nothing holding him back, but he couldn't work. The jinx—Nina's presence seemed to carry it with her—had returned. He worried about her, and about Lauren. He worried about his own relationship to them, and he delivered whispered harangues directed at Nina, rehearsing them for confrontations that would never come. His energy, his freedom, his inspiration, all the things he had had again for one blessed week, were gone. He ate lunch early,

walking from the park to a health-food restaurant, not the one
Nina had worked at for fear she might be socializing there.
He didn't want to see her. He returned to the juice bar for a
quick bit of conversation at four in the afternoon. With the
passing days, the hour became earlier. He believed, or hoped,
that the conversation would stimulate his work. By the end
of two weeks, he was arriving at two in the afternoon, losing
the day in gossip about what had appeared in Variety. Hurriedly, at the end of the afternoon, he would jot some notes
about the script so that he'd have something to show for the
afternoon. It was a disease. He had gotten sick with Nina's
return.

Nina could see the idleness, the lack of progress, but she
said nothing. Writing was a mystery. She didn't want to
disrupt whatever subtle mechanism might be ticking its way
toward first gear inside Alan's head. She had no idea what
the problem was. In bed, with Lauren lying asleep by their
side, Alan told her simply.

"I want to go to New York."

The money was not enough to decrease their debt in any
meaningful way, he explained. He wanted to think about
things. It was his money. Was she angry?

Nina was infuriated, but silent. Temper wouldn't do. She
was quiet for a long time, running through hoops of anger
and disappointment. As her adrenaline pumped and flagged, one
idea kept reasserting itself: this is a boy. I'm living with a little
girl and a little boy. I'm the only one who is no longer a child.
She was at a loss, angry at Alan for what and who he was, who
he had to be.

"Well?" he asked.

"Go," she said.

Every relationship has a power structure. An equal part-
nership is only equal when there is a counterbalancing of
strengths. One of the advantages of a relationship that develops
slowly is the natural learning of the power structure. In Alan

and Nina's case, however, there was no time, and the power
structure was simple. Alan was in charge. He was the "smart"
one; Nina was the "beautiful" one. She had sexuality on her
side and a liberated attitude toward living, but he was the
master of nutritional philosophy, the creative one, and the
man with the potentially explosive career. The power structure in this relationship was so simple, in fact, that it could
not possibly be profound. And when Nina had her baby,
things began to shift.

Without acknowledgment by either party, the emphasis
began to rearrange itself in Nina's favor. As she discovered her
own self-worth through mothering, she began to care less
and less about what Alan thought about things. She began
to recognize herself as independent.

Despite all the advances of the women's movement, we
have found husbands to be the dominating power in almost
every marriage we have studied—until the baby is born. This
is, in part, because young wives see their prebaby days as temporary. They tend to expect that their "real" lives will begin
when they become mothers. Their careers are frequently just
time-passing devices. Understand, we do not applaud this state
of affairs: we have observed it.

Husbands, meanwhile, have begun their careers, the pursuit
of which will take up the major portion of their adult lives.
In other words, they see themselves as already having gotten
serious, while the wives feel that seriousness is just around the
corner. Husbands get used to wives feeling that way, and they
like it. It makes them seem important, and everyone wants to
seem important. And so the power structure is created.

The arrival of the baby throws everything into turmoil. Suddenly wives are working longer, harder hours than their husbands. They begin to demand equal time, equal power, and a
right to do as much complaining about their day, as much
crowing about their achievements, as their husbands. Usually
there is trouble, at least for a time. Husbands no longer feel
they can come home from a hard day and bask in their sense
of achievement/exhaustion in front of an eager audience.

They have to do as much listening as talking, and frequently they don't care all that much about the subject. It's hard to admit that your own child's every progression, the change from hand-sucking to thumb-sucking, for instance, doesn't fascinate you; yet many men are bored by the news of their infant children. Disinterest is probably, in part, a product of guilt; if you haven't been paying enough attention, and if you feel guilty about it, it's best to remain distant.

With this gap in communication comes the power shift. As mothers take on a more dominant role in the relationship, fathers can feel threatened, ignored, and resentful. If they feel that way, they should say so, because the worst aspect of the power shift is that some fathers begin to blame the child. Therein lies a potential lifelong problem. The child does nothing to deserve this resentment and will never be able to understand it or cope with it. This emotional tension between father and child can last into the child's adult life. It is the subject of many great works of literature and drama, which is to say it is serious business, and it all starts with the shift in the marital power structure. Fathers beware: mothers can become quite great women through mothering, and they can find reserves of spiritual strength and innovativeness. To complain about this is to miss the beauty of developing life. Only the most extraordinary men can make this transition smoothly, but there is nothing wrong with a rough passage, as long as you get there.

AT SIX MONTHS

"The Return of the Man-About-Town"

ALAN was gone three weeks. He sat in the parks, relearning his roots and writing love letters to Nina. At a distance of three thousand miles, she seemed irresistible. Unthreatened by her presence, he repeatedly congratulated her on her dawning self-confidence and her new-found satisfaction. He took only partial credit. As he saw it, he had forced her to confront herself by making her a mother.

To Alan, the world was a place of poetical philosophy, and he was in tune with it. A sample text from his trip reads as follows:

There is no boundary to your self-exploration. I can see you in the future, pursuing the world itself, making it your world. The top has blown off; anything you want you can get. It makes me love you even more to think that Lauren has done this for you. The future is yours.

Well, what the hell, Nina thought. The future is now. She took a pad and pencil to the hair salon the afternoon after she received Alan's letter. While she sat under the dryer, she jotted down notes: all the things she was interested in, all the things she had meant to do, all the careers she had dreamed about. Two points compelled her, one generated out of social conscience, the other out of ego. She had seen a lot of girls like herself—strippers, hookers, hangers-on—harassed and mistreated. For the most part, they were represented by male public defenders, who were insensitive to the issues at hand. Nina knew about many bad drug raps, too. P.D.'s liked them best of all: the cases were easy, and plea bargaining made them look good. Nina could be a better lawyer—if she could get the training. Or she could be an actress.

Stripping, as she recalled it in what seemed like the dim past, had begun as a temporary occupation, something to tide her over until her acting career got started. Almost all the girls had begun that way, but none ever moved on. Still, here she was, living in Hollywood with a producer/director/ writer (admittedly self-styled), and if the time was not right now, it never would be. It occurred to her that acting was too self-indulgent. Law was prouder, better for her. Sitting under the dryer, she dreamed up a scenario for each. They were both fuzzy, enjoyably vague, and unrealistic. In her dreams, she had reached the apogee, all the hard work was behind her. Nina was bad at imagining that part. She hadn't thought about it and it had cost her. This time she was going to go looking for advice.

It came from the counseling office at Los Angeles City College. Although almost a month passed before Nina admitted final defeat, the L.A.C.C. counselor dashed all her hopes of becoming an attorney from the start. There were four years of undergraduate work to go through, then three years of law school and the bar exam—and that was if you were unattached, with no responsibilities but school. Alan would have to be a permanent baby-sitter. She knew that would never work. For two weeks, she tried to juggle schedules, tried to make a law career probable by willing it so. Then, with a small pang of regret, she set out to have a composite photo sheet made of herself and find a suitable acting seminar.

Alan returned to California and found Nina working at fever
heat. She had enrolled in a class, found a classmate with a
baby, and the two of them shared the cost of a sitter. There
were scripts all over the apartment. Alan was slightly bewildered. Nina kept changing, kept going him one better. The
light in her was almost visible to the eye, coming up through
her skin. He hadn't meant to start a revolution with his little
rhapsody.

Nina thought he'd be proud, thought he was ready to start
a family at last—two self-sufficient people and their child. She
thought, in short, that Alan had moved ahead, kept in step
with her until several nights after he got home, when she overheard him talking on the phone to an old, long-lost friend.

"Life is real different," Alan said to his friend, within ear-
shot of Nina. "I was dating this stripper in Vegas, and she
got pregnant. So now I have a baby. We're living together."

Nina listened, and finally she understood. She understood
the whole situation. She was still living in a fantasy world,
like the little girl who copied the orgy scene into her diary. It
was a world where the family would meld into a perfect whole,
shaped by the kindly forces of fate. Now, for the first time,
she knew: she was not a real part of Alan's world—his career,
his social plans—and she had no assurance that she would ever
be. Alan could leave her. She was, and might always remain,
the stripper he had knocked up. As soon as he got off the
phone, she threw a fit.

"I don't need you here," she shouted. "I don't feel like
you're doing me a favor, hanging around here!"

Alan looked up from the bed and remained silent.

"If you want to go, go. If you want to stay, stay. But *never*
think for one minute that you're doing it for me. You do it
for you. Whatever you want."

Alan didn't know what he had said, didn't know where
the wrath was coming from, but as long as the gates were
open, he marched through.

"I can't stay and be nursemaid anymore," he said. "I have
my work. I can't spend my days taking care of Lauren. It's
impossible."

"Who the hell asked you?" Nina screamed. "For God's sake, go out! Get work! We don't need a nursemaid—that was your crazy idea. We need money! We always needed money!"

"I can't stand this," Alan said quietly. "You know who I've turned into? I'm the guy at the party who has to use the phone so I can call the baby-sitter, see if everything is okay, is she crying, did she eat? . . . How can I be that guy? I hate that guy! I'm not him. Inside, I'm just not him."

Alan left the next morning. He had been home a week. Even as he went out the door, he knew it was the wrong move. He knew it was all just a tantrum, and his vehemence had already cooled. He did it only to fulfill a promise made in fury. He was back the same night.

"With whatever money we have," he said, "I have to get an office. I have to work."

Through mothering, Nina Degarmo found herself. Unlike Betsy Scheflin, who found her baby a cause of guilt and a deterrent to her career, Nina found that her baby set her free to pursue whatever she wished. The difference in the two women is root simple. Betsy had enormous self-confidence until she became a mother. Nina had none. Nina learned her own worth through mothering, and then nothing could stop her. (Psychologists feel that people in sex-related businesses usually have a poor sense of self-esteem.) By succeeding with Lauren, managing to hold the house together, and realizing that she could do very well without Alan around at all, Nina came to realize her own human value.

She did it by looking outside the family unit for support. Some women feel guilt about admitting that they need help beyond husband and baby; Nina didn't have to think about it. She was isolated, lonely, and frustrated, and she went out in the world. In finding a support group and, more important, a friend with a baby, she certified that all of her problems were real and common, and she began to see that there were solutions.

Alan had taken up with the old, unconfident Nina, and he felt wretched in front of the new, proud one. She was no longer in awe of his talents, his potential, or his accomplishments. Even his ace in the hole, his willingness to become a totally involved parent, had backfired. He couldn't stand being around the house anymore, and his sacrifice to fathering so far had brought the most fruitless business year of his life. All this leads to a common syndrome, one that occurs between the sixth and ninth month of parenting. We call it "the return of the man-about-town." It is nothing more than a father's rebellion against all the constrictions of marriage and family. The rebellion often flourishes in couples who have not been married long, couples who are young, or both; however, it appears to some extent in almost every couple, no matter how mature. Once again, we return to the traditional stereotype of the male: eager to get away from family responsibilities and play big-game hunter in the world of business and leisure. Like a lot of clichés, this one holds water. There are many factors involved. To many men, having a baby provides a handy way to measure the flight of time and youth. Some men fight time all their lives (so do women, to be fair) and see the length of the losing battle represented in the progress of their children. A man who resists marriage is frequently involved in the first step of this lifelong struggle. After having succumbed at last to wedlock (a quaint term under the circumstances), he will almost certainly suffer the "man-about-town" impulse sometime after the birth of his first child.

This can all be quite rough, especially if, as in Alan and Nina's case, the mother is just beginning to glory in the family unit. In extreme cases, husbands will run, as Alan did. More often they will become career-crazy, insist upon constant entertainment in the evening, and try to trivialize the importance of the child in the eyes of their mates. Needless to say, it's a losing battle. Having a child is permanent and *will* change a man's life drastically. The "man-about-town" syndrome is, more than anything else, a rough-and-ready system of adjustment. It is an internal peace negotiation, which, like its counterpart in international politics, involves a lot of blustering demands, bombastic philosophy, petty deceit, and saving of face. It does work, but it can take a week or seven years. The impulse to escape may never fully vanish, but in most cases where the marriage holds, it will be submerged and dormant most of the time.

There is no point in women pretending that they are not part of the syndrome. Their reactions, combative or sympathetic, constructive or destructive, can make a big difference. The syndrome may not be morally defensible, but it is there, and it *must* be dealt with. It is important to understand that a husband's rebellion is not generally directed at a wife or child specifically, but at the whole system. Of course, you will take it personally, but you *shouldn't*. Mothers who become hyper-nesters, who become obsessed with the whole fabric of homemaking and mothering, will arouse more ire than mothers who maintain outside interests and a sense of perspective. The transition from office to home can be a hard one if home is a wellspring of diapers, broken rattles, and clippings from *American Baby*. Wives, although they are not responsible for this outcropping of male independence, can, to some extent, ease the situation if they are sensitive to where the damage is being done.

AT NINE MONTHS

The Money Crisis

SHORTLY after Alan's declaration of independence, the option on his screenplay was renewed. This time he took the money and did what he thought he should have done with it the first time: he rented an office. It was a single room in the kind of dilapidated Hollywood building that the fictional private eyes immortalized. There was nothing there but a desk, a typewriter, and a phone. The filing system consisted of four cardboard boxes labeled in green felt-tip pen. But it was all his. Each morning he awoke, dropped off Lauren at the sitter's house, and went to work. The office rent was right at the edge of impossible. Alan knew he might only have the place a month or two, but he clung to it.

Miraculously, as if the gods were in on it, things began to break for him. Two friends vacated a remote, quiet apartment at half the rent that Alan and Nina were paying. The couple snapped it up and doubled their spending money by making the deal. Alan's financial source sent him to New York for further research, which meant more money. A film Alan had made years before fell into re-release in Texas. A check arrived in the mail from the distributor and did not bounce. Suddenly, there was money.

It wasn't a lot of money, and it wasn't a guaranteed steady income. There might be only three or four easy months ahead —three or four easy months. It seemed like heaven had descended.

No one could have predicted the measure of change that money brought. Poverty is like a migraine, especially for people who are not used to it: it cuts across all levels of comfort and capability. It may seem to be only a headache, but the pressure tells everywhere. Money was relief; with money there were moments of leisure, and the tone of grimness began to lift from the Sheinman/Degarmo household. It was a fog burned away by cash. Boxes of bric-a-brac that had been collected from the various apartments each of them had occupied at different times were, for the first time, unpacked in the new place. Curtains were made. Carpets were shampooed with a machine rented from the supermarket with leftover grocery money. That constant symbol of American domesticity, the family dog, made a premiere appearance. Alan found a sort of springer spaniel awaiting the gas chamber at the local animal shelter and saved her. She was called Scarlett.

NINA: The treat of a lifetime—I went to see Ricky Nelson at the Roxy. A friend of mine and I got tickets. Suddenly I was sixteen again. I was standing and screaming for more, and I realized that I hadn't changed. I was still the same me—still had a crush on Ricky Nelson, still recognized every part of myself, even with the baby and living with Alan, and the life I had been through. I really hadn't changed. Of course, on the way out, some kid, about sixteen, was talking about the show, and he said, "That guy could learn a thing or two from the Sex Pistols." And that's how I've changed—now they have rock groups called the Sex Pistols. Ricky Nelson was part

of Ozzie and Harriet, and I guess I was, too. I'm old.
But I'm still me.

The house was not completely at peace, but combat was
rare. Nina kept her waitressing job and devoted the rest of
her hours to the acting seminar and Lauren. Alan began to
work late and, occasionally, on weekends. The weight of the
schedule seemed to oil their movement; things went smoothly.
Most unusual—absence brought them together. All the hours
lavished on Lauren in the past had made Nina and Alan
claustrophobic, especially Alan. The apartment—the new one—
was home. It was a refuge from everything else that was suddenly going on. When they met there at night, it was like
regular married people home from the day's work. They were
glad to see each other.

Alan's second trip to New York was the first time Nina
missed him. On the first trip she was glad to get rid of him,
glad to be left alone with her baby. She and Lauren seemed
to be the true and complete family unit. Now, however, Alan
was definitely a part. She could tell because something was
missing when he was gone. It felt good to miss him. She no
longer cared too much whether they ever got married.

His return was the occasion for a celebration: Lauren was
standing against the crib for the first time, waving her arms
wildly and falling over backward when she saw her father
enter the room. The trip had gone well. If the movie got
made, there would be a small part for Nina. It was storybook
time.

There was still ambivalence, but there was no time for
analysis, for brooding, or for questioning. For the first time,
Alan didn't feel like it either. It wasn't that he had settled
the whole thing in his mind, because he hadn't; yet the
days seemed to go by painlessly without his thinking about
it. A Vermont farmer once told a young writer who had moved
in next door, "Farmers don't have time to be neurotic." That
was pretty much the story with Alan and Nina. Alan had
deadlines to meet, people to see, and money to raise. Nina

had two careers—actress and mother. They had disagreements, but there was no inclination to let them fester.

They did not attribute the change in their relationship entirely to money, but money was the root of it. Money had provided the impetus, had lifted the burden, had cleared the air. There wasn't that much of it, but the promise of more kept them busy, and activity kept them sane. Lauren, who had begun life as a fretful and difficult preemy, had achieved near perfection by age of nine months. She didn't seem to miss her parents when they let go of her in the morning, and she squealed with delight upon seeing them in the evening. That helped. More significant, however, the overwhelming stagnation and the bitterness, finally hopelessness, of the first six months of Lauren's life was over. A very small sum of money lurched Alan into forward motion, and the first kick was all that was needed.

When we asked the question, "What worries you most about the prospect of becoming a parent?", two answers from husbands were overwhelmingly common: birth defects and money. We've already said most of what we're going to say about the former; there is not enough one can say about the latter. Money is such a nonspiritual subject that it is difficult to be honest about what it can mean to a new family. It is not only the presence or absence of goods and services that comes into question, but issues of pressure, worry, and leisure time. Human beings have certain things in common with automobiles—they heat up, they cool down, they get in and out of tune, and, from time to time, they break down. Psychology tries to explain and sooth all the various symptoms of human disrepair, but generally, people prefer repair to analysis. Much of the time the crucial missing part is money.

To a childless couple, leisure time may seem like a readily available luxury; to new parents, it is an absolute necessity. In other times, families clustered together and a couple in need of a day off could leave a baby with a relative—aunt, mother, grandmother—and be gone. Not one of the couples in this book had such an opportunity. Their parents, grand-parents, and cousins live hundreds, often thousands of miles away. (This is not an entirely fair survey. All the couples lived in Los Angeles—a notoriously transient community.)

Leisure time became a matter of money for all these people. Every time they wanted an evening or a Saturday or Sunday to themselves, it cost money. Relaxation is expensive, especially when you add on the price of a baby-sitter. Tennis, theater, the movies—almost everything has a price.

The baby is an enormous expense as well. There are many guides to budgeting your newborn, and one need not be offered here, but the total sum is substantial. The threat of not meeting it can be more debilitating than anyone admits.

One of the common conflicts husbands and wives get into before children are conceived involves this question: How established should the husband be in his career before adding a child to the family? Wives tend to worry that they will be too old to have a first child by the time their husbands are ready. Husbands, on the other hand, make the argument that they cannot take the pressure of having a newborn who may, figuratively speaking, go hungry. At some point the com-promise is made, the child is conceived, and the race begins.

At the moment, couples seem to be getting married later and later in life, so the vise is often tightening by the time the wedding takes place. There is no "right" solution to the money problem, but it is important to recognize that if such a prob-lem exists, it will not confine itself to factual deficiencies, such as "the baby cannot have a new pair of shoes" or "we cannot afford a maid." It will cut across every aspect of the relation-ship, doing psychological damage every place it hits. It will cut into your confidence, your communication, and your trust. If you must have a baby on a tight budget, make sure you plan carefully. Above all, *do not consider money spent on your own leisure as money wasted.* It may be the most important money of all. It may save you when nothing else can. It's so im-portant it has to be said twice. *Do not consider money spent on your own leisure as money wasted.* Now write it on the blackboard thirty times.

AT ONE YEAR

Living the Conventional Life

DREAMS of the alternative family—the father staying home, the mother sharing all the chores—had danced in Alan Sheinman's head from the beginning. He was glad he had done it, but he was happier that it was over. He wasn't cut out for child care.

ALAN: I thought it would be hard, and bad at times, but I thought I was prepared for that. As it turned out, the bad parts weren't as bad as I expected, but I also wasn't anywhere near as prepared. It wasn't that the tasks were so hard, it was just that I was no good at them, if that makes sense. But ultimately I just had to say to hell with it. I have to go to work every day.

The office became his second home. Often he would get home at two or three in the morning, wake up by the telephone, pick it up and begin making calls. Nina was anything but upset.

NINA: That was the man I fell in love with, the man who works so hard he falls asleep in his clothes. He was what I thought I was getting. I never minded if I had to do more than my share with Lauren. When he started to stay home, and to help me, it was sweet, but I almost stopped loving him. I didn't go for this homebody type. He was doing it for me, and I guess I didn't even understand what was happening, but, little by little, it was like a different man had moved in. He was forcing himself to be what he thought I wanted, but I was in love with what he was before. So it was crazy.

Progress was slow for Alan. As he inched forward, Nina went out for her first union acting role and got it. It was a one-day shoot for three hundred dollars, and she had to call in sick at the restaurant to do it, but there she was—a professional actress. So it went. From the floundering uncertainty in the days of the pregnancy, Alan and Nina had become mates, running a household more or less like any other. Each of their parents told friends and relatives that Alan and Nina were married. For the sake of those very people, the couple had a Fotomat Christmas card made up with a picture of Lauren on it, enigmatically signed: Alan, Nina, and Lauren. No last names. It was a painless step toward reconciliation with the world of convention and commercialism. They missed the old days in a way, but things were going so well that they hardly noticed how familyhood had "normalized" them.

The life that Alan had rebelled against—bottles, baby-sitters, bills from the pediatrician—seemed acceptable now. Alan had work. He was still Alan, and the trappings of his life-style no longer mattered to him. He knew his current behavior was in direct contradiction to everything he had promised himself in the past, but the past was a long time ago. Everything was going well.

Alan, the philosophical one, saw the adjustment as an almost organic process over which we have no control.

"That's what this year is for," he explained. "That's what the year is. It is a year to become a parent, to learn to be that parent, to learn who he is and what he will do in any situation. Anything you do in that year is a part of the learning process."

Nina agreed. For her, the time preceding Lauren's birth seemed to be from a different life, not hers. Stripping was something she could no longer picture; her mind played tricks on her. The men who used to follow her from bar to bar had faces, but she could no longer recall them. The colors and the music began to fade, and, most especially, the impulse to be a sexual animal in public had vanished.

Sex had become private to Nina, and with Lauren in the world, it took on a different meaning. It was more detached from her own ego than ever before. Her sex drive had risen markedly during her pregnancy, when she was most obsessed with being unattractive; it had been tapering off ever since. By Lauren's first birthday, sex had become a sometime thing for Nina. Alan was understanding, but frustrated.

"I'm tired," Nina said. "I'm tired every single night. That's just the way it is. And Lauren gets us up in the morning."

"And if there's one thing everyone should know," Alan added, "it's that nothing kills an erection faster than a baby's cry. Two seconds would be about average. Of course, this will only go on for another seventeen years or so."

As far as Nina was concerned, she was without sexual stimulus. There were no parties, she was not drinking or dancing, and she was surrounded by diapers and baby food. Somehow, she just didn't feel sexy, didn't feel like a courtship was going on or would ever go on again. What made it worse for Alan was that the sexual lull didn't distress her. It seemed to be a natural phase. She didn't picture it lasting seventeen years at all, but she was in no hurry to put an end to it. She just hoped Alan would last.

The sexual inequity problem was different in a fundamental way from all the other problems Alan and Nina had encountered during their first year. They talked about it. They had rational discussions. They tried alternate methods of satisfaction, and although none worked well, there was no argument, no apparent bitterness. Where all other disagreements were solved by private warfare, gloom, and temperamental outbursts, this one was met head-on and handled in a nondramatic forum. The problem itself was never solved. Something more important happened: they succeeded in keeping it from bleeding into other areas of their life. To some extent, they felt, maturity had gripped them.

It seems unfair to leave Alan Sheinman and Nina Degarmo in the lurch. One feels their sex life might resolve itself at any minute if one were to wait around, but, of course, it won't because sex never resolves itself. It always changes; sex depends upon everything else, depends upon who the partners are at any given moment. If Alan and Nina's sex life was in a state of flux at the end of a year, it is hardly any wonder. Of all the people in this book, these two had undergone the most radical, unpredictable, and important growth spurt during their first year as parents.

The raggedness of their progress is nothing to sneer at; they began at wild loose ends and ended in some kind of conventional harmony. If there is a sadness in the loss of their earlier life-style, then it is a sadness in which all of us can share. Becoming parents involves loss or, more accurately, trade. We lose a powerful and thrilling selfishness. We lose the right to be unpredictable, irresponsible, spontaneous. Most parents feel, at the end of the year, that they have traded these attributes for something just as valuable—a deep understanding of what it is to be part of the ongoing human race. Still, what they have given up is gone forever. There is no question about that. Speaking statistically, three couples in this book felt that they could keep their life-style and become parents at the same time. Of the others, one was dissatisfied with married life to begin with and felt that adding a child might help. One never thought about life-style at all, and one felt that five years of selfishness was enough, that they had done everything they wanted to do, and that they would totally change their lives when the child came along. Only the last one escaped serious, traumatic difficulties during the first year.

In Luis Bunuel's movie, *That Obscure Object of Desire*, a man falls hopelessly in love with a woman who remains unattainable. Not only is she unattainable, she is played by two different actresses who change places seemingly at random. The point is made that we are all more than one person, that a different me will show up at a cocktail party than the me who goes to the typewriter each day, or the me who goes to the ball park. When children enter a couple relationship, parents begin to find new persons everywhere. As many faces as we have tried on during courtship and marriage, there are hundreds more waiting. The more we reveal, the more we learn about each other and ourselves, and the more vulnerable we become. The more we show, the less we are hiding. Before our children are born, we tend to hide a lot. Perhaps we're worried that our mates will not like our uglier or more brutal sides, so we bury them. There is only the bare beginning of honesty in many relationships. With children, the pressure becomes greater. We are called upon to work harder, under more stress, for longer hours than ever before. The best-hidden facets of who we are begin to escape. This can work well or not. An insecure woman like Nina Degarmo can discover unexpected strengths of character and self-assurance, while a blustery philosopher like Alan Sheinman may find a raging adolescent inside. The comings and goings of these characters can be most disturbing, but there is no advantage in keeping them buried. They're going to have to come out, and your relationship will stand or fall on whether the additional you's can find common ground with the old you's. For this reason, couples who have been together only a short time tend to fail. Not enough aspects of character have been dealt with before the child, and the flood afterwards can drown both parties.

Alan and Nina achieved a major victory by lasting the year. Statistics were all against them. Our guess would have to be that if they had not had some financial success, which gave them a direction to pursue, they wouldn't have made it.

Their failure to create a new kind of family is another sadness, both for them and for us. They wanted badly to live up to an ideal they believed in, that of the father taking on 50 percent of the parenting chores. That they failed is probably partly a matter of temperament—Alan's—but it is as much a matter of practicality. It's very difficult to survive in a society that operates one way when you operate a different way. We are not talking about discrimination here —certainly no one in Los Angeles cared remotely how Alan and Nina were living. We're talking about systems: systems for making money, for keeping house, for advancing in a career. Unless you live in complete isolation, you interact with other people. You depend upon them for your own livelihood; they have no desire to conform to your way of life. When he was taking care of Lauren, Alan was only about 50 percent as efficient as he might have been, and his is too tough a profession for him to succeed at that efficiency rate. There were too many other film makers who were better than Alan merely because they could spend twice as much time at it as he could. He couldn't meet the competition. That was the sad fact of life. Alan had to conform to the rules of the profession that was feeding him, and so do most men.

He was never sorry he had spent the year trying to do it differently. He only regretted his failure. To all future parents with similar ideals, Alan's first year as a parent should serve as a cautionary tale. If you cannot afford to give a year away, you probably cannot be a full-time father.

The other side of the coin is equally important: the money Alan earned when he finally went back to work did much more to ease the anxiety in the household than his devoted presence had ever done. Earning money *is* parenting. It's one of the parenting chores, and to see it any other way is to misplace one of the greatest responsibilities a parent has— providing a comfortable atmosphere in which nurturing can naturally take place.

THE
FIFTH
FAMILY

Hal and Susan Bradford

AND ERIC

THE NEW MARRIAGE

For Hal and Susan Bradford, life seemed to turn sunny all at once. Their arrival in Southern California marked the beginning of an unexpected adventure in romance. Both were just out of bad, young marriages. They worked on opposite coasts in pressure-cooker worlds—the New York art gallery scene and the rapidly advancing world of computer technology. Susan, the New Yorker, red-haired, freckled with a model's bones and green eyes, knew a lot of men. But men were just a thing to be around. She wasn't thinking of love or marriage: she was still feeling the exhilaration of reprieve.

On the West Coast lived Hal, her opposite number—a born Californian with shaggy dark hair, easy movements, and a ready smile. His tan was permanent, highlighting the few strands of white in his sideburns. There were no lines on the face; nothing to worry about, yet.

They met in a bar, like a thousand other meetings, but this one was it. Uncalled for, their number had come up. Hal was in New York for four days of business, and the time limit made him feel like a sailor on leave. He and Susan did everything but sleep. They did things no one ever did—the boat tour of Manhattan, the bus tour of Chinatown. This was the most ardent, the most playful either one of them had felt since their first love in high school. There was a difference, however. They were old enough to do something about it. At the end of the four days, when Hal went back to California, he took Susan with him. She made hasty arrangements for a leave of absence from her position (she was a buyer for a Madison Avenue litho gallery), and they just flew away. It was all too amazing. A month later, they were married.

They moved into a nearly hidden apartment in the Los Feliz hills with beamed ceilings and a living room stuffed with plants—a place from the forties. The neighborhood was only a short drive from the Sunset Strip's frenzy, but it seemed to be a hundred miles away. This was where the people who escaped, escaped to. Regularly, Hal and Susan would go back to the discos, the clubs, and the restaurants, but it was different now. They weren't looking for anything but entertainment. They already had everything else. The nagging inner dissatisfaction, which had become so much a part of each of them that it was no longer noticeable, suddenly gave way to euphoria. Life became extravagantly pleasurable. There was pleasure everywhere; they would shop the all-night supermarkets at two in the morning, make omelettes at six, and sleep all day Saturday. Honeymoon and marriage, career and vacation all blended together, and neither sunrise nor sunset could hold them. At thirty-four and thirty-two, they were too old for this kind of intense romance, which made it all that much better; they were born-again lovers.

After two months, it was too good not to share. They had proclaimed each other the perfect mate, and each wanted the other's child. Twelve weeks later, Susan was pregnant. Hal came home from the office with a dozen red roses, a brown teddy bear, and a savings bond.

A well-known gambler once explained his own folly: "There comes a moment," he said, "when you've had a string of winners, and something clicks in your head—you begin to believe it's you and not the dice that's doing the winning."

Hal and Susan had been on such long losing streaks that they had become numb to the feeling of their own emptiness. The onslaught of winning made them remember. They savored the pregnancy as a golden time—every event led to laughter, and many led to lovemaking. At one dinner with friends, it was suggested that the scientific method for determining the sex of the unborn infant involved a box of Drano and an empty tin can. The Drano was to be sprinkled on the bottom of the can, then mixed with water. The color of the can after the chemical reaction had taken place would reveal the child's sex. Drano was provided by a bewildered but curious neighbor. A can of cling peaches was quickly turned into peach daiquiris, which were consumed during the experiment. Hissing smoke emerged from the can and the water frothed, causing a momentary retreat of the guest. When it was all over, the inner tin was nearly black. No one, alas, could remember whether that meant boy or girl.

Separate experiments were undertaken involving apple peels; wedding rings rolled down bellies, and bracelets tossed over the shoulder. The results were inconclusive. Hal and Susan wanted a girl, but they really didn't care.

Hal thought Susan was beautiful with her new belly. Lovemaking became better even as it got more physically awkward. They had known each other such a short time that sex had never settled into a routine; Susan's body was just another innovation. As she grew, Hal was able to imagine her as a new woman each week, eager to experiment and get comfortable. The pregnancy was the greatest kick of their young relationship. Having a child, they could only assume, would make things even better. As they lay in bed, their descriptions of the future grew increasingly florid. The links between sex and child, and themselves and the universe around them all seemed to be closing in a chain. It was amateur philosophy, and they knew it, but it warmed them.

Two couples with babies were among their friends. One was

getting divorced. The other seemed happy enough, but was generally unavailable for any but the most elaborately arranged outings. There was the matter of baby-sitters, who frequently had to be picked up and dropped off, and then there were days when these people were just tired. Hal and Susan understood. But they felt that their friends' 100 percent devotion to the child was responsible for these problems.

Hal did not expect to give up his independence to his son or daughter in quite that way. He felt that a child could be taken almost anywhere. Susan, who was a little more realistic about the baby, was not opposed to doing more than her share. She understood that Hal was "just that kind of man," and she had fallen in love with him, so what could she do? She was determined that the baby would not become a drag, holding her back, turning her into the women in the laundry commercial. She had no fears of that happening. Because she was aware of the problem, she could control it. The baby would be fun for her. Both partners announced that they were willing to make sacrifices. Hal would help with the housework, although he would not, except in an emergency, do the dishes. That was a quirk. The conference on shared child care responsibilities lasted about five minutes. Hal would do anything for the baby, but he would object to handling the baby's diapers if they contained a bowel movement. There was no negotiation. This constituted an undisputed agreement.

The Bradfords chose a progressive delivery room technique named for the man who devised it, Frederick Leboyer. Using Leboyer, the delivery experience is approached from the newborn's point of view. Lights in the delivery room are dimmed to make the transition from the womb to the outside world as gradual and free of trauma as possible. Music is played throughout the delivery (the Bradfords chose Mozart). The newborn is placed on the mother's abdomen, massaged by both parents, and then, after the umbilical cord has been cut, immersed in a water bath the same temperature as the amniotic fluid that has surrounded him/her for nine months. The aim is to ease the

newborn into its new status. To Hal and Susan, it seemed a
perfect choice. It represented the right way to come into the
world, and symbolized their determination to give this child
more love and devotion than any other child had ever had. The
hospital had prepared one delivery room for Leboyer births.
The Bradfords' obstetrician remained neutral on the question
of whether the Leboyer technique had any real measurable
value, but he was willing to use it, barring any unusual developments during labor. Hal and Susan dreamed about it. It seemed
perfect.

Two weeks before the baby was due, Susan's mother went
on call in New York City. She was prepared to fly westward
the moment her daughter went into labor and stay for as long
as she was needed. Despite the income from Hal's growing
computer analysis firm, the couple could not afford a live-in
nurse, but they wouldn't have wanted a stranger in the house
anyhow. Hal liked his mother-in-law. He appreciated her willingness to help, but he also saw it as something she *wanted*
to do. He didn't feel he owed her anything, and he didn't
think her presence would affect the household that much.
Most of the time-saving would benefit his wife, not him, because it was she who would have to attend to the baby's daily
needs. He was glad mother and daughter would have each
other's company, too, because it would free him to attend to
business without guilt. He and Susan had never lived in a
household of three before, let alone four, but in some crazy
sense, Hal believed that his mother-in-law and the baby would
cancel each other out, occupying each other's time and needs,
leaving Susan and him alone as a twosome. However it worked
out, it would be another adventure.

Susan's due date approached and she quit her job. There was
the baby's room to attend to, and like a last-minute Christmas shopper, she began to panic. She stayed up all night
hemming and pleating curtains. Hal would come home at
night to find her on the floor with her legs spread, assembling
clown lampshades and picking Styrofoam-packing shreds out
of the fur of newly arrived stuffed animals. More than once

she found she could not get off the floor without help. It was a handsome nursery, and even before the baby's arrival, it had become their favorite room in the house.

The big day came and went, and the baby did not arrive. There was no depression. There was, in fact, a small sigh of relief. Things were not quite ready. Hal and Susan were not quite ready. The reprieve was welcome, and it built suspense. At midnight that night, when the labor pains had not started, Susan turned down Johnny Carson by remote control and said something to Hal that was to trouble her later.

"Everyday the baby doesn't come," she said, "gives us one more day to gaze at each other."

For one brief moment, she felt like a five-year-old, looking around the living room after a spree, realizing how many, many things have been broken. Then she turned out the light.

The question facing Hal and Susan Bradford was like the tag line from a radio soap opera of the thirties: Can a newlywed couple find happiness and romance with a newborn baby in the house and a mother-in-law waiting in the wings? This couple saw their life together as a dream come true. Obviously, dreams also come to an end.

The Bradfords had one thing going for them; they were very much in love. Each was consumed with concern for the other. They were ready for ecstasy and could create it on a moment's notice, if necessary.

The Duke, Theseus, in A Midsummer Night's Dream, listens to the ardorous, amorous babble of two pairs of lovers and describes their dialogue as "more strange than true." This is what lovers have to watch out for. They do, indeed, seem strange to the rest of us, and we envy them for their high spirits and impaired judgment. There are very few experiences that compare with the full force of romantic love, maybe none, but high times can be dangerous times. The Bradfords took the wildest chance of all in deciding to have a child immediately. They heard the warnings from friends, and undoubtedly had read of other couples who had failed to incorporate children into a brand-new marriage, but there are two sides to the coin. Lots of couples get married *because* they are going to have a baby, and other couples have a baby without getting married, and many of these couples live to a ripe old age together. So Hal and Susan were taking a chance. Life is a chance. They didn't see it as any big deal.

As the months went by, they became more and more convinced of the wisdom of their decision. Susan's pregnancy brought more joy and hilarity than anything the romance had seen yet. It was stimulating sexually, conversationally, and in every other way. They believed they had the game beat, because if there was going to be trouble, surely there would be signs.

They are the one couple in this book who expressed no fears about either money or having an imperfect child. They just didn't believe such things were possible for them. They were on a hot streak. We can't discourage this kind of thinking because worry is usually pointless, and what will be will be. The Bradfords were not really thinking realistically. They admitted it. They believed in the power of positive thinking. Even though they weren't being realistic, they would make their own reality; they would shape the baby and their lives around a world they could control. There's a benefit to this kind of thinking: it carries a tremendous surge of energy with it. There's also a liability: there's no margin for error.

AT ONE WEEK

Breast-feeding Failure

THE FIRST cautionary moments came in the hospital. The Bardfords were in for a long labor. They hated their nurse, and their doctor was out of town. They were shunted into the wrong delivery room where no preparations had been made for a Leboyer birth. It was too cold. The bath had to be arranged while Susan was on the table. No one seemed to care. Nothing was working out.

Still, Susan gave birth. Euphoria was restored with the last good push, and as their son was placed carefully on Susan's abdomen, both husband and wife burst into tears. Hal's glasses fogged up and his nose became stuffed as he wept over the infant. Susan was unable to help much with the massage. She was exhausted, and the anesthesia had left her immobile from the waist down. Her attention was riveted on the doctor who was stitching her up, and the whole scene was confusing.

The baby, Eric, wasn't crazy about the bath and was chilled

by the cool air of the delivery room. Somehow the poetry just wasn't there this time, not the way they had expected. While it was a moving experience and they let their tears flow, it wasn't exactly what they had bargained for.

To Hal and Susan, nothing about the hospital seemed satisfactory. The nurses in recovery were conducting a loud card game, and the nurses in the infant nursery tossed Eric around with an abandon that caused all the blood to drain from Hal's face. No one seemed aware of the importance of this event. Hal and Susan took their lumps and waited to get out. Next time, they said (they were already thinking of next time), they would retain complete control of things.

At home, waiting for them now, was Susan's mother, Lillian, called Ma by her daughter and Lilly by her son-in-law. She was a game woman, in her middle fifties, who looked ten years younger. She liked to dance, she laughed easily, and she had every intention of staying in the Bradford house until everything was 100 percent normal again. She hadn't had a baby in her arms in twenty-eight years, and she was looking forward to it. When Hal and Susan walked out the hospital doors, she was waiting to take the baby, to usher Susan into the car, to tuck her into bed, and to set a platter of cold cuts in front of her son-in-law. She had the house dust-free and polished to within an inch of its life. And she loved her grandson.

Susan's milk came in quickly, but Eric was sluggish at the breast, reluctant to get involved. Susan didn't know whether there was something wrong with the milk, whether he was just a slow learner, or whether it just wouldn't come out. She expressed some with a hand pump, an agonizing two ounces. It hurt and vaguely disgusted her. The swelling grew with each unsuccessful nursing, and as Susan's breasts expanded so did her sense of panic. At first weakened and painful between her legs, she now experienced a top-heavy ache that was quickly becoming unbearable. She worked and fretted over the breasts with a waning confidence. The milk just wouldn't come out. Another two ounces was diluted with water and fed to Eric from a bottle. At her breast he became at first diffident, then balky. And her breasts continued to grow. On the second morning, she discovered her nipples had inverted; her alarm was now augmented by a sense of freakishness. The problem was running away from her. The implications were overwhelming. She was not facing simple failure; Susan knew that she carried more than the responsibility for Eric's nourishment in her breast. There were egos and theories at stake. There had been much talk about nursing.

Hal had been speaking romantically about Madonna and Child for the last eight months. He believed breast-feeding to be the most important thing a mother could do. The advantages were all-encompassing—health, emotion, the natural order of things, and the bonding process between parent and child. It was the fundamental parenting process. Susan had to do it for him.

Her mother, Lilly, had a more blasé attitude. Nursing was all right with Lilly, she had done it herself; however, it meant no one could feed your baby for you, you had to get up all the time, and you'd be exhausted. It wouldn't be good for you. In other words, it wouldn't allow grandmother to do her part. Susan had a lot at stake with her husband and mother. There was only one thing to do, and she had to do it. As for Eric, without nursing, he'd starve. Susan started making phone calls the second morning.

Her pediatrician, her gynecologist, anyone who might help was contacted, but there was an undercurrent of failure and discord around the house. Lilly went out and bought two big cans of formula and got into an argument with Hal about them when she got home. The two of them woke Susan by mistake and felt terrible. Susan was in agony. Eric was drinking unsweetened water from a bottle, and each time he would try Susan's breast the same thing would take place. He could get just enough milk to taste it, then no more. He would howl with frustration, and the sound of his outrage, of his mother's failure, would drive her wild.

"I don't know what to do," she wept to Hal in the middle of the night. Pain and fear prevented sleep. Her breasts seemed huge beyond possibility, as hard as a regulation football, and straining from her body as if at any moment they would tear. It couldn't go on.

Hal looked at her seriously before he spoke.

"Only you know if you've tried your best," he said.

It was the first horrible, chilling moment of their marriage. He had betrayed her.

He didn't know what he'd said, and wouldn't for the rest of the week, because at that exact moment Eric woke with a howl, demanding nourishment and love. Hal paced by the side of the bed while Susan tried the usual, desperate, inadequate ritual. The baby's squalling awakened Lilly, who stood like a ghost at the half-opened bedroom door, her hair a fright, her sleep-heavy eyes held wide open by the noise. To Susan it seemed like something out of late Tennessee Williams: the family in sudden collapse, with herself as the helpless, pathetic heroine. She waited as long as she could. She let there be time to amply prove that this was not going to be the one session where, miraculously, it all worked. Then she just began to cry, pitiful sobs joining the baby's angry, hungry howls. For a moment there was no movement, just the sound in the dark. Finally, Hal spoke.

"Jesus," he said. "I can't stand this." He looked to Lilly who nodded at him, and then he slipped out of the room, passing her in the doorway. When he was gone, Lilly took Eric from her daughter and kissed her on the top of the head.

"I'm sorry, honey," she said. "But this boy needs food."

Susan nodded. Her arms lay limp at her side. She stared off into space, through a dark window. Lilly took the baby out of the room and into the kitchen, where there was already a pot on the stove for the bottle of formula. In the distance, Susan heard the sounds: pot clanking against the stove and counter, mother's expert, experienced coos and kisses, and the baby's sudden calm. She knew he was eating, taking some nourishment out of a can. She was relieved.

Hal came back in the room sheepishly, but angry inside.

"I hope you know what you're doing," he said, "what this means for Eric."

Susan fell softly back on the bed, her breasts raging with a ponderous ache.

"Don't talk to me till tomorrow," she said. "I can't take it."

The idea of bottle-feeding took some getting used to. The next morning Susan took her enormous breasts between toweling and cloths and bound them up, according to her doctor's instructions. It was a sight Hal didn't want to see. Her baby drinking formula from a bottle: there was nothing less likely, nothing she could have had more trouble predicting. The sense of failure was total. Only the baby, Eric, seemed not to notice it. Hal watched her with some suspicion; her mother was a picture of happiness, meddling with the bottles, pots and pans. Susan couldn't shake it; where had she gone wrong? Why was this her fault?

"You put some pretty strong guilt on me," she finally told Hal, a week later, when the size and the pain of her breasts had at last subsided. He seemed stunned.

"I only wanted what was best for everyone." He was not tuned in. "I have to tell you that breast-feeding is an important thing as far as I'm concerned. You couldn't do it. I honestly believe you *couldn't*. But I still think it's important. I wish it was different than it is for Eric."

So. Hal just wasn't going to be the pillar for this one. He didn't know what she needed, and he didn't know how to find out. And Lilly, of course, had won a small moral victory. She was all sympathy and concern, but there was something fishy about it, and Susan didn't like it. She wanted someone there who didn't have a stake in the matter. She needed someone who would just understand what she had been through, how her confederates and her infant son and her body had deserted her, and how awful it had been. It was over now, but she wanted some acknowledgment, some official recognition of her struggle. That was, of course, the one thing she would not get.

Nursing may be the single biggest wedge driven into most marriages during the early months of parenthood. The reason is that nursing is so much more than it appears to be. It *appears* to be an efficient method for mammals to feed their young, but that's like describing a handgun as a good tool for putting holes in things.

Briefly, here's why:

1.) *The natural way.* Nursing is "the natural way" to feed your baby, and getting back to nature is a strong moral and political issue these days. Consequently, breast-feeding becomes a way of advocating certain views and condemning others. Frankly, this has gone a little far. There are all kinds of reasons for nursing, but saving the whales is not one of them. Still, couples feel strongly that nursing is a way of taking a certain stance in the community. When there is a disagreement with a parent or mate about the merits of nursing, it can often be a disagreement that cuts to the heart of a differing world view. Sometimes women choose to nurse or not to nurse as a way of proving something to their husbands or parents. Unfortunately, husbands and parents tend to be more than willing to play this game.

2.) *Nursing means "I am a mother."* Since mothers nurse, there is a subconscious feeling among some women that people who don't nurse are somehow not mothers. The decision not to nurse, whether because of a physical dysfunction, an emotional unease, or simple convenience or preference, is seen by many women as an omen; they will never be real mothers, never be able to take on the most basic tasks of child-rearing. This human tendency to turn everything into a symbol is widespread and, in this case, unfortunate. Nursing is "in" at the moment, but it was "out" twenty years ago. Whether we like it or not, we are products of our own times and victims of our own trends. The authors of this book advocate nursing, and both are raising children who were nursed, but our advocacy is emotional as much as it is anything else. We believe it's the healthy thing to do, but that's because we did it.

One thing is certain: with a newborn baby, the healthy thing to do is to keep a peaceful, emotionally stable home. If you don't want to nurse because you're maintaining a career, or because you don't like what it does to your breasts, or because it leaks all over your mate and he doesn't enjoy it, these things should be taken into consideration. They may mean that in your case, formula is healthier for everyone, including your baby.

3.) *Men have nothing to compare with nursing.* Men, for the most part, do not understand nursing. There is no need to explain it to them because they will never understand. This is part of life. Asking a man to join you in the deep emotional well that nursing leads to is like asking a German shepard to sing "Sweet Sue." Men have no experience, ever, that is equivalent to nursing. They may bond themselves to their children in all different ways—feeding, playing, hugging, singing, whatever they can do—but they do not nurse, and they cannot comprehend what it is to nurse. You must give them the right not to understand. A thoughtful man who is emotionally in-touch with his woman will be extremely careful in dealing with a nursing failure. Hal Bradford, who wanted his son to be breast-fed, took it as a personal affront when things didn't work out his way. He was concerned about his son, but it was his wife who was suffering the damage. If a nursing failure occurs, it is the mother, not the child, who needs tending, because the depth of that failure is unimaginable to someone who sees it from the outside. In that moment of failure, if it happens, a mother may be at the most emotionally vulnerable point of her life.

The reasons for nursing failure are varied, and we can only speculate on what happened to Susan Bradford. Undoubtedly, the failure was both physical and emotional. Physically, she had not prepared her breasts and nipples prior to the birth. (Doctors have several recommended procedures which you should ask about.) Also, the pain and sudden engorgement of her breasts came as a surprise. She was unprepared for anything beyond a little swelling, which she was actually looking forward to. What happened instead (as it often does) was an enormous change in her breasts that included pressure, acute discomfort, and radical enlargement. This brought on fear and shook her confidence.

Emotionally, Susan was trying to do more than feed her baby. She was trying to please her husband and prove something to her mother. This is a serious and crucial mistake. Only one woman in a thousand could have overcome the emotional pressure combined with the physical pressure that confronted Susan.

The real question at hand here is: Why did Susan make the decision to nurse? Nowhere in her interviews does she mention that she actually *wanted* to nurse. Her ambivalence, if there was any, was steamrolled by Hal's enthusiasm. She had a lot of external reasons for nursing, but possibly no internal reasons. When things began to turn difficult, she had little conviction with which to fight back.

Every decision regarding parenting should be made by both father and mother. But in the case of nursing, we feel that the mother's inner conviction should tip the scale. For nursing to be successful, she has to *want* to nurse. While she may not be free of fear or confident about the facts of nursing, these inadequacies can be overcome. But a lack of desire is likely to result in failure. Ultimately, our advice would be: if you don't want to nurse—*DON'T*. And don't be cowed by all the fashionable nonsense that has been designed to make you feel guilty.

Having mother in the house, even though both Susan and Hal wanted her there and enjoyed her company, again made life harder for the couple. She was helpful, but she didn't let them establish a separate identity as a family, and she got tangled up in the nursing issue just when she wasn't needed. In the case of this couple, it is unclear what would have happened without her. Hal was so out of touch with Susan's needs during this first week that there might have been no improvement, but the presence of a third party, with a philosophical difference of opinion on the nursing issue, certainly didn't help. It is impossible to measure the emotional damage caused by the failure. Ultimately, Susan got over it. She came to believe that nursing is nice for those who can, but not important for those who can't, or don't want to. However, at the time she was going through it, she saw it as the first big "mother-test" and gave herself a failing grade.

It is imperative that men understand the importance of this private activity between mother and child. They can never understand *what* it is, but they must be aware *that* it is. When and if a crisis occurs, it must be recognized as a crisis, not simply a short squabble. At that time, men must lead a blind crusade in support of their women's emotional health. Otherwise, as the gangsters say, they pay.

AT ONE MONTH

The Baby as a New Toy

EVERYTHING subsided with the pain. As Susan's breasts gradually returned to their normal size, and her stitches healed, her strength returned. With strength came her sense of humor and her self-esteem. It was as if everything had been physical—the shame, the depression, and the anger—just extra symptoms, additional post-partum wounds. Each day she felt better and got stronger. After the baby's first week of formula feedings, she even forgave Hal everything, the way lovers do. He was a poor misguided fool when it came to nursing, but what was she to expect. She didn't know him all that well, and he was only trying to say and do the right things.

Lilly was a godsend. She fed the baby at night so that Susan and Hal slept a full, regenerating sleep. Each morning they awoke refreshed, and there was Eric—the greatest toy doll ever invented. As toys go he was expensive, but he was better than a sailboat or a video-cassette player could ever be. He was human. Susan and Hal now had it all. Hal went to work each morning with a bounce in his step that made him look like he was about to burst into song. And Susan, who had been ready to die two weeks earlier, was the picture of perfect motherhood. She had a long linen caftan that she wore until noon. While the baby slept, she would bathe and change. In the afternoon, a sitter would arrive so that she and Lilly could go out shopping, or they would have coffee and cookies in the living room. They talked that month as they had never talked in all Susan's years growing up. She learned her family heritage, her mother's tricks for child-rearing, some good horror stories about her parents' best friends, and the story of her mother's suffering during the last years of her father's life. The two women traded secrets like schoolgirls, and Susan had a friend to help with Eric. It was better than she could possibly have imagined, like a vacation plus a new career adventure. She had everything she wanted.

Hal couldn't believe his good fortune. Every night when he came home he found an immaculate house, a well-rested wife, a friendly mother-in-law, and, best of all, his toy-boy. Work was going well, and people from the office stopped by regularly to have a glass of wine and poke little Eric in the chest. Eric was a beautifully behaved child. He slept two and a half hours at a time, which wasn't quite enough, but the bottle comforted him. Lilly was a master of the art of feeding. Even when Hal or Susan would hear the baby's cry at two or four in the morning and bound out of bed eager to be of some assistance, they would get there too late.

"I was already up" was Lilly's self-effacing explanation as she popped the bottle into Eric's mouth. "Isn't he a doll?"

Everybody was a doll as far as Hal was concerned. He was living the dream life that California promised to everybody but delivered so rarely.

On weekends, there was sports on television, barbecues, and the occasional party. Hal felt no pangs of guilt about leaving Lilly to oversee Eric's evening, nor did Lilly ever show signs of wear and tear. If Susan would occasionally wonder whether they were depending too much on her mother, Hal would say to her:

"Ask her. That's between you and her. If she wants to change things, we'll change them."

Susan hinted several times to Lilly that she didn't feel entirely comfortable about how complete their dependence upon her had become. Lilly had only one answer.

"Don't be silly," she said each time the subject was raised. She saved up all the energy of the sentence for the first syllable of "silly."

"Don't be *silly*."

So, with her permission, they used her. They went disco dancing and took in a couple of movie premieres. When a big musical opened, they took their tickets and sent Lilly in their stead, dressing her up and shipping her off to have a good time while they stayed home. They didn't much like musicals. While she was gone, Eric awakened them and had to be fed. It was, Susan realized with some surprise, the first time she had had to get out of bed and feed her child at night in almost four weeks. The thought chilled her. Hal turned on the TV while she was gone and kept it low. As she came back into the bedroom, he clicked it off.

"Was that any fun?" he asked, as Susan climbed under the covers next to him.

"I don't know," she said seriously. She really didn't. Hal was snoring fifteen minutes later when Lilly let herself in downstairs.

The Bradfords had one capacity that many of us can envy; they knew how to have fun. When things were going well, they took advantage. Having someone live in, taking care of your needs, giving you time to yourself, can make these good stretches longer and more frequent. Live-in help is hard to find, however, and many people are uncomfortable with it. Having a mother/mother-in-law live in may be fine, but as we have stressed over and over, it tends to be a loaded situation. During the first week, Susan's mother was a catastrophic influence. During the next three, she was a constant delight. The Bradfords had it both ways, which is common when you have an emotional tie to the person who is helping you out. The first month of Eric Bradford's life, barring the first seven days, was the happiest time of Hal and Susan's marriage. They rode the good times as hard as they could and came out of it the way most people come home from vacation. You need these carefree periods. They are there for the taking. Few couples have them so soon because few can lay off all of the night feeding on a third party. The Bradfords were lucky. They were also unlucky because there had to come a time when Lilly would go home, and neither one of them could face wondering what in the world would happen then.

AT THREE MONTHS

The Father as Boy

When Eric was six weeks old, Lilly went back to New York: Hal and Susan had their baby to themselves. They were expecting to have some fun with him, to carry him around, and take him to Palm Springs for the weekend, but there wasn't time. Hal was at the office late each night, and Susan could barely keep the house together during the day. Immediately, she sought help.

There was a twelve-year-old girl on the block who, for a small fee, was willing to ride around town with Susan on errands and watch Eric in the car. This would theoretically reduce the shopping time. However, the second time Susan had to scold the girl for reading *Celebrity* magazine while Eric howled for his bottle, she decided it wasn't working out. The plan had lasted a total of one shopping trip.

"I'm at the edge," she told Hal after one week of full-time mothering. "I'm slipping into the abyss." She was smiling when she said it, acting the heroine in distress, but Hal understood it to be no joke.

"Say no more," he assured her. "Tell me how to help."

Susan wasn't sure how or why she resented him so bitterly for taking a shower after dinner. She had managed to shower just that morning herself, the usual two-minute affair. Hal's shower seemed to be without end and was followed by "Monday Night Football." At nine-thirty, as Susan was looking over the morning paper, Eric awakened, hungry and in a snit.

"Honey—," Hal called to her from the TV room.

"But," she protested gamely, "what about the abyss? Remember?" She knew he couldn't hear her with the sound turned up.

"It's three minutes left," he explained, whining over Eric's bellowing. "It's twenty-one to nineteen."

By the time she heard the score, there was already a bottle simmering on the stove.

Hal had talked about all this with Susan before the baby was born. The division of labor. He would make the money; she would raise the child. He was certainly keeping up his end of the bargain. Business was good, but it required his concentration. His firm provided computer analysis for several enormous corporations. There was no margin for error. The pressure was always on. He needed to air out his brain and body when he wasn't working them. Given his ideal schedule, he was a close-to-perfect work machine. His schedule, unfortunately, did not include Eric, except as a miscellaneous entertainment. There was no room for him. Hal needed to awaken refreshed, to breakfast, to work, to play handball for forty-five minutes at midday, to spend the afternoon double-checking his employees' work, and to relax after supper. This formula resulted in success, and Hal had no desire to change it. His wife's emotional emergency was not a welcome addition to his life.

He promised to take a day off the following week, a day when Susan could do whatever she wanted and he would handle the baby. Unfortunately, work heated up, new clients materialized, and that week was impossible. The next three weeks were impossible. Susan, he realized, had begun to look at him differently, like an unfamiliar, possibly hostile, stranger. As far as he was concerned, this just wasn't his fault. The more he thought about it, the angrier he got. He had taken a whole week off when the baby was born, and now he had responsibilities. He was holding up his end, and it wasn't his fault that Susan was totally wrapped up and tied to the baby. That was the deal they had made. They hardly saw each other anymore. Dinner had become irregular and frequently interrupted. There was neither the time nor the energy for sex. Even *without* leaving work for a day, the whole thing was a titanic inconvenience.

He could see the problem was real, however. It just didn't *seem* real. There were times in life when emergencies occurred, and this was one of them. He would have to make the free day he hadn't been able to find. Ultimately, he decided it would be easier to take a week.

A week was a big, planned vacation, much less likely to evaporate before it happened than a day off. He and Susan would spend a week in Palm Springs with Eric, and rekindle things. In advance of their departure, they worked out a hard and fast schedule: Susan sunbathing in the early morning (gentle sun for pale skin), while Hal takes care of Eric; Hal sunbathing in the midday (strong) sun, while Susan takes care of Eric; lunch during Eric's nap; late dinner after Eric goes to sleep; turns taken playing tennis if partners were available. They had the loan of a one-bedroom condominium, and it seemed ideal.

There was a lot of free time on the schedule, and the free time killed them. Palm Springs was treacherously hot. Eric had to stay indoors, and someone had to stay with him. Confined to three borrowed rooms, Hal began to go mad. If Susan swam or shopped, he would sit with a book, gritting his teeth, waiting for the inevitable cry from his son. He would read the same sentence ten times or more, comprehending nothing but his own edgy misery. This defenseless eleven-pound person, who needed only to eat and sleep, was running his life.

He kept quiet about his feelings, believing that Susan had

enough on her mind, and he tried not to take it out on Eric, who was so little. But from time to time he would lose all control and shout "For Christ's sake, shut up!" at the top of his lungs.

Eric, on an infant seat on the kitchen counter, waiting for his formula to warm, would only shriek back at a comparable level. He was hungry. It wasn't his fault either.

Susan played tennis on the first day and found Hal a partner for the second. The silence, as Hal rode out to the courts, was thunderous. There was no way to get enough of it—it was like spring water at the edge of the desert. Hal could feel the tendons in his neck, in his lower back and thighs, loosen gratefully as he put distance between his family and himself. But there was a screw-up at the club; reservations had been crossed. There was no court for Hal and his middle-aged opponent. Had he known the people well enough to feel comfortable he would have lost his temper. But since he was a stranger, he acquiesced quietly to a round of golf, at which he did not excel.

The course was trimmed and pampered, the air crackling dry in the low nineties. Hal, in sunglasses, with borrowed clubs, worked out on the links. There was a good male rhythm to his stroke, even to his stride as he moved from green to tee. The conversation was sparse—financial notes, show-biz gossip, and sports: four players who didn't know each other and risked nothing. They were unevenly matched, but Hal was in the middle—good enough in a sport he considered not his own—and at the end of nine holes the relaxation was just beginning to come to him.

Two partners dropped out, but two more were picked up. They had been out more than two hours. The nearest phone was in the clubhouse. Hal thought about Susan and the baby, then he looked at the tenth tee. There were people waiting behind him already, and more behind those. It was impossible to call. Besides, Hal thought, I need this. I'll be great tonight and tomorrow if I can relax today. It wasn't just idle play. It was medicine.

So fortified, Hal knocked off a near-perfect tee shot and

birdied the tenth. It was not until he came up over the rise toward the eighteenth green that he could see, silhouetted against
the late-afternoon lavender of the mountains, her female form,
swayback as she held Eric on one hip. Hal had not told her he
was on the golf course. That meant, he reasoned, that she had
been out looking for him, asking questions and searching. As
he stood over his chip shot to the green, it all began to come
together in his head. He could not help but see the face of
his watch as he looked down at the ball. Six hours since he
left Susan and Eric. She would be angry: how angry? And how
had he let this happen? How had he reduced himself to the
level of a five-year-old child who hides in the attic? Well, the
crime was committed now. Mommy was pounding at the attic
door and there was no explanation. As he leaned over the ball,
he could feel it all coming back, the tightness in the neck and
back, the anger pumping in his arteries. He swung. The ball
swooped up over the green and down a slope into a trap, hugging the underside of a grass overhang. Hal dropped his club.
Then without acknowledging any of his three companions, he
hoisted the clubs off the cart and strode off toward the clubhouse. The ball lay where it had dropped. The game was over.

There was an icy decorum about Susan's greeting to him as
she gracefully evaded a kiss he had no business giving her.
She would not give him the baby, would not let him lay off
any of his guilt by having him take over the chore at this late
date. Eric looked at him with innocent wonder. Hal wondered
how he could be so stupid. How could he not see the dog-
house that was being constructed around his daddy? Susan
was silent until they were inside the car. Even then she was
not loud.

"You want to be single," she said, as Hal turned the corner
and pushed toward the town. He was silent.

"I can't believe this happened," she said.

"I couldn't stop playing," Hal said, as if it all made sense.
"It won't happen again."

"No, it won't," Susan agreed. He had never seen her so
angry—so quiet. They rode on for a mile, blood racing. There
should have been a sudden storm—lightning, black thunder—

but the air was placid and the sky clear. At a red light Hal glanced over at Susan, who was staring down at the sleeping baby in her lap. There was a look of outrage, of exhaustion on her face, and it appeared to be chiseled there, permanent and unchangeable. In that look, Hal saw that his life had become something irrevocably different. He could divorce Susan, he could move to the other side of the world and expunge Eric from his personal records, but that look on Susan's face was forever, no matter what he did, and it made his options very narrow. He had ruined her life, their life together, their romance. Now, mixed in with his sorrow for Susan and his sense of abject apology and guilt was a creeping sense of self-pity. He felt so terrible about what he had done that he thought he would need help to get over it. Insanely, he turned to Susan, his victim. He didn't know anyone else.

"Honey," he said.

But she was hard.

"I don't know why I rock the baby to sleep at night," she said. "I might as well rock you to sleep and send him off to work. He may not be grown up yet, but at least he's growing."

When the Bradfords began to crack apart, they cracked hard and fast. This, we suppose, is a reflection of the people they are and the life-style they unwittingly chose. They capitalized on the high spirits of impulsive behavior, and they suffered the results. Parenthood was tough for them for several reasons, at least two of which were matters of choice:

1.) *Lilly.* Lilly came when the baby was born and stayed six weeks. Once the nursing problem was out of the way, she was great—she took on all the responsibility. The flip side of this is, of course, that Hal and Susan inherited a six-week-old instead of a newborn, and they were unprepared and resentful. They had gotten used to the baby being there and being no trouble. This dream life was the result of Lilly. This problem is probably overstated, however, because—

2.) *They had a baby too soon.* This sounds like moralistic

twaddle, and very old-fashioned, but it comes across strongly
in our small study, and we feel it's common sense. Couples
who get pregnant when they're still really in a phase of courtship (even if they're married) have a hard time with the
resulting children. We talked about this in the section on Alan
Sheinman and Nina Degarmo, and it is interesting to note the
identical reactions of the two men, Alan and Hal. Each, according to his own social habits, demanded independence in a
completely unrealistic way and resorted to the tactics of childhood. Both women had the same reaction, too. They both
began to think of their mates as additional babies and belittled
them as such.

There's nothing very special to be said about Hal's round
of golf. It should be pointed out that Susan was a less satisfied mother than most, that she asked for more help sooner
than most mothers married to highly motivated career men.
But her dissatisfaction boils down to a common problem with
newlyweds who have children: the Bradfords were entertainment experts. They were in search of a year's entertainment
when they decided to have a baby. Instead, they got parenthood, with its commitment, its deep sense of responsibility,
and its call to adulthood. Hal and Susan needed lighthearted-
ness—they were young and in love. They deserved it, and they
could have had it. But now it was too late, and the seriousness of the situation was roaring in their heads.

AT SIX MONTHS

Synchronization—"It's
Not in My Contract"

THE BRADFORDS were action people. They were not given to siting around; so when things got bad, they moved away from those things. They had one session with a marriage counselor who didn't seem to know what he was talking about or what their problem was; he suggested sex counseling. Their sex life was indeed terrible at the time, but they were convinced that that was a product of the problem, and not a cause. How could you make love under the circumstances?

Having dismissed the idea of counseling, they took an analytical step on their own; they summoned Lilly back from New York. This, they reasoned, was the right way to begin. Things had been fine when Susan's mother was there. They went back to when things were fine. They started again, slower this time.

Lilly arrived two days after the call went out and took command. She stayed out of the advice-giving business, although she had a lot to say. She took over the baby almost totally

for a day or two and let Hal and Susan work things out
themselves. Even as they plotted, she could see the mistakes.
At least *she* thought they were mistakes; they would have been
mistakes for her when she was a young mother, but it was
none of her business. She kept silent.

The plan was exact, on paper, based on a series of discussions and negotiations. It was a peace treaty. It drained the
last ounces of spontaneity out of their lives. The plan called
for hours of child care, recreation, and sleep, Hal's work,
Susan's chores . . . everything was taken care of in the plan.
Here is some of it:

Susan will do all the shopping, cleaning, etc., but will
not shop on the weekend. If groceries or other sundries
are needed on the weekend, Hal will shop.

Hal will take late (11:30 P.M.) feeding every night,
since he is up anyhow, while Susan sleeps.

Susan will buy alarm clock so she doesn't have to be
responsible for getting Hal up in the morning. Alarm
clock will be loud and ring until shut off.

Hal will mind baby for minimum two and maximum
three hours, alone, one weekend day, to be worked out
each weekend.

Hal will be undisturbed after home from work for two
hours, including dinner (time to unwind).

Hal will pick up his own clothes.

It went on for eighteen provisions and seemed to cover
everything. Hal definitely got the light end of the child care
and chores, but since Susan had no career, it seemed fair.
Grudgingly, Hal agreed to change diapers of all descriptions
during his one weekend stint and to help with the dishes on
the weekends.

"It's not in my contract," he said in mock outrage. "But
I'll do it sometimes."

The list looked good on paper; it looked workable. In action,
it began as an improvement, but within a week something
became clear. They had scheduled themselves out of each

other's lives. They had found no time for themselves, and it never occurred to them to look for any because at the time they made up the plan, they really didn't miss each other. On some days they hardly even liked each other.

Lilly had seen it coming and now she ventured a suggestion: "Schedule one night a week alone, just the two of you. I'll sit."

It was the first time she had opened up on the subject of parents. They hadn't wanted her to know how tough things were, but, of course, she knew. She knew they didn't just "miss" her when she was summoned to the West Coast. She knew there was something more serious, too: she couldn't stay forever, and she didn't want to. No one could hold this marriage together but Hal and Susan. For their own sake, she would have to get out soon and let them rebuild their own house.

Hal and Susan tried it. They picked a restaurant and a show. However, Hal began to get the jitters by midafternoon at the office. He called Susan on the phone.

"Why don't we cancel dinner?" he asked. "Just go to a show. Dinner costs a fortune these days, and it's always lousy."

Susan thought this was curious. "Where'll we eat?" She wanted to know.

"I'll pick up a pizza," Hal said. "We'll eat with Lilly. Then we'll go out."

It all sounded strange. Susan was silent on the phone for a moment, and the quiet drove Hal to explain further, in a manic, shotgun delivery.

"I'm really looking forward to tonight," he said. "I mean it. I really want to enjoy it a lot. The show'll be good, and the tickets cost a lot, and . . . I don't want to have dinner and dredge up all the . . . everything that's gone on and arrive at the theater ready to kill each other and leave halfway through. I just want to have a good time. Like we're supposed to do. I don't want to talk about anything."

For Susan, this was the big revelation. Hal had to keep the wheels turning. He didn't want to talk. He wanted to go out on their night alone and sit in the dark. For the first time, she understood they were in real trouble—big trouble.

"I'll cancel the restaurant," she said. It was as if someone else had taken over her voice.

"That'd be fine," he said. He sounded genuinely happy about it.

She had just gotten off the phone with the restaurant when Lilly came in to find out what was going on.

"Don't even ask me what this means," her daughter told her, "but you're joining us for pizza tonight."

Synchronizing your life with a baby can be difficult. It's like having a checkbook that's not quite balanced: your urge to leave it unbalanced increases with your instinct that the balance is not going to be a happy one. Most marriages spin out of control for a while after the baby arrives. Some of it is fun, much of it is frustrating, but the instinct not to measure is very strong. Who can afford to go out seeking bad news?

There comes a time when it gets harder to let things run on than to take them in hand. (Understand, this is not true of every couple; those who are very much in tune with their decision to become parents have already achieved an instinctive balance. Can you name one?) Synchronizing your life as a couple requires systematic thinking and, too often, pencil and paper.

Now, no one likes to think that his or her romance needs to be charted like the Dow-Jones Industrials, and that's why synchronization can be so painful. All the love that's in the air, making the world go 'round, so to speak, gets plopped down on the pad as hours of child care, privacy, shopping, sleeping, etc. Even without pad and pencil, you'll find you're doing a lot of negotiating with your mate, having the kind of conversation you used to save for the car salesman and the man who ripped off all the buttons on your shirt at the dry cleaner. This, it turns out, is part of growing up and becoming an adult, and there is no way of convincing any young couple of the next point: it isn't bad. You have to be ready for it, and you have to look at it with as much a sense of humor as possible. Everyone enjoys playing grown-up from time to time—children do it all the time. Well, no one ever really feels grown up, according to our parents who are all in their sixties, but having children allows you to play at it practically full-time.

When we were in college, we used to try to pinpoint the moment when you would know you were grown up. The best one we came up with was that you were grown up when your dentist lived in the same town as you, instead of the town your parents lived in. None of us, for some strange reason, ever suggested that having children might mark the turning point. It doesn't, but it probably comes closer than any other single event.

The Bradfords, as we have stated previously, were not ready to grow up. They were still new lovers, and new lovers are not grown-ups no matter how old they are. Consequently, the planned synchronization, which was intended to help them through the transition, functioned instead as a kind of grim day of reckoning. Suddenly it became clear on paper just how large their problem was and just how much they didn't want to solve it. Set down in black and white, the next months of their lives became all too clear and frightening.

It became obvious that the account could not be allowed to run uncontrolled any further. Hal and Susan had reached a point common to couples who have children right away: they were having lovers' quarrels about parenting. Full of passion, self-assertion, and egocentricity, their arguments were not really intended to solve problems. Unfortunately, with problems as severe as the Bradford's, that was a bad sign.

Synchronization *always* takes place whether it be on paper, in discussion, or through instinctive adjustment. It may solve problems and it may not, but the moment of truth arrives, and usually at about this six-month period. It need not be a horror to set up systems for the care of your child and each other; if you can accept it as a game, it can be like planning a trip, like grown-ups do. In making their plans, the Bradfords subconsciously squeezed their private relationship down to nothing, an act which can only be seen as a symptom of a failing marriage. We have stressed elsewhere the importance of keeping the private couple relationship warm during these first months. Synchronization needn't mean that you work and sleep in shifts so as never to see each other; it simply means that those private parts of your relationship—dinners, window-shopping, even sex—may have to be planned in with everything else.

This is particularly painful in the case of sex. Many women refuse to use the diaphragm because it takes all the spontaneity out of sex. Well, just wait: babies make the diaphragm seem like the greatest of erotic poetry by comparison. That leaves you in a tough position. You can do what the Bradfords did—maintain a stiff position that if there won't be spontaneous sex, there won't be any sex at all. That led, quite simply, to there being no sex at all. Or, you can try to plan a positive sexual experience.

One of the authors of this book made the following arrangement, more or less out of desperation: on Tuesday nights the couple would cook dinner together (both were cooks). This required the husband to be home early from work, and that was a hard and fast rule, unbreakable except in utter and total emergency. Husband had to be home at four forty-five for cooking. Dinner was not to be served until the baby was down for the night. Dishes were to be left in sink. Wife was not to clean kitchen floor that afternoon, which always resulted in a cranky mood. Husband was not to read magazines or anything other than personal mail after dinner. There was to be wine with dinner, no matter what. No chores were to be done after dinner, no matter what (only allowable exceptions: evacuation to hotel in case of flood or fire). A wife soon became a mistress, and Tuesday soon became the focal point of the adult week. It was a game, and it was silly, but it was a game that worked.

So synchronization can go either way. It is never much fun to realize how systematized your life has become, but the initial shock can be relatively brief if you're ready for it. The Bradfords shouldn't have been asked to handle systems, they were too new. They found themselves in open revolt, but even open revolt couldn't change the situation for them. They had their marriage and their baby and those things were permanent. They might have walked away from each other, but they weren't ready for that either. Every step was too big for the Bradfords because no step would take them back to what they had been.

AT NINE MONTHS

On Strike

IT BEGAN by coincidence. There was a Halloween party—costumes and contests—at the Bradfords' house. It went on until all hours. When Eric began to whine for his bottle at six-twenty in the morning, Susan rolled over and stared glassy-eyed at the clock. After only three hours and fifteen minutes of sleep, she felt as if there were a knife-point sticking into her gut, and the room was spinning. Unfortunately, Eric didn't know that; he just wanted milk.

In the kitchen, as she prepared his bottle, the remnants of the party brought her awake with disgust. The air was thick with the grime of old smoke. The sink was full of plates smeared with hard chocolate and drizzled with melted ice cream. She could count seventeen dirty glasses. Someone had left the oven on. It was Hal's morning to sleep late.

As she rushed toward Eric's room with the bottle, the remains of someone's costume caught her eye. It had been left behind: a homemade picket sign. The sign said, simply, ON

STRIKE. The person carrying it had come as a modern Lysistrata, and the sign had been a joke. Lysistrata, Susan remembered while feeding Eric, led a sexual strike to keep men from going to war, and she started a revolution. Susan didn't have anything that complicated in mind. When Eric was rebedded, and just beginning what she knew would be a fotry-five-minute rest period, she dressed quickly. Hal did not stir in bed. He was impossible to rouse at this hour. When Susan was showered, dressed, and reluctantly awake, she went back out to the kitchen and rinsed Eric's bottle. She picked up the ON STRIKE sign and carried it into the bedroom, where she propped it up in front of the bureau, blocking the mirror. Then she tapped Hal on the shoulder. It took more than one tap. Finally, after a good shove, he rolled over and spoke without opening his eyes.

"What's wrong?" he asked. He was never awakened without a catastrophe awaiting him.

"Nothing," Susan replied. "I'm going out today. You take care of Eric."

It was said so innocently that it aroused not a wrinkle across Hal's brow. He mumbled something and was already asleep again before she reached the bedroom door. She let herself out: out of the bedroom, out of the house. The sun was just up. Even dressed and clean, she knew she was exhausted. She could not imagine what to do. What she needed was to sleep, to rest. She weighed several possibilities and finally decided on a simple one. At seven-fifteen, she checked into a Holiday Inn near the airport, where a room was already made up. She watched twenty minutes of the "Today" show, then drew the blinds and fell into a long, untroubled sleep.

Eric's panic-driven shrieks awakened Hal at seven-thirty, just as Susan was getting ready to drift off, over at the hotel. His first instinct was that Susan had died, or collapsed, but there was no time to look for her. He went to Eric's room and picked him up, trying desperately to comfort him, having no idea what to do. He was still half-asleep, still totally confused.

"Where's your mom?" he kept saying, more to himself than to his son. This did little to comfort Eric, and a bottle did only about half the job. As Eric whined with uncertainty, looking around, Hal picked through his memory, trying to isolate what could have happened. He was on his second cup of coffee, still holding the insecure baby to his side when he went back into the bedroom to look for Susan's purse on the bureau. There he confronted the sign.

"Shit," he said. The sign reminded him. The bedroom, his rolling over and listening to her say something. She had awakened him. Why? While thinking over all these hazy circumstances, he called his office to report that he would not be in. Then he sat on the floor with his son and spent twenty minutes trying without success to teach him to clap his hands.

The longer he sat, the more he knew. He knew Susan would come back, and he knew why she had gone. The last few days had been rough. He should have seen that she was not bearing up well under the pressure. His work had been totally absorbing. He hadn't been doing even the rudimentary things she had always asked him to do, but he thought she understood. This was a special occasion. Soon work would let up, and he'd get back to the household. They had almost made it to that magic time. Now it was all gone. Eric had calmed down finally and was playing with two shoe boxes on the floor. He seemed reasonably comfortable in his father's company, but Hal didn't know what in the world to do with him.

"You think the Rams'll make the playoffs?" he asked forlornly. Eric did not even look up. He was busy.

"Come on, pally," Hal told his son. "You and I are going out."

There was a piece of property Hal wanted to visit, an old investment he used to camp out on before he met Susan. Susan thought the outdoors was for animals. It now occurred to him that Eric had never seen this plot of land he would someday own. It might be nice to take him, since they had the day to themselves, under whatever foul circumstances. All Hal needed was a shower and a shave, a fresh pair of jeans, and they'd be off. He calculated it at thirty minutes. It took ninety.

He tried to take an uninterrupted shower, but Eric pulled

a plant down by the tendrils from the bureau. The pot missed him (Hal didn't know by how much), leaving him only frightened and covered with dirt. Dripping and in a rage, Hal cleaned dirt first from Eric, then from the floor. Sweeping Chinese porcelain into the garbage, he put Eric in the crib and let him scream for the next ten minutes, while he hastily washed his hair and shaved. He was suffering from the beginnings of a headache by the time he threw his clothes on his back and raced to the crib to rescue his now red-faced and unforgiving child. Eric was in his pajamas. He had to be changed. Now began a search of the hampers, washing machine, and bureau for suitable clothes. Hal had no idea where anything was kept. In the middle of it all, Eric had diarrhea. Hal's worst fear had been realized. It was all over everything.

"I've done this to myself," Hal said with self-mockery. "I've brought the house down around myself. But you didn't help."

Holding his nose and attempting to avert his eyes, he managed to clean Eric up without becoming ill, but he'd had it with style. He dressed him in yesterday's clothes, whatever was at the top of the hamper, and away they went.

They got as far as the driveway. Before Hal had time to turn his head and look, he knew what was going to happen. He knew what would be there. It was all too perfect. She had taken the car with the baby seat and left him on his own. There was no way to carry Eric to the mountains, or anywhere else.

At eleven-thirty, Susan's feet began to sweat, and she awakened naturally, dazed by her unfamiliar surroundings. Where was Eric? Why had she done this radical thing? Her body broke with perspiration, she reached for the phone, but then she changed her mind. She had done it, and she was going to have her day. She knew if she called, it would be a matter of moments before she went back, and she was not going back. Her hand never touched the receiver. She took a long bath instead, something she could hardly remember ever doing before. She put on her clothes and had a late breakfast in the restaurant below. She wanted to shop in Beverly Hills, to take in an afternoon movie, to have a drink in the bar of the Beverly Wilshire. Or, in another plan, she would play tennis and eat a hamburger at the club, then change and window-shop the antique stores. Anything would be okay—but she couldn't get Eric out of her mind, and she couldn't feel free to enjoy her rebellion. A movie seemed like it would divert her attention the most, put her in another world until she got straightened out. There was something with a big ad in the paper that she had never heard of, but it starred Jane Fonda, and it went on at twelve-thirty. So she went and sat in the dark.

At home, Hal made do. He played with Eric until eleven, and then, when nothing would amuse him anymore, he fed him a bottle and plopped him facedown in his crib. After five minutes of screaming, he was asleep. Hal sat down to have a minute by himself, picked up the paper, and got his own coffee.

A strangeness was creeping into his mind, though. He wasn't worried about Susan, and he wasn't stunned by the turn of events. That seemed odd. How could he have known this was coming? Maybe it was that he just didn't care about Susan anymore, didn't care where she was or what happened to her. Certainly he felt on the sensible side of the event: it was she, after all, who had done the crazy thing, and he who had to pick up the pieces until she came back to her senses. There was a certain amount of satisfaction to be savored from that. No one could criticize him for today's events.

For a full half-hour he was engulfed in these trivialities, chalking up little points for himself and putting little black marks by Susan's name. However, when he had totally satisfied himself that this would be worse for her than for him, he began to think about the important things, about the future, about the resolution of today. It would have to be fought out hand to hand, no matter who was at fault. The more he ran over the possible scenarios in his mind, the more depressed he became. He had been a terrible father and husband. He saw it all too clearly. On second thought, he hadn't been so bad. There were two ways to look at it. He had made

this deal: he would bring home the bacon; Susan would raise
Eric. Simple, no fine print, a two-way split. He had done his
part. Why should he be responsible if she couldn't do hers?
Even at first blush, the above reasoning seemed patently ab-
surd. Susan was his wife, the love of his life, and Eric was
his own flesh and blood. He had to stop looking at them like
a pair of defaulted contracts. His own life and happiness were
at stake. What had he done wrong?

1. Been inflexible.
2. Retreated into the comfort of his own problems.
3. Become a workaholic to avoid the family at home.
4. Stood on ceremony about his duties, never offering to
   do one thing he hadn't agreed to.
5. Managed to forget to do practically any favor that
   was asked of him.

Yes, he sounded like a garden-variety heel, all right, like the
cad who always turns up in the soap operas. He was a cad.
A word he had never used before described him perfectly.
You cad! He found all this very amusing as he sat amid the
rubble of last night's party, alone, his wife having run away
to get a night's sleep and be alone, his son sleeping a precious
two hours. It was hilarious.

"My life could come to an end right now," he said to himself, and something rang a certain bell inside his head that he
had never heard before. It was a bell that said: this is the
moment. Inside here, you always knew things would finally get
so bad that they couldn't be any more dangerous. You always
knew the moment of truth would come, and that you didn't
have to lift a finger until it arrived. Well, this is it.

Hal looked around and honestly felt something inside was
changing. He stood up and did something it never would have
occurred to him to do before, something that came so unnat-
urally to him that he felt like someone else was moving his
limbs for him. He began to collect glassware and ashtrays, and
do the dishes.

Susan lasted until two-thirty. After sitting through the movie

and treating herself to an ice-cream soda, she realized that
any more time away from home would amount to torture.
She got in the car and drove back, ready for the confrontation.
She was loaded down with ammunition, certain she would find
the house a mess, Eric wandering naked on his hands and
knees through the garbage, and Hal asleep on the couch,
surrounded by peanut shells, with the television going. She
was disappointed.

The house was not immaculate, because Hal didn't know
where anything went, but it wasn't bad. The dishes were done,
the carpet was vacuumed, the garbage taken out, and the
ashtrays cleaned and redistributed. Eric was wearing one red
bootie and one white bootie, but his clothes were clean, and
his diaper dry. Susan had, in fact, affected the change she was
asking for by walking out—but she was furious with the results
anyway. She had been ready to confront a set of horrible circumstances, a breakdown in her life that she could pin on
Hal, and now her husband had double-crossed her. Now she
was in midair. It knocked the wind out of her.

"I'm changing," Hal announced when she looked over the
house. "Honest to God. I know you think I'm a bum, but I'm
changing."

Susan was only speechless a moment.

"I've heard this all before," she began, but Hal held up his
hand to stop her.

"I didn't say, 'I'm changing, what do you think?' I didn't
ask for a reaction."

Susan eyed him suspiciously. "You've said it before."

"Yeah, but this time I'm doing it. Because all of this is
too important to me, and you've got too much hostility, so I'm
changing."

"We'll see."

It took a lot of power for Hal to swallow this skepticism
whole, but he'd made a deal with himself. "I'm changing," he
repeated. "And I'm going to change for long enough and
completely enough so that you won't be able to say anything
about we'll see, or I've heard it before."

"Why now?" Susan wanted to know. "What's different now?"

"What's different is, I don't have any choice anymore. It's change me or get a divorce, and I'd rather change me. I don't want a divorce."

Susan looked around the room and suddenly felt exhausted again.

"I don't know what I want," she said as she collapsed into an easy chair.

"Well," Hal said. "I know what I want."

We are in no position to give advice about a relationship in as rocky condition as the Bradfords'. By the time their baby was nine months old, they were in deep trouble, and they knew it. The only point we wish to make is that their situation should be no surprise to anyone but themselves. The Bradfords lacked a sense of reality. Their approach to childbearing and child-rearing was that it would be a wild, carefree plunge into unknown entertainments. Now, put that way, it sounds silly; it sounds impossible that any couple could really think that. The Bradfords would have denied that the above statement captured their emotions during their pregnancy. However, the subtext of what they were thinking comes through in every word of their early interviews.

"We know what we want," they kept insisting, but their description of parenting was so far removed from the reality that it provoked an almost irresistible temptation to shout back, "You know what you want, but there isn't any place in this world where you can get it!"

The Bradfords had a lord and master/servant and devotee relationship. Beneath the guise of modern Southern California life-style, this couple was as old-fashioned as the couples of three generations ago. Hal expected to be cared for in every way. He wanted his breakfast on the table and his coffee steaming in a pot when he emerged from the bedroom. He wanted his shirts lightly starched, and his underwear picked up at night—and he got it all because Susan wanted to treat him that way. It was part game, part resignation. There were so many fine things about Hal—his sense of openness, his emotionalism, his ability to laugh and cry—things so rare in a man that she was willing to live with his essentially dictatorial rule. He promised he would make a lot of money, too. Susan wouldn't have help in the house, however (this seems to be becoming a common obsession among people with enough money to afford help), and when Eric was born, it became clear that she could not be servant and mistress to two people. The game was up. If she had clearly seen how much of her day was devoted to pleasing Hal, she would have gotten the message before the baby arrived. But since she enjoyed that part of the day and didn't really consider it painful, she never bothered to calculate it. To her, it seemed like a lot of little favors. She never realized Hal saw it as an essential part of the marriage.

The Bradford marriage never had time to get organized. It was a dazed romance (the best kind) that got deep-sixed by parenthood. Then, and no one will ever know why, Hal decided to come to the rescue. Maybe it was because it gave him the chance to play hero. More charitably, it may have been that he just didn't want to lose Susan and Eric. Instinctively, he realized that only he—the *culprit*—could take action. Susan was totally beaten down. Hal was the cause of a lot of it, and he decided to change. It was like raising the *Andrea Doria*—things were pretty far gone—but at the moment of truth (which he had the great perception and/or good fortune to recognize), he made his move. It was unilateral, unsupported by his wife, and it was a long swim upstream for a man with whom it was hard to sympathize. Perhaps he was just trying to undo his own negative self-image with heroics. Whatever the reasons, he spun himself around and began heaving against the current.

AT ONE YEAR

Romantic Love / Parent Love

IT WOULD be nice to report that Hal Bradford's unilateral
resolve resulted in the sudden righting of the Bradford marriage—happily ever after always makes a good story. What
can be said is that Hal did try, but the results were no
better than fair. He hated the lists and all the instructions.
He had lived through a ream of printed resolves, negotiated
peace agreements, do's and don't's, enumerated "ways to be
helpful" pinned to the mirror in the closet: the whole experience had made him feel like a ten-year-old, and he certainly
didn't want to hear any more about it.

"With me," he announced, "it has to come spontaneously.
Otherwise, I resent it, and pretty soon, I don't do it."

So Susan took down the lists and just let things happen.
Hal got to like Eric more as the weeks went by. He learned
that feeding a baby only takes five minutes, no matter how
much you hate it. He learned the organization of his son's
clothes and toys. He learned to do things Susan's way, since

it was too hard to devise his own. But he only did some of what he was supposed to do because that spontaneous willingness still dried up after particularly tough days at work. It hardly functioned at all on weekend mornings, when Susan would try to physically push him out of bed to awaken him. The Bradfords were quiet with each other, but they lacked affection. They had no sex life and practically no meaningful conversation. Things weren't threatening, but they weren't great either. Then one night, they became newly serious.

Susan had a new bra that fit the first time she wore it, but suddenly, on a second wearing, it was uncomfortable. It pulled and felt lopsided. She was reaching around to change it when she froze, her arms stretched back. She stared in horror at the mirror. It wasn't the bra that had changed shape, but her breasts. It was barely noticeable, and when she dropped her arms it *wasn't* noticeable. But lifting her right arm high above her head, she could reach over and feel it—a small knot resting up under the underside of the breast. That thing you always checked for: the lump. She could see it—actually see it.

Her throat was without moisture, and she barked out the only words she could think of.

"Hal, come here."

He looked, watched in silence as she moved her deft fingers around the spot, making it jump out into relief. She didn't have to say anything, and she didn't.

"Put a sweater on," Hal told her. "We'll go to the hospital. She looked at him dumbly. Did people turn up at the emergency room with lumps in their breasts? What would they think?

"What about dinner?" she asked in a dull voice. Hal looked at her like she was crazy.

"Get dressed," he said. "Put on a sweater!"

They drove to the hospital, and Hal got on the phone to the gynecologist while she was being examined by the resident on duty in the emergency room. Hal wanted to check her into the hospital for the night, as if no evil malignancy would dare grow within its walls, and they would be safe;

however, the hospital wouldn't have them because there was
nothing to be done that night. They were sent home with a
terrifyingly neutral report: there was something there all right,
but no one knew what.

The baby-sitter, who had agreed to take absolute charge of
Eric in this emergency, stayed all night. Susan took a sleeping
pill, but there was no drug invented that would have given
Hal any rest. He read in the living room while Susan, Eric,
and the sitter slept: magazines, the backs of record covers, any
trivial nonsense to occupy his brain and combat the sense of
disaster that threatened to engulf him. As the evening wore
on, he found himself speaking to a God in whom he believed
only marginally. "Get me out of this," he said, "and I'll never
be bad again. I'll treat that woman right." The naïveté of
it was appalling even to himself, but desperate men do odd
things in the middle of the night.

Susan went into the hospital the next day, suffering from
a level of panic that can only be induced by fear of imminent
death. It flooded all the logic from her brain. Her doctor had
told her not to worry, that hundreds of women found harm-
less lumps in their breasts, and that the statistics were on her
side—but he wouldn't say it was benign. That far he would not
go, and she knew better. The Bradfords had sinned. They had
messed up their lives, their marriage, their son's first year of
life, and now they were going to pay.

Hal was very good. He took her tears, her anguish, her irra-
tionality in stride. He never left her room, except to check on
the baby at home. He brought back glowing reports. He was
stoic, almost cheerful at times, and, of course, it was all a
phony, ridiculous act, but she was able to believe it. She was
going to die, and it made her lightheaded. She found herself
involved in completely inane conversations, pursuing them
from point to point, to fill up the silence. Hal was always
with her. And in this bizarre, unreal world, where it seemed
impossible that any of it was happening, she realized that she
loved him, despite everything.

He loved her, too. He found out when they wheeled her

away. He had reserved this time for himself. The time, the shorter the better, was all his alone. He closed the door to her private room and wept for most of an hour. Totally losing control, he wept for everything, all the horror and innocence in the world. He touched himself with his magnanimity, and wept over that. He was so filled with emotion that he felt himself on a wave of humanity, turning and sputtering, riding toward the crash at the shoreline with everyone else. Everyone should weep so. All he wanted out of this was his family back again. He would take them and embrace them. He would never leave them.

Even as he said it, he could feel the melancholy lack of truth. He had a career and outside interests, and friends, and he was impatient by nature. There would be further fights. For a moment, he almost hoped for fate to take Susan away, so he would never have to go back to being the failed family man he was. However, he wanted them all back together more, and he would face up to his failure somehow. He would live with inadequacy.

At one-fifteen in the afternoon (Hal was watching the second hand sweep twelve when the door opened), they came and told him his wife was all right. She would have a pencil-line scar on the underside of the breast, and there was nothing to worry about. There was no malignancy, just a small cystetic tumor. It was out. The next morning they were home.

It was like a lost weekend; the horror was encapsulated between the moment Susan had put on her bra and the moment when the second hand swept past twelve on the hospital room clock. They could wrap it up and bury it, the horror of thirty-six hours. There was, at least for the moment, a different feeling in the house, a feeling that had been absent since sometime in Eric's fourth month of life. It was a feeling that all three of them were actually alive in the house, living with each other for a purpose, to build a family, however imperfect. They were quite surprised to be there, quite surprised that the emergency had proved how much they valued the life they were living. Both had somewhere, subconsciously, begun to look for a way out. Now they clung to each other in desperate relief. Interestingly, they made no foolish promises. They knew what was in store. When the bitterness began to crawl back in, which it undoubtedly would, they would have to try to remember.

From how far down can a couple rebound? There must come a point at which no recovery is possible, when the bitterness gets so acute and the desire for revenge so strong that nothing can ever grow between two people again. The Bradfords may have been headed for that black place, but they were rescued by a brush with death. That's what it took: the biggest scare in the world. What were they left with when it was all over?

They were sobered. They were possibly beyond ever recapturing the giddiness of their first months together. Their marriage was probably safe, but the elation was gone. That isn't unusual—the madness of young love usually recedes with time, but the Bradfords' gentle madness didn't recede. It was murdered—and therein lies a tragedy which many couples court.

The following is a very traditional sentiment, a personal statement. It can be argued and it can be laughed at. It cannot be proved; however, it cannot be disproved. The emotional periods of our lives have a natural duration. We do not make emotions out of nothing, and we cannot control them, although they can control us. There are some emotions that are extraordinarily powerful: mourning the dead, fearing death, a child's love for a parent, the romantic love of one human being for another, a parent's love for a child. When these emotions occur, they want to live out a natural life. We cannot control the emotions, but we *can* sometimes control the events that give birth to them.

Hal and Susan Bradford were in the thrall of new romantic love when they decided to switch gears and have a child. For this couple, at that particular time, this was a mistake of such mammoth proportions that there is no way to overemphasize it. They simply didn't know what having a child entailed. Not only did they not know the rigorous work involved, or the loss of privacy, or any of the other specific requirements and realities, they did not know the most fundamental thing: that having a baby means dropping one kind of love and picking up another. We do not mean to imply that a couple must stop loving in order for their parenthood to be smooth; there is enough love to go around. However, for new lovers, the exhilaration of having a playmate and a soulmate to share in a brand-new, untarnished, all-consuming love is a particular emotion that is incompatible with the reality of parenting. So the Bradfords had to drop it.

But how can you drop it? It's as big as all outdoors, and it may never come again. People don't simply let go of a joyful state of mind; it has to be torn from them. Inadvertently, Eric ripped apart the romance his parents were building, but he was surely not to blame. Hal and Susan had chosen him, and in so doing, they cheated themselves. They had killed their first love, and in that wary state of bitterness and suspicion, they could not very well manufacture the parent-love that is supposed to come. They were cheated twice. Parent-love, to coin a phrase, does not simply mean a parent's love for a child. It is the love that parents have for each other, and it can be deep and tender, related as it is to the way you or your mate infuse a child with yourself. It is as romantic, as fine, and as satisfying as the first blush of new love. We recommend it. *But it is not the same thing as new love.* It has a different season in life, and it deserves to be properly placed. We believe that parenting can be an expression of love, but only if the wild kick of new love is allowed to run its course. New love can satisfy itself in a year or a month or a decade. We suggest no timetable, but rather a keen inner sounding. If you want children, the time will usually come by itself—not necessarily without conversation, or even debate, but it will come. To force its arrival is to cheat it and to court disaster.

THE
SIXTH
FAMILY

Ben and Sally McCadden

AND BRIAN

GETTING PREGNANT

When You Can't

IN SEPTEMBER, when the days began to grow noticeably shorter, the tomatoes along the walk lost their last traces of orange speckling and turned a burnished, deep red. It was just at this time that Sally McCadden became too large to reach down and pick them. Toward evening, when Ben came home from work, he would grab a small armload of them on his way in the house. One he would plunge under the tap, so that it would hold some salt, and pop it into his mouth. The others were lined up along the windowsill above the sink, and the freshest he took out to the backyard. Sally was always there, stretching the fibers of a nylon-mesh lawn chaise. She waited for him daily, ate her tomato, and accepted his two hands to help her up.

It was hot in Santa Monica in September, and the hour on the lawn chaise really meant something to Sally. She walked home from work at five, taking a little longer every day now, and flopped down in the shade of the house. There she thought about all manner of things, things connected with the baby. The mundane mingled with the profound in her mind— everything from the rise in heating costs with the extra room to the pleasurable speculations on the future courtship and marriage of her unborn baby. Thoughts visited Sally in the backyard, stayed awhile, and wandered away. It was a pleasurable time.

In the evening, Ben would disappear down to the garage while she cooked dinner. The landlord had let him set up a workshop there. Well-used tools hung from a pegboard and littered a gouged wooden bench where the basic pieces of a pine bassinet were being assembled. Ben had grown up at a workbench.

The kitchen had become pleasantly littered as well; recipes clipped from *Redbook* and *Family Circle* were held to the refrigerator by little glass turtles whose undersides were magnetic. The recipes were of two varieties. The first were vegetarian. Sally and Ben had never been vegetarians, but it had been impossible to keep up with the flow of tomatoes through the house. Green beans and zucchini had been coming in for nearly a month. Sally had weeded and nurtured the garden through the withering summer, and she was damned if she was going to give away the fruits of her labor. Ben was a chop and roast man, so the McCaddens were eating some pretty fancy side dishes. Only once a week could she prevail upon him to take a supper entirely of fresh vegetables and cheese. Catholicism made it easier for them—Friday became meatless again.

The second set of recipes, which were tacked to a cork bulletin board, were for the future. They instructed the interested homemaker on the art of making baby food. Sally would not need them for at least another six months, but she couldn't bring herself to put them away. They made the best browsing.

The peace in the household—Ben's jigsaw whining below, Sally's pots rattling on the stove—was something neither of them was used to, even after eight months. Truly, it was like the end of a war: getting Sally pregnant had nearly broken them, spirit and body. Looking back from the comfortable vantage point of success, Ben could not pinpoint the moment when he had first felt the marriage slipping from his grasp. The panic, the oppressive gloom, had just been there one day. It was impossible to analyze. Ben and Sally were not analytical by nature, and it was just as well. They had survived. Without turning each other's psyche inside out and picking through the rubble, without psychotherapy, without self-help groups, they had managed to learn a good deal about each other. There were things that had never come up in the first four years of marriage. There were things that never seemed serious until problems confronted them. Still, Ben couldn't say that life would have been better if they had asked more depth of each other before the marriage. They might not have gotten married at all, and that would have been a mistake. Despite the problems, Ben and Sally were sure they had done the right thing. They wanted to make a life together.

The Vietnam War had made them stronger; they were only dating when Ben was called up, but being apart had made their love seem very real. The grim possibility that they might never be reunited worked a powerful spell. When Ben came home, eager to remain silent about his battlefield experiences, anxious to get the sound of mortar fire out of his ears, Sally remained by him. Never hurrying his slow re-entry, she paced herself; she saw it as a mission. They waited six months to announce their engagement.

The wedding was held in church. The priest had known Sally from birth, and he did his best to acquaint himself with Ben in two short sessions. He was gratified that the young people had embraced Catholicism as a way of life. So many others had run from the fold. He did not encourage theological discussion, however, much to the couple's relief. They were church-going Catholics, with a fondness for the religious holidays and sound of the choir, but they had already seen a doctor about birth control and couldn't lie to a priest. Sally dreaded a lecture or, worse, a fight, possibly a public denunciation. The church could intimidate as well as comfort. Ben found her mounting panic more amusing than anything else, and, in the end, it made no difference. The subject never came up. The pomp of the ceremony rolled heavily over any questions in Sally's mind. By the time it was over, Ben and Sally knew they were married for good.

Their wedding photo, propped up on an end table back in Santa Monica, is a wonderful, out-of-time thing. The McCaddens are out of the 1940s. A tall, thin man with a bony face and rimless spectacles squints into the sun. By his side is a woman who does not reach his shoulders. Her dark, sculpted hair is hidden by a veil worked with baby's breath. There is immodest happiness in her face. Behind the pair, a Gothic church door threatens to swallow them whole, but their smiles betray no awareness of this ominous backdrop. They look like the world is just beginning.

The honeymoon brought them across the country from Sally's home in Connecticut to Santa Monica. Sally had lived there during Ben's active duty, and they made it their home. Sally's old job was waiting—a file clerk/secretary's position at the world headquarters of Pioneer Fried Chicken.

Ben took a long look at the possibilities of putting his wartime medical experience to some use. Medical schools were beyond his means and, he felt, beyond his ability. There would be no financial return for at least four years. He enrolled in nursing school, taking a simultaneous B.S. degree. It seemed realistic.

They felt young and independent, attached only to each other and this new existence they were building together. Ben took his degree, found a job, and security began to descend upon them. Little improvements were made. A rattan coffee table, pulled to shreds by cats, was replaced with glass and wrought iron. There were new sheets and lamps. On weekends, they bicycled to the beach and went to the movies. Ben and Sally felt that life had played fair. From time to time, Sally missed the roar of her Italian family back East, but she knew the marriage needed its own plot to grow in. She was happy to be where she was.

With the passing of their fourth anniversary, life had reached a point of comfort from which there seemed no danger of slipping back. Ben had become a consultant at Children's Hospital of Los Angeles, and Sally's job was secure. Her income paid for a new car and bought almost all the groceries. The garden saved them more than a few dollars in the fall. They stayed in the little apartment near the beach, and only one extravagant idea crossed their minds: it was time for the baby.

Sally had always wanted it, had always expected that mothering would be her primary occupation in life. She had no great complaints about sex, but looked forward to the time when it could be used for procreation. No one had ever taught her to enjoy it for its own sake. She was an old-fashioned girl. Ben had gotten used to this quality in Sally. There were worse things in the world.

The disaster of unwanted pregnancy had so obsessed her parents' generation that Sally had grown up fearing a good-night kiss. The ominous dangers of petting were discussed only in hushed tones and with many obscure gestures. Thus it was with a free heart and many expectations that Sally tossed out almost an entire month's supply of pills, compact and all. No adjustment was made in her sex life; it never occurred to her that one might be necessary. Ben and Sally made love on weekends. A month passed. Nothing happened.

In the second month, a new plan was conceived: sex every twenty-four hours, no excuses or exceptions. This was not Ben's idea of a good time, but how could it not be? Suddenly his wife wanted him practically every time he turned around. He had dreamed of such things, but the reality was a disappointment. It did not take him long to discover that it wasn't him she wanted. All she really wanted was the use of his potency. By the end of the month, it had more than lost its charm. When Sally awoke with menstrual cramps at the end of the thirty days, Ben was practically elated. It was a temporary respite, but it was something. The twenty-four-hour plan had failed and could be abandoned! Sally was crushed There was a rare, long talk, a day or two of pouting, some distance put between them.

Ben took a medical posture. Failure to get pregnant after

a month of steady sex could hardly be called failure. Three to six months was the minimum one should expect to wait for a missed period. Sally was not comforted.

"What about all those girls who lay down next to boys once in a barn and end up having abortions in Tijuana?" she asked.

"Just lucky," Ben said, but Sally was in no mood for scoffing. Ben brought home statistical reports from the hospital. She read, with some alarm, a theory that failure to conceive is frequently the result of emotional imbalance caused by earlier failure to conceive. In other words, the more she worried, the harder it would be. This she swallowed hard. She resolved to hold on for six months, burying her fear. She resolved not to ask herself what she would do if she failed.

The six-month menstruation was the hardest. Sally felt the pains mocking her. Ben only fretted. He had gambled and lost. In the process, they had grown distant; there was only one thing to talk about, and neither one could stand to hear about it anymore. At Sally's insistence, tests were arranged. If nothing else, they served to comfort her. They represented a positive step, and progress in any direction was what she craved. Her life was losing meaning by the day.

It was simple enough at the beginning: every morning, before she moved a muscle, Ben would pop a thermometer in her mouth and graph her temperature. It was supposed to rise, then fall below normal once a month, at the time of ovulation. This it did. Sally demurred in asking Ben to have a sperm count. She didn't want to hurt his pride or attack his masculinity. She had caused him so much trouble already that it seemed like an uncalled-for insult, asking him to masturbate into a bottle for her sake. Besides, she was sure it was all her fault, her inadequacy. Bolstering her courage with wine, she put the question as obtusely as possible, and Ben laughed. The next morning, he stopped off at the lab on the way to work and watched them run the analysis. His count was normal.

Their sex life was a total wreck, and now the tests came to be painful and humiliating. Sally had to show up at the doctor's office immediately after intercourse to have her cervix examined and slides prepared from the contents. Her fallopian tubes were injected with dye to check for undiscovered blockage. Nothing was found, but an odd change had come over Sally; she had become convinced she was sterile. All she wanted was the confirmation, to put the whole thing to rest. The battery of negative test results began to distress, rather than comfort, her. She just wanted it all over.

When the tests were completed, Sally's doctor summoned both of them for an office consultation. There was one course left, he explained: hormone treatments. Results were often gratifying. Ben excused himself from the meeting at this suggestion. Children's Hospital had its share of newborns who had been conceived with the aid of artificial hormones. Ben had seen tiny quadruplets lose breath and color over a period of days, dying one by one. He drove from the doctor's office to the hospital and asked for a few minutes with a colleague. He badly needed someone to talk to, and Sally was not the one.

The story came out in jagged bits, from the carefree beginnings of a great adventure to the solitude and rancor of now. Life didn't look good.

Ben's colleague had heard it all before. He was an obstetrician with a separate degree in human sexuality and communications. Ben didn't know him well; they had played handball once, and Ben had watched him work the clinic. The man understood things. He understood Ben immediately. Sally agreed to a visit. Pursuing her pregnancy had become a way of life for her. However, this was not to be a doctor's appointment, she was told. This man wanted to talk to the McCaddens as a matter of human concern.

The office was austere—a white cubicle at Children's Hospital, its dust-spattered window facing an alley—but the atmosphere was warm. The doctor had looked over the test results, and he had four simple things to say.

1.) Fully 50 percent of all couples have enough trouble getting pregnant that they end up consulting professional help.

2.) Any couple that has *any* difficulty getting pregnant goes through a period of really rotten sex. This may be God's best joke on mankind, since sex is supposedly there only to make procreation possible.

3). Psychological distress is the most frequent cause of conception failure.

4.) There was no reason that Ben and Sally had not conceived except that panic had become a way of life for them. They should begin again, forgetting all about the testing and the measuring, just going to bed as many times as they comfortably could, beginning twelve days after Sally's next period.

"Don't expect to enjoy it," the doctor cautioned. "God's little joke is foolproof. Just try to be good-spirited about it."

There was nothing in this advice to startle—no revelations, no shocks—but somehow the sympathy, the understanding that came from this brief meeting made them feel more human toward each other. They felt blessed by the knowledge that not only were they not unique, they were not even particularly rare. They saw for the first time how far off base they had gone in their attempt to do a simple thing. They went home and talked, as best they could. There was a good deal of self-recrimination and apology. They ate, and drank, and they tried.

Sally missed her next period.

Like a fierce tide that retreats without warning, the anxiety and the depression pulled smoothly away. The excitement of success banished their anger, their feeling that life had singled them out. They awoke as if from a real dream to find themselves in Santa Monica, by the sea, with a garden to tend and work to be done.

Ben and Sally McCadden are a common kind of couple who only appear to be rare because pop culture has left them behind. They live as close to *Our Town* as anyone can in the 1970s. They uphold a way of life that is a warm relic of a simpler America. Religion, tradition, and the work ethic do not seem outmoded or passé to the McCaddens; these things hold their life together.

They came from strong families and hoped to create one. Life's path did not seem to be land mined or crossed with confusing sidetracks. They knew what they wanted, and it was essentially the same thing their parents and grandparents had wanted: to work, to raise a family, to live in peace and harmony. The unwavering simplicity of their needs made the pregnancy failure into a major catastrophe; the McCaddens are not variable people. Sally McCadden couldn't say, "Well, I'm having trouble getting pregnant, so I think I'll start a bookstore." Being a mother was not only all there was for her, it was the only way she had to measure herself. From her earliest days, she had planned to spend her life mothering. Her inability to get pregnant meant that there would be nothing for her to do or be for the next sixty years.

Probably, her passion helped her fail. Probably, the obsession with becoming pregnant ruined her internal timing and her body's receptiveness to the sperm cell. No one knows how this works. The link between mind and body is one of the most impenetrable mysteries of science. Where life and death are concerned, there seems to be some truth to the "mind over matter" philosophy that has been appropriated by hypnotists and charlatans, as well as psychiatrists and physicians. There is no way of knowing, at the present time, how much mental attitude has to do with the ease or difficulty of conception. It seems foolish to dismiss the idea, however.

Sally's problem did not begin with mental attitude, however; it began with misinformation. She believed that without birth control she would become pregnant instantly. She did not know how long it takes most couples to conceive, and she knew nothing about the cycles of her own body—the best and worst times to engage in intercourse to encourage pregnancy. This information is available. Start twelve days after the first day of your menstruation, and expect to wait a minimum of three months, commonly six, before you will miss a period.* If

* This information was supplied to the authors by Dr. Phillip Brooks of Los Angeles, California. The number of days may vary, depending on the length of a woman's menstrual cycle.

you've been on birth-control pills, your body may be a little less reliable, and it may take longer. This means your timing has to be very general; you can't select the month for your baby's birthday with any accuracy, nor can you make sure he won't be born the day before Christmas, thus ruining his schedule for receiving birthday and Christmas presents. In beginning to try to get pregnant, you are taking on the mantle of a natural order. The timetable is no longer yours, nor are the possible turns of events. You are embracing a tradition that has led to the creation of much of the symbolism, religion, mythology, and otherwise nonrational thought and substance in the world. Having a baby isn't like anything else. If it gives you anything, it should give you a sense of the power humanity at large succumbs to: one time, unlike all the others, and for no apparent reason, the sperm penetrates the ovum, and everything is suddenly different than it has ever been in the world. The rigidity of your own thinking cannot control these events, and neither can your plans or desires. When that baby is conceived, he will be conceived—not before or after that, and no one knows why. As for what he or she will be, you have very little control over those things as well. In embarking on parenthood, you are starting to wander into one of the last bastions of mystery in the human experience.

AT ONE WEEK

Hospital Emergency—Labor Pain

SALLY McCADDEN began to fall apart thirteen hours into her active labor. She had been feeling contractions for almost twenty-four hours, but they had been mild and irregular for a while. At four in the morning, they had checked into the hospital with serious contractions, and it was now approaching the cocktail hour. Things just kept getting worse. At first Sally could handle the discomfort without employing any Lamaze techniques at all, and she was pretty proud. Finally, at around ten in the morning, she began using the simplest of the breathing exercises. By then she had been getting twelve contractions an hour for four hours. It was starting to wear her out. By three o'clock, she was on the most advanced of the breathing techniques, and delivery was nowhere in sight. At five, she began to crack.

She began to pray that the contractions wouldn't come. She felt like a rag.

"Tell them to give me a Caesarean," she told Ben in a whisper. "I can't do this."

Ben realized she was not thinking straight. He was pouring out support.

"You're doing fine," he told her. "It won't be long."

"You don't know that!" she screamed. "Nobody knows! I can't stand this!"

No one had told her to expect this. She expected it to be painful, to be like nothing else she had ever felt, but it was all for a purpose: to have a baby. By this time, the baby had faded into oblivion in her fogged mind. What people kept referring to throughout her pregnancy as "discomfort" was not discomfort or anything like it. It was agonizing, a series of wild surges of attack upon her body, a vise-grip of shock. There was no mental attitude or physical effort that could make it bearable. And there was no baby—just the hours ahead with this animal of pain tearing at her. She began to scream at twenty minutes before six.

Still, she wouldn't have drugs. She knew who she was supposed to be, and she was supposed to have been born for this thing, this event. She had had a mild sedative. That was all she would take.

Ben remained in a professional posture. He was a nurse, after all, and he had seen nearly a thousand people in this kind of pain. There was nothing to be done if she wouldn't have drugs, and he concerned himself with the health aspects of the event. He read the fetal monitor, listened to the baby's heartbeat, talked technical language with the doctor, and kept up a first-rate front. The labor was long and worrisome. He knew, but didn't say, that it could not go on much longer without the issue of a Caesarean section being raised, and he didn't like the idea of surgery no matter how simple. So he was relieved when, at six-fifteen, after more than fourteen hours in the small, cramped quarters of the labor room, after living with and comforting almost an hour of Sally's mounting panic, the doctor moved them to delivery. It would all be over soon.

Sally knew nothing. They pushed her from her bed onto

the delivery table as gingerly as possible, instructing her, coaxing her, making her try to perform. She was wild-eyed every time the clamping spasm of contraction grabbed her. Now they were doubling up on one another, leaving her no spare moment to breathe. Sally saw the end of her life near at hand, felt death approaching. It was a very real instinct. No one could endure this harrowing pain; she would die.

Ben, watching the procedure like a flight controller, caught sight of the monitor's tape a split second before a nurse and saw the heart rate dropping, a common occurrence.

"His heartbeat's down," he said quietly, just as the nurse noticed the signal and reached for the oxygen mask.

Sally's mind jolted. Suddenly it was clear to her what was happening. Her instinct had erred. It was not she who would die.

"It's dead!" she screamed. "Oh my God, it's dead! Take it out of me! It's dead! It's dead!"

"The baby's not dead," Ben said, looking straight into her eyes. "The baby's fine."

The oxygen mask was slapped across her nose and mouth, and Ben told her to breathe and be quiet.

"The baby's fine," he said again. "Now push!"

But even beneath the mask, the rush in Sally's mind could not be quelled. Her baby was dead. She had been carrying him dead for months. All this pain was for nothing, for a corpse born out of fear, a body, a lifeless infant tragedy. Her baby was dead.

"Push!" The doctor and Ben were coaxing her, their faces imploring her in concert. "Push!"

Rough arms pulled at her and tilted her head. In a mirror she could see what must have been herself, spread open grotesquely, pried apart and swollen.

"Push!"

Against her will she saw the head, still, lifeless, emerging from between her thighs. Why were they doing this to her, showing her this nonexistent child? Still, she watched, blindly obeying orders barked from distant throats. Push. Stop pushing. Little push. Stop. Push. She didn't care. She was not really in the room anymore. Pain and panic had driven her into herself, into a private enclave where nothing existed. Push. One hard push.

And it snapped. She felt it glide from within her—the pain, the belly, the sureness of death, everything slipped away. The doctor was holding a little thing in his hand that was unrecognizable.

"It's a boy," he said. Had she seen it come out in the mirror? She would never know.

She heard the cry and looked up to Ben, who was beaming like a boy of eight. Then she looked down. She was just coming back, back in the room, back to her senses. On her breast was a little baby boy, living, squirming, his eyes looking vaguely around the room. Ben's man's hand descended on the tiny back and began to rub color into it. Sally raised an exhausted hand and joined his.

"Hello, sweetie," she said.

"Sally, you're a champ," her doctor proclaimed. Sally tried to focus on him with a weak smile. He'd done a job for them, but he was a terrible liar.

Ben saw Sally through recovery and into her room. She was given a sleeping pill while she stared at Brian, eight pounds even, who was asleep at her side in a Lucite bassinet. The ordeal had been too much for her. Even with the excitement, the emotional charge, and the baby right there, the pill took action within the hour, and Sally drifted off. Ben checked everything and went home. Mission accomplished. He was tired.

The phone rang at five forty-five in the morning. Looking outside at the dark, Ben knew it was bad news. It was too early for good.

"Sorry to wake you, Ben . . . we've got some problems here: Sally's lost a lot of blood during the last few hours and developed a hematoma. We need to take her into surgery kinda fast. Could you get . . ."

Ben was out the door in a daze. His satisfaction at the evening's activities vanished and he felt as if he'd been knifed in the back. He was headed back into nightmare time, and now he knew it could be serious. Hematoma, an internal blood hemorrhage in the uterine wall, meant, at the very least, a lot of blood gone, a drop in blood pressure that was equivalent to severe shock, and a long, slow recovery. At worst, it could be the very worst—Ben would be a widower with a newborn to raise. His brain was swamped with anxiety by the time he pulled into the hospital parking lot. All through the pregnancy, labor, and the delivery, he had bolstered himself with his professional posture. He knew what everything meant, and he knew there was nothing to worry about. Now the knowledge that went with his training wouldn't go away. He knew Sally might die.

The surgeon was not encouraging. "It's touch and go in there," he said to Ben, as if Ben were a fellow professional and not the husband and father that he felt like. "We'll see."

Sally was back in her room by ten. She was conscious, vaguely aware that things were not normal, but unclear as to what had been done. She had no idea she was really ill.

"Why won't they bring Brian?" she asked Ben. "I want to see him."

"You've got a fever," Ben told her. He had to pull the words out of his throat one by one. "It wouldn't be good for him."

"Tonight can I see him?"

"I hope so."

For three days, they watched her and lied to her. She was sedated, dazed, and uncomprehending. They would show her the baby at a distance, hold him up, wheel her bed to the nursery window, but that was all. Sally could not get out of bed, had barely the strength to raise an arm. She had an I.V. bottle feeding into her left forearm, a blood bottle feeding into her right forearm, and a catheter. Practically speaking, she was wired to the bed. She had no idea what was going on and was so sleepy it seemed as if she didn't care.

Underneath the fog of apparent indifference, however, she

was mournful and bewildered. She wanted her baby, and no one seemed to be able to make sense of why she could not have him. They contradicted themselves, said nonsensical things to her as if she were an infant herself, and generally kept her as dazed with their reasoning as they did with their drugs. She fretted throughout the night, unable to make her brain work right, unable to put one thought after another and march them along to a conclusion. Where was her baby? That one ran over and over in her head, no matter what. Asleep and awake: Where was the baby? Somehow the desperation in her plea got lost between her brain and her mouth. No one seemed to notice how much she wanted a coherent answer.

Ben had to work. Children's Hospital, just across Vermont Avenue from the hospital where Sally was recovering, had a row of windows in its connective passageways from which you could look out and see Sally's room, counting up and over from the southeast corner of the building. Ben could not walk the corridor easily. He turned his head from the windows and watched the opposing wall as he walked. He went through his duties with more indifference than could be concealed and was reprimanded harshly several times. He thought he'd be fired, and he thought he wouldn't care. As he looked around the bustling corridors of the hospital, he felt the heart-stopping insignificance of his life and Sally's, of any one human life against the tide of sick, dying, childbearing, being born people who were coming and going every day right before his eyes. He would have liked to matter more than that, more than someone just coming and going, but he couldn't convince himself that he did. It seemed likely that Sally would die of the insignificance of her disease and her life, as much as anything else.

On the third day, however, she began to come around. She started to be awake more, and her fever dropped. At 10:00 P.M., a sympathetic nurse popped a thermometer into Sally's mouth and pulled it out immediately, looked at it, and said: "You're normal. Let me tell the doctor to bring in your baby."

Ben arrived ten minutes after Brian; he'd been telephoned by the doctor. He was speechless, afraid to come out of the shock that had kept him in control through sleepless nights and pointless days. He was wary of good news and final curtains. No one knew about these things really. There could be a relapse. There could be complications later. Nothing was settled. But when he saw Sally with Brian, he could tell that was all that mattered to her, so he was happy—at the edge of happiness anyhow.

Cautiously, the hours going by on tiptoes, the predictions began to firm up. Sally was all right. Nothing bad was going to happen to her. She kept Brian in the room with her for two days, and at the end of a six-day hospital stay, she was allowed to leave. She wept real tears of gratitude at the news, and when Ben walked her out to the car, there was a smile practically paralyzed on her face. She chattered all the way home, overexerting herself and running on adrenaline. Brian rested in her arms, awake but comfortable, being perfect in the car.

She needed help to the front door, and more to get up the stairs. Listening to her talk, Ben, at her arm, realized that she had never known what he had been going through or what the doctors had been saying about her. She was still in a private world, gripping her life tightly, but without concern.

"You haven't exactly been a perfect housewife," she said to him, noting a stack of frozen pizza tins in the kitchen sink and six days of trash waiting to be taken out.

It was all so blasé that Ben didn't know what to say.

"I've got to rest," she admitted, settling down onto the bed.

"That's the idea," he told her. "You've been through a lot."

"Just an hour though," she said. The baby was asleep in the bassinet at her side. "Wake me in an hour, even if he doesn't get up."

"What for?" Ben wanted to know.

"People will be coming over."

"Yeah, but not today . . ."

"I've got to get this house clean, get things ready. We want things to be nice."

Ben stared at her as if she were out of her mind.

"Well, don't we?" she asked.

"I guess," he said. "I guess we do."

The rate of emergency connected with childbirth is so low that it is not something you should spend much time preparing for. Understand that there is *always* the possibility that your delivery will not leave mother and child in perfect shape, but you have no control over the matter beyond taking good prenatal care of yourself, eating intelligently, and so forth. Once you are in the hospital, there is nothing much you can do to protect yourself. Thinking about the possibilities for a difficult and protracted labor, however, is quite another matter. When we asked people being interviewed for this book what they would most like to see in it, more than half the mothers said they wanted the truth to be told about labor and delivery, that they had never seen it in print. We would very much like to tell the truth about those subjects. The trouble is, there is no truth about them. They are individual experiences, and no two women feel the same way about them. Given that warning, here goes.

The physical sensations of the early and middle parts of labor are hardly worth talking about. There is some discomfort, and some disruption of your normal activity, but there's also a lot of excitement, and the two usually cancel each other out. It is the last phases of labor and the delivery experience that are physically awesome.

There is a great reluctance on the part of people in the childbirth industry to talk about the sensation of labor as "pain," and the old phrase "labor pain" is not in use at the moment. We are certainly not afraid to call labor "painful," and we'd do so if that were a word unanimously used by women who have gone through it, but it's not. Some women we interviewed were angry about the unwillingness of their doctors and nurses to acknowledge what they felt as "pain," and said that labor was without doubt the most painful thing that had ever happened to them. Other women *refused* to describe what they were feeling as "pain" and simply perceived it as an overwhelming physical experience. The contractions hurt, they said, but the hurt was not "pain." There is no way to adequately explain that statement, but it was made by so many women that it must have some meaning to a good number of them.

When you start talking about the sensations of childbirth, two myths normally enter the conversation. The first is that "labor pain" is "beautiful" even though it hurts. The other is that it is impossible to remember the sensation. Both myths seem to have been constructed by people who did not want to confront the realities of the situation. By calling hard labor a "beautiful pain," the entire issue is clouded and placed beyond discussion. In "beautiful pain" you have a self-contradictory coinage that really has no discernable meaning. Telling someone that labor is "beautiful pain" amounts to telling them that you don't want to hear about what they're going through or be responsible for giving them any hard information.

The idea that pain is not memorable is extremely comforting, and turns out to be utter garbage. At least a good number of women in our sample remembered their labor clearly enough to state that nothing would make them go through it again, except the prospect of having another baby. So the two myths don't help much, and perhaps nothing we can say about the sensations of childbirth will help much either. Whether they help or not, however, there are a few points that are often overlooked and should be made.

When a woman is in labor, whether she perceives it as "pain" or "hurt" or simply "sensation," it *can* be agonizing, scary, and it *can* overpower her mental processes. Women say that there is no way to approximate the sensation in words, that it cannot be compared to any other experience in life. Men nod sagely at this, and the most honest of them admit that they have no idea about what is being said. Labor is simply one of the few elemental physical sensations a woman experiences in her life. To call it "discomfort" is to cheat the expectant mother. Whether she chooses to call it pain or not, it is more important than discomfort. It is bigger. If we are reluctant to use the phrase "labor pain," it is not because the sensation of childbirth is small or trivial or unimportant, but because, as big as it is, only some women feel it as pain.

The whole "pain" issue brings up the subject of drugless delivery, a much-argued topic among women and doctors these days. With the increasing popularity of childbirth preparation classes, more and more women are going through delivery without the use of anesthetic drugs. It is becoming clearer and clearer that, from a purely physiological point of view, this is a good thing *when the mother is up to it.*

What do you have to be to be up to it? You have to be physically able to deliver the baby without suffering so much agony that drugs are virtually a necessity. This depends upon everything from the position of the baby to your pelvic bone structure, to your physical condition and your stamina. With the exception of the last two, these factors are uncontrollable, and you won't know what's happening until the time comes. The emotional side is more complex and depends a lot more on prenatal thought and planning. To be "up to" a drugless delivery, you have to *want to have* a drugless delivery—not think it's the right or chic thing to do, nor do it to accommodate your husband or your childbirth instructor, or your parents, or the math teacher who once told you you'd never amount to anything. You have to *want it for you.* Without the conviction, the chances for success are greatly reduced.

The reason your conviction is so essential comes back to the overwhelming sensation of hard labor. As we stated earlier, every woman, at some point, wants to escape her labor. If drugs are offered, they will be an almost irresistible temptation. You won't be able to think clearly about the matter, but if you know you don't want them before the whole process begins, you may very well remember what you *do* want when you are emotionally pulled toward escape.

How much safer or "better" is a drugless delivery? It's a question that will be continually debated for some years to come. It's certainly healthier for the mother and for the baby because *all* drug use is potentially harmful. The degree of danger is a matter of disagreement, and there are cases where a drugless delivery may be more harmful than drugs if a woman is not capable of withstanding the duration of a long labor. As advocates of drugless birth, we feel there is an added dimension that should be mentioned.

Years ago, women were given all kinds of anesthetics for labor and delivery—drugs that clouded their minds, numbed their senses, and depressed the responses of their babies. Those days are over, for the most part, and anesthetic drugs for delivery have been greatly refined: they numb specific areas of your body and depending upon the dosage, may or may not affect the responses of your baby. Still, some part of you is missing. Some part of the experience is lost. Many women who have gone without drugs report that, health reasons aside, they were grateful for the fullness of the experience and concerned that they might never have perceived it in its totality had they been drugged, no matter how locally.

Even so, we think the drug question is a personal one, and no amount of "right-minded" thinking ought to influence your decision. Labor hurts, all right, but although it may not be a "beautiful" pain, it's a very special pain, if it is pain at all. Describing it is impossible, and living through it may be a match for anything you have yet done. Still, you may not want to miss it.

AT ONE MONTH

The Madison Avenue Mother

BEN expected Sally to recover slowly, but he didn't expect her to stop being Sally. Something strange was happening in the house. Within a week of the return home from the hospital, Ben began to see that Sally had entered the tunnel of illness with one personality and emerged with another. The second Sally was not unrelated to the first. She was, as a matter of fact, simply a passionate rendering. What had been quirks were now obsessions. Happiness became hysteria. Depression verged on despair. Sally was zealous on all subjects, most especially propriety in the house and with the child. Ben thought she would calm down in a day or two, so he said nothing. After all, she had been very sick.

Sally seemed to like herself this way, however. It occurred to Ben that he might have a permanently transformed woman on his hands. She would not let him watch her while she nursed (nursing had been his idea); she would not let him dress the baby without standing over him to see that it was done properly. She cleaned each glass and butter plate as it was dirtied in the kitchen, and the oven each time it was used for anything more than warming a pot pie. Ben suspected there was a name for this in psychiatric parlance, but he didn't want to know. Sally had the house ready for guests every morning at seven-thirty, just in case. She was not getting her strength back.

Brian was cared for in private. It seemed to Ben that Sally was deliberately keeping the baby away from him, as if he might harm him or steal his affection. When he could stand it no longer, he put it to her as gently as possible.

"I'm worried about you," he said.

"Me, too," she confessed.

He breathed a sigh of relief, but it was short-lived.

"I'm sleeping so much," she said.

"What?"

"I'm sleeping too much, and I can't keep up the way I used to. It's got me scared."

Ben probed. It seemed that Sally had an image in her mind. It was a picture of a new mother she had seen in an ad for some baby product. In the picture, this woman was wearing a baby-blue wool robe and a pair of fluffy slippers. Her hair was flowing carelessly but perfectly over one shoulder, and her face was fresh and smiling. She was young motherhood personified on glossy paper, and she was selling something. Sally kept comparing herself to this woman.

"I'm probably younger than she is," she insisted. "She looks like she has a beautiful house, puts her husband's meals on the table on time, and gives him some Scotch and a big kiss when he gets home."

"What are you talking about?" Ben asked, seriously perplexed.

"I'm a terrible failure," Sally said. "That's what. Can't you even tell?"

In fact, Ben could tell. As obsessed as Sally had become with housework and baby care, she was getting less and less of it done each day. She would pick specks of dirt off the window-sills, but the bathroom would remain untouched as a result. She began to disregard her own hygiene for the sake of keeping the laundry load down to a manageable bulk. On one afternoon Ben returned home to find the curtains drawn, the house sweltering in the upper nineties, the baby crying in the bassinet, and Sally still in the bathrobe she had been wearing at seven-thirty in the morning when he had left for work.

"What in the hell is happening here?" he said.

"I'm tired," she replied. "Why am I so tired?"

He put her to bed and threw open the windows. He changed the baby and took him away from the house for a ride. He was glad to be alone with him, bewildered but safe. He sang an Irish tune, the only one he knew, as he rode around Los Angeles in the car with the baby by his side in the car seat. It was getting dark out. The baby fell asleep. Ben thought about *his* equivalent of the lady in the blue robe— his own imagined picture of himself as father. He was thinking about the Little League. He looked over at Brian, barely the size of a high-priced first baseman's glove. The Little League would have to wait. What came before the Little League? Disneyland. And before that? Ben was stumped. What was he supposed to do with this baby?

"I think we're in trouble," Ben said aloud. Brian refused to acknowledge him, except with an all-but-inaudible snort.

"That's the spirit," Ben said.

They got home at seven. Sally was not in bed. Ben couldn't find her. She was not in the kitchen or the living room. There was a light on in the bathroom, but the door was open—not one of Sally's habits. With a cautious eye, Ben looked around the corner. Sally was standing in the shower. She was dressed in jeans and an old shirt of Ben's. There was a toothbrush in one hand and a can of Comet cleanser in the other. She was brushing at the little lines of graying putty between the tiles. She was cleaning them. She looked up at Ben with an impassive face. She was caught in the act.

"I'm sorry," she said. "You were gone with the baby. It was such a good opportunity. It's needed doing a long time."

Looking back some time later, Sally tried to figure out what she had been doing. What she came up with was this:

"I had this good job; I was good at it and was getting promoted little by little. My life was very simple and stable, and then I had a baby. Suddenly, I had a job I didn't know the first thing about, I had no boss, no training program, I wasn't getting paid. At this other job, I knew I was doing well 'cause my salary kept going up, but now there was no way to know if I was doing good or bad. I was just out there, floating around. So I started to do everything. I figured if I did everything, no one could complain. I'm like that anyhow. But I guess I wasn't seeing myself. I was going crazy in a way."

Ben wanted to help, but he didn't. He resented the way Sally closeted herself up with the baby, and he resented it when she so obviously couldn't cope. He wanted her to handle everything like a normal, mature, cogent woman, and he wanted to be included in all the ways that fathers like to be included. He didn't care about the house, the neighbors, the guests—he wanted the family put in shape, and he saw Sally's activity as so much wasted energy. Furtively, he went to colleagues on the hospital staff who had children and badgered them. Had they gone crazy during the first weeks? Did their wives become strangers? Were they jealous of all the attention lavished on the baby? Everyone more or less answered in the affirmative, and they all said it would pass, eventually.

He had tried to help by taking the baby, by insisting that Sally do less, by suggesting everything from counseling to group therapy. Sally was not so much opposed as unresponsive. She was tired. She didn't see why she should take on something else. She was just waiting to get better. Ben couldn't get through to her because, inside, she was just too scared to let him. He didn't want to know that, so he quietly backed out, closed the door, and stopped trying to peek in. Sally was going to have to solve this one herself.

Post-partum recovery is one of the less cheerful mysteries of human behavior. For some people, it is a week or two of rest, no bad moods, and back out into the world. For others, it can be a time of almost unbearable stress, to which reactions are unpredictable. It is, in any case, one of those times when the physiological and psychological get all twisted up together in a tangle no one has ever fully put straight.

THE PHYSICAL SIDE

A woman's hormones are in a state of flux from the time she gets pregnant until she stops nursing (if she nurses). These hormonal shifts, which sometimes account for moodiness just before or during menstrual periods, go on day and night for as long as twenty months or more, instead of the five or so days it takes to have a period. They are at a particularly intense pitch just after the birth, when they are adjusting to nonpregnancy and possibly to nursing. They can spin you all around, make you behave in completely irrational ways, and give you physical symptoms of varying sorts (headache, nausea, etc.). They can cause acute depression (new mothers have been known to attempt and commit suicide) or giddy periods of overactivity. There is no way to control hormonal rebalancing. You wait it out. In all but the most extreme cases, things will, in fact, settle down.

One point should be emphasized for husbands, however. As stated previously, most women hate being told that their emotional state is due to menstruation. The reason should be obvious. When you tell a woman this, you are telling her that what she is feeling is not valid, that it is somehow inferior to a "real" feeling. This is insulting and degrading. More to the point, it accomplishes nothing, except to assure the man that he does not have to bother sympathizing with the emotion, since it is not real. It's a self-serving thing to do. The same goes for this post-partum period. The fact that women are influenced in their feelings by physiological events in their bodies does not mean you can discount or ignore those feelings. Of course, you can't spend twenty months pretending that there is *no* hormonal influence on your mate just because you don't want to hurt her feelings, so tact is required. Bring up the subject when both of you are feeling well and affectionate toward each other. Try to come to a state of mind where the irregularities of personality are recognized and accommodated. They aren't likely to be welcomed by the male, but if they are understood, at least they cease to be a threat.

THE PSYCHOLOGICAL SIDE

This has to do with myths, public relations, advertising, and the American mother's self-image. At the moment of birth, all the dreaming you have done about being a mother suddenly becomes real. How happy you are going to be with the results depends a lot upon what you have been dreaming. There is always a moment of terrible anxiety when you arrive at a spot you have anticipated for a long time. In what ways will you be disappointed?

Sally McCadden had a fairly overstuffed dream. We live so much in the thrall of media and popular culture that we are almost all suffering from an extraglossy image of ourselves. It's hard to be a glossy mother. There's too much work involved. It's hard to be knowledgeable, authoritative, sure of yourself, or strong-willed when you have no idea what to do. One of the things that makes popular culture popular is that it comforts us. It makes us believe everything will come naturally; we'll all be beautiful and clean and energetic all the time. Then, when we fail to live up to this image, we look around and say, "Well, everyone else is all these things, why not me?" Only no one is any of those things. Everyone is like you, half-scared, semicompetent, only beautiful from time to time, and tired all the time. So part of the psychological letdown of post-partum is that your dream comes around to haunt you, and laugh at you, and belittle you.

The only way to get around this problem is not to buy into the dream to start with. The lady in the blue bathrobe with the hair-do and the grinning infant is not you. You are the one with the robe that needs cleaning every two days because of the spills and the spit, the one with the hair that's been needing a washing for longer than you'd care to imagine, the one who is still bleeding, and who sleeps with one eye open in three-hour shifts. The lady in blue is a model. She's twenty-three years old, unmarried, neurotic, and the last time she held a baby not in front of a camera was when she was seven, and the baby was made out of rubber. She was thought up during a three-martini lunch in a little bistro off Madison Avenue, and any time you spend worrying about her is surely time wasted.

AT THREE MONTHS

Infatuated with the Baby

As BRIAN grew, Sally found herself quite mesmerized by him. It was hard to describe, even to herself. When she nursed, something much more than milk flowed out of her. It was not sexual, exactly, but it was more than devotion. She was enthralled, distracted by his moods, and consumed with satisfying him. It was something close to being in love. In her darker moments, she admitted that it *was* being in love. She poured herself out to this infant, and she cared only for him. It was a feeling she had never quite had for Ben, and while one is not supposed to feel the same way about a husband as a child, Sally began to think she had the proper feelings reversed. She was carrying on a secret love affair with her child, in her head. As her personality began to stabilize, she realized that everything was for Brian, the housework, the cooking, the nursing, and handling—whether he benefited directly or not, she was doing it for him. The inequity of it had to bleed into Ben's consciousness eventually.

Ben had stopped badgering her. He had begun to leave her on her own, to work and rest as much as she wished. He came home each night, they described their days to each other, ate, watched a little television, and went to bed. Exhausted as she was at six in the morning, when Brian would awaken her with his cry, she rushed from bed to see him, to hold him, and bring him to her breast. And when Ben left in the morning, she was alone in her own domain—her house, her baby, her work. She grew to feel possessive, began to see Ben as an outsider, an interruption of her inner world. She knew these feelings were dangerous, that they could suck her into a pattern of life where Ben would have no place at all, but she didn't feel the danger near enough yet. She still loved Ben, still cared about him, and thought about him. He was her husband, and she didn't want to be rid of him or apart from him, except during the workday, when she could have her own life and think her own thoughts. It was the best part of her life.

Brian was still too young to cause any trouble. He would sit quietly in an infant seat wherever she put him and just look around; Sally began to see the house through infant eyes. Often she stopped work to watch him stare. He was beautiful—his face becalmed by security, his eyes roving and shining with curiosity. Half the day her heart was in her throat just from looking at him. When Ben's car rolled into the garage each evening, heralding his arrival, the adrenaline would start flowing in Sally's body, as if Ben might catch on to her true feelings.

It was a worrisome time. Sally gave the baby over to Ben for a few minutes in the evening, let Ben feed him supper some nights, and then put him to bed. Twice a night she would check on him, and more than once Ben had entered the room and found her staring down at Brian's little body, hypnotized by the soft, regular breathing. Ben seemed to think this was a normal thing for a mother to be doing. He wasn't disturbed by it, but Sally was embarrassed.

Ben wasn't sure what was disturbing him. It didn't seem to be any particular thing, but something was causing ambivalence to grow in him. There was nothing much to this child, as far as he could see—just change him, feed him, put him down, and pick him up. There were times when he didn't much like Brian, when he thought Brian brought a lot more trouble than happiness into the house. He was willing to let Sally be distracted for a while, and he was glad she had stopped seeming so crazy, but he sort of wanted his life back the way it was.

There were silences in the house that hadn't been there before, and Ben didn't know how to break them. With Sally so wrapped up in Brian, he sensed how little his workday meant to her. Events he might once have reported died on his lips. He excised the kinds of conversations they used to have, and there was nothing left. Sally didn't help. She only wanted to talk about the baby, and there was nothing to say about him. He cut a tooth months before he was supposed to. That was good for a paragraph. His first solid food took up almost an entire evening meal to describe. Ben had been there for that experience, and he didn't care to rehash the details. It wasn't that Brian hadn't been cute, but it was over. Ben was a little tired of Brian.

If he was jealous of anything, it was not Sally's attention, but the concern of visitors. Sally had been sick, and Brian was adorable, and guests seemed to have a hard time deciding what was interesting about Ben, if anything. He found himself sitting in silence for hours at a time, while the conversation swirled around him on subjects he had long since exhausted in his own mind. The air was dusty with his indifference. And he was hurt. No one, including Sally, seemed to think that fathers had much to do with parenthood. There were some jokes about Ben "getting to do the fun part" and then having to watch Sally suffer, and Ben did his best to give a charming little snort of laughter when such comments were made, but he had about had it with the whole situation. He was lonely.

He was hungry for physical love, too. They had tried to have sex only once since the birth, and it had been painful for Sally. But Ben didn't need intercourse. He didn't need any sexual satisfaction at all. He wanted to be hugged, and he wanted to feel love going back and forth again. Sex had never been that important to him, and Sally had never lost herself to it, but they used to love. They used to look at each other.

On a Saturday night when guests had been over, Ben piled dishes into the sink and ran scalding water over them, letting them soak while Sally went in to nurse Brian, who had been awakened by the noisy farewells. It was eleven, and Ben had had three glasses of wine. As he watched the suds mushroom in the sink, he grew sad and finally morose. It seemed to him that when Sally was in the baby's room, with the baby, the house was really empty. He was all alone. From the kitchen, he heard Brian moan as Sally laid him down on his stomach in the crib, then the patter of her feet on the hallway tiles let him know that the nursing was over. He dried his hands and stepped out of the kitchen. Sally was turning on the light in the bedroom. Coming up behind her, Ben reached around and gripped her lightly. She jumped, pulling free and spinning away.

"What?" he asked.

It took her a moment to respond. "You just scared me," she said finally. "It's nothing."

He watched her eyes for a moment, until they drifted.

"I didn't scare you," he said.

"Sort of you did," she said.

"What does that mean?"

Sally had to think what it meant. "I just . . . don't want you touching me so soon after . . ." she gestured to Brian's room, where a heater was humming placidly. "It's just that there's two of you, and only one of me. I can't handle all the touching."

The McCaddens were not naturally communicative. They were middle-class people of good intentions, who only wanted the darker sides of life to leave them alone. They were not especially passionate, argumentative, dreamy, or secretive by nature. Their emotions were held tightly in check. Professionals would probably have called them repressed, but it was nothing so flamboyant; they were just quiet people, until Brian came along. Up to that crucial moment, every emotional event in either of their lives had been an event of choice. They chose each other; they chose to get married and to make a life together. Nothing was thrust on them before Brian, and they were able to mete out their emotional involvement as they saw fit. Brian changed all that. It was a choice to conceive him, but, after that, nothing was a choice. He tapped the major vein of Sally's core, a part of her that she had no idea existed. She was less than thrilled to discover her capacity for love. She liked love the way it had been with Ben, where the risks were small and the rewards predictable. Brian took away her safety margin; she was perplexed and excited.

What happened to Sally happens to a lot of mothers, and we suspect it happens more often with boy babies than with girl babies, although we have no statistics to back up our suspicion. Women can experience feelings toward their infants which are very much like romantic love. Those who are unaccustomed to letting their emotions run wild sense a danger in this love, which is probably overstated.

There is always a danger in love. Love leading to emotional, financial, and physical ruin is one of the most popular themes of literature. Everyone is afraid of love because it rules us, instead of the other way around. Love makes people mad, and, indeed, the overprotective mother smothering her child with affection and disrupting his emotional development is another popular literary theme, especially in America. Mothers who have this sudden, wild rush of devotion to, and obsession with, their newborns usually fear for both their own emotional lives and the safety of their children. In reality, most of the rush wears off. Not that you will stop loving your children—you won't—but that first outpouring of devotion does, generally speaking, taper down somewhat. Newborns are new, remember, and the "crush" is often a function of meeting a new person, especially a dependent new person. Just as romantic entanglements tend to eventually come to a simmer from a furious boil, so do crushes on new babies.

They can be problematic, however, if husbands are unaware, or if wives seek to keep them unaware. If you are a new mother, and you find yourself obsessed with your baby, and the obsession makes you feel guilty, there is bound to be trouble. Like Sally McCadden, you run the risk of becoming furtive in your devotion, trying to deny it, and pretending that everything in the household is "normal." Like alcoholics, who keep bottles stored in secret hiding places all around the house, you may begin to keep little spots of time hidden away for yourself, and even though your mate may not know what is wrong, he will certainly sense the distance you have put between yourself and him. Remember that the first months of having a new child in the house are months where the couple's relationship is being overhauled. You will be establishing a whole set of new patterns. Secretiveness shouldn't be one of them.

Ben McCadden didn't know what was wrong, but he knew something was, and he didn't even know how to go about locating it. Somehow the sense of betrayal came through, but the details eluded him. Sally spent her time covering her tracks, and the couple was bound to drift.

As a new mother, you should recognize the potential for an overwhelming, disturbingly all-encompassing relationship with your newborn, and you should try to talk about your feelings. The fear that a husband will become jealous is a real one, but there is no way to avoid the jealousy. He will be more jealous if you are hiding from him than if you are talking to him. The feelings are not uncommon, unnatural, or morally evil; you are supposed to love your child, and love has a way of making your head spin, no matter what kind of love it is.

Husbands, facing the distancing process from their wives, should be aware of the complexity of the situation. The easiest thing to do is become difficult and intractable. At any given moment in a relationship, one partner is in a stronger position than the other; in this situation, the husband is definitely the stronger. Understanding your mate's "baby crush" requires a suppression of your own ego for a time, but if the relationship is solid, that is not too much to ask. Husbands are crucial, of course, and fathers virtually essential, but during the early months of parenting, their role is sometimes passive. That does not mean worthless. One of the main things husbands are there for is to monitor wives, to keep track of the emotional flow of things, the physical rejuvenation that can be slow, and the adjustment of mother to child. This is worthwhile work. It requires a perceptive mind and as high a degree of sensitivity as you can muster. If your mate seems to be having an affair with her baby, that's something worth talking about. She may be far more concerned about it than you are, and she may be frightened. But it is *she*, not you, who is likely to be in an emotional vise-grip during the first three months or so of parenting, and you who must seek and discover, and soothe.

AT SIX MONTHS

Sex after Childbirth

AFTER six months of motherhood, Sally decided she owed Ben
a sex life. She was frightened of it; the last time they had
tried, it had been painful and she had bled a little. The whole
thing had been distasteful, and it projected a gloomy picture
of the future. Sally's views about sex had never been more
confused. She had never gotten much out of sex. She was
timid; she learned sex with Ben the way a fourth-grader learns
fractions. After awhile, she was pleased with herself that she
had mastered it. She enjoyed it in a subdued way, but she was
not especially anxious to get back to it after Brian's birth.
Brian was loving her without sex.

If anything drew her back to sex, it was a sense of slipping
family stability. Sally believed in making the family work,
and sex was a part of the family. While this view bordered on
the Victorian, it was what finally drove her back into Ben's
arms. She had been so unresponsive for so long that now she
had to be the aggressor; Ben had long since given up his pursuit

of her, dogged by lack of success. Sally felt silly calculating the seduction of her husband; what was she supposed to do— dance naked on the coffee table? She didn't carry herself around like a sexual being. Sally felt that some women just saw themselves that way, and walked, talked, touched, and gazed with sexual awareness. For them it would be easy—the shift from passive to active allure would come naturally. This was not true for Sally. She had to think about these things.

She bought a new nightgown. It wasn't exactly flamboyant, but it had nice, lacy sleeves and a low V-neckline. It remained hidden in a box on top of the closet for a week. Once, when Ben was at work, she put it on in broad daylight in the bathroom, just to check it out. It looked all right. It went back in the box. Even a new nightgown seemed artificial, a foolish way to tell a man something so important. Where had she gotten such an idea? Magazines, probably.

On a Sunday night, after a rainy day, a day Ben had spent in the shop working on closet shelving for the baby's room, Sally decided she had to try. They were both rested, at peace with each other, and Brian had been good all day. He had eaten his supper and gone to bed. The fireplace was turned on (it sent a gas flame over a concrete log, and vaguely disgusted her), and the room was warm. Sally had a glass of sherry and listened to Ben humming the tuneless little dirge that always accompanied his work. Sex had never been this hard to face, not even the first time, as she recalled. She wasn't sure about that. As she sat and listened, Ben seemed essential to her, a husband building something, going out and working the week away, coming home to be fed and tended, taking the baby in the early mornings without complaint. He was a good husband in the most traditional ways. That was what Sally had been looking for. If he didn't understand her, that was part of what husbands were all about; at least it seemed so on this particular night.

When the light in the workroom went out, Sally got up and took her sherry glass into the kitchen, washed it out, and left it on the drainboard. She gave the floor a quick mopping and

let the door swing shut behind her. Ben was already in the
bathroom, brushing his teeth. Sally went quickly to the closet
and got out the nightgown, draping her robe over it to hide it.
When Ben came out, she went in. She put it on and looked
at herself in the mirror. It was ridiculous. She couldn't wear
such a thing. It made an idiot out of her. She felt like a child
wearing her mother's high heels. Ben would have heart failure
if he ever saw her in such a getup. The tags were still on it,
and, fingering them, she knew that she always meant to return
it. There had never been any chance that she would wear it.
It was a brave, stupid gesture, and she could never have gone
through with it.

She moved from bathroom to closet with speed; the switch
was made. Ben noticed nothing. She appeared in the bedroom
with her flannel nightgown, tied at the top with a ribbon.
Ben looked up from bed just as she doused the light. He didn't
know what was going on, didn't see the confusion in her head
as she slid in beside him and wrapped her arms around him.
It was all numb fumbling to her, but Ben was receptive. He
was more than receptive, and it was different. It was wonderful in a way. Sex for Sally had always transported her out
of the room, to somewhere else, where it was safe. Tonight
she stayed in the room. After this long build-up of fear, here
was a simple, loving sexual encounter, with a husband who had
been missing something. The pain was gone, and it was such
a relief not to have it that she relaxed. She didn't know who
or what was responsible for this new situation, but sex was
fun. Even Ben noticed the change in her reactions, the strength
in her limbs, and the smoothness of her movements. They
talked afterwards, and the distance returned. It was no fun to
talk about. They lay silent in bed for a time, not disturbing
each other. Sally didn't know what Ben was thinking. Ben
didn't know what had happened to Sally. He dozed for a few
minutes while trying to figure it out, and woke up to find
Sally's head on his chest. She was crying, just like in the
movies. Words sprung up to Ben's lips and died there. He
was crafty. Within moments they were making love again.

It took a few days for Sally to talk about it. She didn't understand what had happened to her. She hadn't become a nymphomaniac. She just enjoyed sex for the first time. It had to do with Brian, she thought, but that didn't make sense to her. It had to do with her new health and with balance. She was pulling out of a six-month nose dive, and her values were being straightened. Husbands and babies, families, her public image, and her private world—they were all filtering down and settling to rest, like snowflakes in a glass sphere. She had waited so long to go back to being the old Sally. Now, for the first time, she sensed that the old Sally no longer existed, that becoming a mother had changed her forever, that all the things she had meant to keep inside forever were going to come out, and she would have to prepare to welcome them.

Sex plays a big part in most marriages, and sex after childbirth causes a lot of worry, discomfort, and embarrassment. Some of the problems have already been dealt with, relating to sex and nursing and sex and exhaustion. But one of the greatest difficulties couples have in adjusting to post-childbirth sex is purely emotional. Sex seems to mean something different to parents than it does to nonparents. They indulge in it less often (especially at the beginning); they do not, for the most part, report drastic changes in the physical act or the sensations it causes; yet after childbirth, sex is often better. Everyone is surprised. Our explanation is simple, and some may find it sentimental, but we feel the cause is obvious: the profundity of the act is visible for the first time.

For years now, since marriage began to become less and less popular in this country, men and women have been reporting a kind of sexual despair brought on by too many partners, each for too short a time. Sex quickly becomes meaningless given the casual circumstances. That's not to say the physical need isn't there anymore. There is just a general feeling of hopelessness that sets in when physical pleasure is at a peak and emotional involvement is at an ebb.

With a steady relationship, sex can become pretty terrific. Some couples do not find it so, as a look at the divorce statistics will show, but we would guess that more often than not, bad sex is a product of bad something-else, and not a cause in itself. When a couple has a baby, there is usually a lot of bad something-else. Women feel pain, or men feel ambivalent about their wives' sexual organs after seeing them in childbearing; nursing causes problems, jealousy sets in, and so forth. All the things dealt with in this book can lead to a downturn in sexual interest and activity, but when things settle, even tentatively, sexual attraction can return with a new set of specifications. There is a baby—the product of the sex act—to remind you of what it is you are doing. What you are doing is this: you are shaking the foundations of the human race. No one thinks about it quite that way before the baby is born, and it would be surprising if you ever thought about it directly during the sex act, but this sense of primal importance to what you are doing is there—and it can make sex into something it never was before.

This is not one of those books that ends up telling you it's a sin to have sex without the intent to procreate, and nothing in the previous paragraph should be misinterpreted. Obviously, a very small percentage of the sexual encounters in the world are intended to produce pregnancy. There's no reason why it should be otherwise, but in an attempt to justify all this random sexual activity (as if it needed justifying), the pendulum of sexual liberation has swung into an extreme position; we now think of sex and babies as natural enemies. Birth control and a freer attitude toward sex have made us liberated, but they have also deemphasized the importance of sex to couples who create families. We think of young, beautiful, physically perfect human specimens whose activity leads to nothing but physical satisfaction. Contrarily, for Sally McCadden, sex didn't even *start* to make sense until she was a mother.

Perhaps hers is an extreme case. Perhaps her conservative upbringing led her to be repressed. But even for a couple with a terrific pre-baby sex life, there can be potential improvements after the baby is born. Babies and sex are not necessarily bad for each other. There are sexual problems aplenty with new parents because there are relationship adjustments going on all the time during the early years of parenting, but along with the problems is the possibility that sex will become a more profound act than it has ever been.

AT NINE MONTHS

The Work Ethic

THE SEASONS hardly change in Southern California. There is little sense of the passage of time, which may be why so many youth cultists have moved there. All that happens is that the time changes, it begins to get dark at five o'clock, the smog blows away from the mountains, and the nights turn cool. It is the subtlest hint that the world is spinning, aging everyone at the same pace. Sally McCadden didn't feel older; she didn't even feel changed. She just felt as though she had bobbed up to the surface of her troubles and could see again.

On one of those dark early evenings, she stepped out of her car at a fashionable restaurant in Westwood and looked over at Ben in a tuxedo, taking a ticket from a red-vested attendant. She was in heels, a long, black velvet dress, and more makeup than she had had on in almost a year. It felt good to be out, but Sally was intimidated. The elevator leading to the rooftop restaurant was filled with older couples, conversing easily in hushed voices. Sally didn't know who they were, but several of them looked famous. The cocktail benefit for Children's Hospital was something she had been anticipating with a mixture of fear and excitement. They could not afford it, even at twenty-five dollars. There was tuxedo rental and baby-sitting to be added in, and it was all very extravagant, but she had wanted to go, and Ben thought it would be a good professional move.

She had never seen anything like it, at least that she could remember. Everyone had dressed formally at her wedding, but somehow, with folding tables and chairs, it just wasn't as formal. The restaurant had mirrored walls, giving the impression that thousands were in attendance. The McCaddens found themselves seated around a plate of nuts with a movie critic and his girlfriend. Sally had never heard the man's name, which embarrassed her, but he talked and talked, and she decided her naïveté wasn't showing. The chatter was fascinating. Movie stars' names jumped in the air like popcorn, and all the dirt about all the popular television shows was dragged out gleefully.

"And what do you kids do?" asked the critic finally. He was perhaps ten years older than the McCaddens.

"Nothing," Sally blurted out. The word was out in the open before she could do anything about it. "I do nothing," she corrected herself. "Ben works for the hospital. I'm a mother."

"That's plenty!" the movie critic said in a hearty tone of voice, but it was clear that discussion of Sally had ended.

"Are you a doctor?" the critic asked, turning to Ben. Sally didn't feel too hurt; she understood that this man and she were worlds apart, that he lived a fast, thrilling life while she stayed home and took care of Brian. The longer she sat, however, the angrier she got. She began to picture this man's life. As far as she could tell, someone paid him to go to the movies. He would sit down for a few minutes afterwards and talk into a tape machine, saying what he thought of the movie. His review would then be printed in a newspaper and he'd receive a check—and for that he got to interview Robert Redford and

Faye Dunaway. What had he ever done besides be in the right place at the right time?

Sally had worked harder than that, and her life was no movie. She had suffered pain and danger, and there was a living creature in her house while she flitted around some high-tone restaurant with a bunch of celebrities. The drink was going to her head, or something was. She excused herself and went to the ladies room.

Ben was waiting by the door when she came out, curious, knowing something was wrong.

"I'm sorry," she said. "I don't feel well."

"Should we go?"

"No. You'll meet some people. You don't want to be seen leaving this early. It wouldn't be good."

Ben nodded and the two of them ricocheted their way into the crowd in search of other company.

"I'd like to be like that," Sally said when they were anonymous again. She didn't know why she said it. She hated the critic, but his life did seem to be genuinely glamorous. She wouldn't have minded the glamorous part.

"Like what?" Ben asked.

"Going around all the time," Sally said.

"Would you turn into a jerk?" Ben asked. He hadn't liked the movie critic either.

"I guess I would," Sally said.

As soon as they noticed people departing, the McCaddens followed suit. The party was getting hilariously loud. No one had mentioned a word about Children's Hospital.

It took Ben two days to confront Sally about what she had said, that she did "nothing."

"Do you think of yourself as doing nothing?" he asked.

"Sometimes," she said. "We just live this little life. I guess, when you're near Hollywood, when everybody has her name in the paper, it seems smaller."

It was true. Sally thought of herself as one of the little people who always turn up on the late movie—little people struggling to make good, to pay the rent, to get medicine for their baby, to get a promotion at work. Being a little person was a hard job, harder than being a movie critic. There wasn't much glamor in it, and being a mother was the littlest little-people job of all. Sally felt guilty for being satisfied by it, and guiltier whenever she was gripped by envy. Given the alternatives, however, she could see it was the right life for her. Ultimately, she felt guilty about being Sally. One thought and one thought only got her through these periods: what movie critic could possibly have survived the past nine months?

The image of the good, old-fashioned American family is in bad repair these days. The women's movement, divorce statistics, and the new world of self-realization have exposed the inequities of many families and have brought about a great deal of self-recrimination. When Tom Wolfe dubbed us "the ME generation," it became clear that the family concepts of harmony, sacrifice, and unity weren't washing anymore. For many people who participated in an era of symbol-smashing in the sixties, the seventies have been a wandering time, and not altogether happy. As the eighties approach, we begin to hear rumblings of the return to traditional values—and if traditional values return, millions of people like Ben and Sally McCadden are going to breathe easily for the first time since the middle of the Vietnam War.

POLITICS TIME

This book is about a lot of things, but politics isn't one of them. We are trying to say what we sense is happening. We don't know what will happen when the women's movement meets the eighties. We don't know whether divorce statistics are really leveling off as some claim. We are both feminist and family-oriented, and we see no implied contradiction in those beliefs. The family is not now, nor has it ever been, all it might be in terms of equality. On the other hand, the women's movement has its failings as well, particularly in the area of dealing with the home-oriented married mother. (See The First Family—Frank and Betsy Scheflin.)

For six of her nine months, Sally McCadden had been a troubled parent. Her behavior was erratic, her relationship with Ben strained, her sex life complex and unappealing. What got her through the rough times was not self-help or support from women's consciousness-raising groups. It was nothing more or less than the old-time work ethic. Busy hands make light work. An idle brain is the devil's playground. These are the kinds of homilies that have been thrashed to death by the sophisticated seventies. They *are* foolish-sounding, simplistic adages. Sally never said them to herself, or thought of them for that matter, but her life is lived along those old-time lines. She is subjected to a lot of scoffing as a result. What is important, however, is that for her, this approach worked. Mindlessly, waiting for the troubles to be over, she toiled her way through six months, and at the end of that time, she was rewarded. Sally wasn't up to a lot of philosophizing about things. She did what she had been brought up to do.

This attitude is by no means universal. We do not mean to belittle the rebellion many women have gone through regarding their parents' values. The work ethic and all the traditional philosophical (and often religious) beliefs that go with it may be abhorrent to you, but it isn't dangerous, and you shouldn't feel unchic if you believe in an old-fashioned family. Raising children is an old, honorable, and difficult profession. It involves much unchallenging work: feeding, changing, keeping children out of danger, and so forth. *Someone has to do it,* however, just as someone has to sweep the streets, change your oil filter, and check out groceries. If you hate the mundane tasks, that's fine. But if you see them as all part of the job (every good job is a hard job), you may find yourself in danger because the ME generation has spoken; it has dictated that we must all be fulfilled and entertained all the time. You may be shamed out of doing the hard work on the grounds that because it's boring, it's unworthy.

Well, it isn't. It's good, uninteresting work, and it's balanced by the rewards that come from knowing your children inside and out. If your upbringing has been traditional, and if you believe that your children should have basically the same upbringing you had (admittedly, a big "if"), then don't be outfoxed by any of the trends. Remember, too, that it is a grand old American tradition to be out of step with the times, marching to your own beat. If that beat seems like a nineteenth-century beat and you believe in it, have courage. Some of the pioneers were very successful.

AT ONE YEAR

Beginning Again

EVERYTHING had settled. Brian's first birthday party was in the planning stages for a month. There would be a turkey, a preordered cake with designs and a birthday message written out in icing, pointed hats, streamers, and favors. The party was for adults, and those with young children were invited to bring them. Sally and Ben were feeling very much like parents. The party planning came naturally to them. Ben's work was going well. Sally had the house in good enough shape so that she, too, had gone to work as a part-time bookkeeper. Brian was secure, and there was a regular sitter with whom he flirted shamelessly.

As the date approached, Sally began to weaken in little ways. With no outward signs of difficulty or stress, she found it almost impossible to get out of bed in the morning. For four days in a row, Ben got up with Brian. Sally wasn't sick, but she wasn't herself. On the fifth morning, she threw up and was seized with a fearful premonition.

"My God," she said to Ben, returning to bed and throwing the covers over herself, head and all. "I'm pregnant."

"That's silly," Ben said. "That's nonsense." But his throat was suddenly parched by the possibility. They had not been using birth control, but Sally had had no periods. And last time was so difficult. It couldn't be.

Two hours later, Sally was at her doctor's office, and by the end of the day, she knew. Never was there a quieter evening. Brian's mumblings in the playpen seemed to rattle the house with noise. Ben looked into the fireplace, with its synthetic logs, and tried to bring into focus a picture of the future.

"When's it due?" he asked finally.

"No one knows," Sally said. "There's no way to estimate, since I haven't had a period in almost two years. March, sometime, I guess."

Ben took a calendar out of his wallet and put his glasses on. He did some quick calculating and drew a circle around June 30. Figuring the baby would be born March 30, and adding up to its third-month birthday.

"What's June 30th?" Sally wanted to know.

"That's the first time I can expect to smile after this baby's born," Ben said. "There's not many sure things in this life, but I want to remember that when this baby is born, no matter what happens, no matter how awful it gets, June 30 will come. It *will* come. There's no doubt about it. And on June 30, he'll be three months old and things will turn nice again. No way I'm looking forward to those three months."

"It's going to be a girl this time," Sally said.

Ben shrugged. Torpor weighed him down. Sally was predicting again. As far as he could tell, looking at it from that particularly rough evening, they had learned nothing. Idiotic thoughts danced in his head; they wouldn't need to buy anything, except a house. Business was going well. This child wouldn't break up the marriage. Vague generalities clattered together, maneuvering for position in Ben's brain, while Sally stared dumbly at a novel she was absolutely not reading. This was some night. Just as you get everything in order, tidy up the ship, get the engines tuned . . . what more could happen to them? Sally thought about her incoherent week in the hospital, her labor pain, her crazy struggle to balance her devotion to husband and child.

"Well," Ben said. "This way the tied-down part of parenting will all be out of the way at the same time. It might be for the best." His words hung in the air like targets at a shooting gallery.

"I'm going to bed," Sally said.

It all seemed better as the weeks passed. The party happened and was a grand success. Brian got up one day and took three tentative steps without holding on. He was a little boy after that, and it was possible there might be room for a baby in the house. And how did they forsee the future?

"Aside from the first three months," Ben said in an interview, "which no one is ever going to convince me are any fun, aside from that, I can see that it's going to be better because we know all the things that can't be done. We know how you have to rest, and we know how little babies react when they're little."

"And we know you bleed," Sally added. "We know you go crazy, and the most important thing is that we know it ends— all the insane parts and the pain. And the napping, which I now do without complaint, and leaving the housework for a few hours when I'm dizzy from being tired, and all that stuff, it all comes to an end."

"There's a lot of hard work, and we're very close as a family, really closer than before we had Brian," Ben said. "But the worst part is gone forever. That was when, in the thick of those first three months, I would have a nagging thought that it would be like this for the rest of my life. People kept telling me it would change, but I hadn't seen it for myself. Now I've seen it for myself, and I *know*. On June 30, it'll change. And if it doesn't, I'm going to ask for my money back."

By Sally's second month of pregnancy, things had already changed. She and Ben stopped making love, more or less without complaint. Ben was afraid of hurting the fetus, which as a nurse he knew to be an utterly groundless fear.

"But it bothers me, and now I know I can succumb to those dumb things and the world won't stop. Our sex life was terrific, but it stopped being terrific, and we stopped making love. And that's the beautiful part of this second pregnancy. I know I'm crazy, and I know I'll stop being crazy. I can afford to let myself be, as long as it doesn't bother Sally."

Sally kind of missed sex, which flattered Ben, but she wasn't complaining. "We don't know what'll hapepn," she said, "but if he's bothered, then that's more important to me than my own satisfaction. How could I *get* any satisfaction, knowing he's bothered? This baby's going to be a lot of trouble. But the difference is, I know it's not going to be impossible. I know the day will never come when I'll die from it. The truth is, we're in pretty good shape."

A couple of things should be self-evident from the closing days of the McCaddens' first year.

1.) *You can get pregnant even when you aren't menstruating.* This is obviously an important point. Here's how it works.

Your system goes through a lot of physiological changes when you get pregnant. These continue if you are breast-feeding. You certainly won't have your period for a few months, possibly not for a year or more, but you may be ovulating regularly. Because there is no cycle of menstruation, you won't know *when* you're ovulating, so birth control becomes crucial if you do not want to get pregnant.

Sally felt that she wouldn't get pregnant because she had had so much trouble the first time. Obviously, this belief was unfounded, as logical as it might have seemed at the time. *Be careful.* If you are a family planner, and if you believe in the necessity of carefully considering the addition of each child to your family unit, heed this: the time following birth can be a fertile time in the female, even though there are no outward signs of it.

2.) *People do learn.* Of course, they learn about diapering and bathing and bottles and breast-feeding, but most of those topics can be fully disposed of in less than a week. What they really learn, and what's worth learning, is that you *can* have and raise children. It is still possible, even with the world flying apart, dissolving into a dither of self-help jargon and tenuous relationships. Almost every one of the couples we talked to reported that there was intense curiosity on the part of their single and childless friends about their post-child lives.

"Our baby," one mother told us, "was an experiment for everyone we knew. They wanted to know if it was possible—this traditional, square way of doing things. We didn't know ourselves if it was possible. Everything has been so crazy for so long in this country, and marriage seemed pretty old-fashioned when we started. I guess we just came from stable households, and we wanted to duplicate them. The people who came from unsuccessful households can't picture *why* anyone would want to create such a thing. Well, we like it."

It seems odd that having a baby should make one a curiosity, but having a baby, once thought the "natural" thing, may not be natural anymore. There are groups of people to whom it is not in any way appealing, and others who see it as a dangerous experiment with the only life they possess. It is certainly true that if you have a baby, that baby may well serve as a model for your friends and acquaintances. You may feel defensive about having taken such a "traditional" route, and you may be besieged by a lot of personal questions. In answering them, if you answer them, you will be involved in self-analysis, and if you are like the McCaddens, here is what you may find:

At the end of a year you are quite different. Your values are changed, your sense of responsibility is greater, your options are, at least temporarily, narrower. Your relationship with your mate has changed, and you have grown a whole new devotional arm to handle your feelings about your child. However, the simple question—Is it possible to lead today's life and still be a parent?—may have the most complex answer. When you have a baby, you change. Mothers tend to change more than fathers (a common cause of friction), but everyone changes. When you have children, you choose to deal with humanity at its simplest and most complex. You buy in to a lot of drudge work and a lot of emotional responsibility and a tremendous amount of sacrifice. There's no nicer word for it; you give up a lot.

It then becomes a question of reward: What do you get for what you give up? It would be nice to say, as most child-care manuals do, that the rewards far outweigh the demands. Unfortunately, most people we talked to found that, on many days, it just wasn't so. It takes a year, sometimes more, for many people to be sure. Ultimately, no one in our sample regretted becoming a parent. Most were thinking of doing it again. But there was nothing lighthearted about their descriptions of the process. When people told us that they were being besieged by friends for information about the parenting experience, *we* asked *them* what they said to their friends. There was one overwhelmingly popular answer: it's worth it. Not "it's great." Not "you'll never regret it." Not even "despite everything, it's swell." We think the response is carefully measured and quite accurate.

It's worth it.

Postscript: The McCaddens' second child, a girl, was born three days before her official due date. Labor was four hours long, and neither mother nor child suffered complications.

FINAL WORD

We HAVE searched this book for common denominators, knowing that in dealing with twelve individual parents it would be difficult to find any. Throughout the period of writing, friends, interviewees, and relatives badgered us with the same question: What are you finding? What is the truth about parenting? We could not answer them because what was true for one couple on Monday was always nonsense to another couple on Wednesday. It has made this book more complicated than it might have been, but, frankly, we're grateful for that. It would be sad to think that life had become so homogenized that everything was the same for everyone all the time.

If one general theme did seem to recur in our interviews, it was a very broad one, and a difficult one to talk about: the maturation process. The struggle to become parents is a struggle to become grown. And although no one ever stops growing, the particular growth spurt associated with the first year of parenting is probably the most intense, compact, and pressurized period of growth in a young adult life. The physical act of coping with baby and mate is arduous enough, but what seems to reach almost every new parent, and make the process so alarming and so difficult, is the maturation of emotional outlook.

If there is one, single sobering thing about becoming parents, it is that it makes sense out of the human lifespan. Not happy sense, necessarily, but visible sense. The metaphor has been overworked in literature since the time of Dickens, but infants *do* look like the elderly. Visit a nursing home with a child in a stroller and walk beside an old man in a wheelchair and the irony will be so crushingly obvious that you will need some air. The cycle of things is presented in such graphic detail by the arrival of a child that your life is never quite the same. Many find the comparisons odious or, at the very least, depressing. We find them exhilarating. The awesome power of the human life cycle, stretching in an endless chain, seems to us an impressive concept. It is so powerful, in fact, that it changes us. The evidence of it in our own families humbles us and causes us to relearn who we are. Coping with the emotional and philosophical implications of giving birth to a new child is the essential stress confronting a parent. The child, so overpowering to our own lives, and so monumentally insignificant in the grand scheme of things, is the ultimate tool in bringing us to maturity. Some of us (many of us) go kicking and screaming. We are asked to work harder, sacrifice more, understand the incomprehensible, and sympathize with the unreasonable. We are more than asked; we're given no choice. The period that follows birth, the next months, or year, or years, is given over to coping with these demands. It's a messy job, ill-defined, with bad hours and uncertain conditions. It is, after all, the riskiest job you can get.

It is also a job that is in danger in our society, and this is a shame. We have been through rough times. The family is not in the best of shape. As an occupation, motherhood has taken a beating. We have kicked apart a good deal of family and child-rearing tradition in the last fifteen years, and we seem to be having a hard time building anything in its place. The seventies has been a self-absorbed, shell-shocked decade, and our children have no doubt suffered for it; but to face the problem of bringing up our children is only to face ourselves in a mirror of time. In becoming parents, we become ourselves in a clearer, brighter light. It is in that light that we must learn to live.

INDEX

About the Authors

Since 1971, SANDRA SOHN JAFFE has been a Certified Childbirth Educator, teaching the Lamaze method in Los Angeles, California. She is currently Chairperson of the Standards and Ethics committee of the Los Angeles chapter of the American Society of Psychoprophylaxis in Obstetrics, the professional organization of certified Lamaze instructors.

Ms. Jaffe has lectured at the University of Southern California in the School of Social Work, and in the Beverly Hills and Los Angeles school systems on human sexuality and sex education. In connection with her work, she has appeared on nationally televised segments of "Special Edition" (ABC) and "America Alive" (NBC).

She is the mother of three children.

JACK VIERTEL is a journalist and screenwriter. His work has appeared in *The Harvard Crimson*, *The Richmond Mercury*, *New Times* magazine, *New West* magazine, and the Los Angeles *Times*. He is also the coauthor of a book on snorkeling and scuba diving, *Underwater Holidays*.

Mr. Viertel is the father of a son.